Teaching Science in the Elementary School

Teaching Science in the Elementary School

THIRD EDITION

JOHN W. RENNER
UNIVERSITY OF OKLAHOMA

DON G. STAFFORD
EAST CENTRAL OKLAHOMA STATE UNIVERSITY

HARPER & ROW, Publishers
New York, Philadelphia, Hagerstown, San Francisco, London

Sponsoring Editor: George A. Middendorf
Project Editor: Joyce Marshall
Designer: Robert Sugar
Production Manager: Marion A. Palen
Compositor: Maryland Linotype Composition Co., Inc.
Printer and Binder: The Maple Press Company
Art Studio: Danmark & Michaels Inc.

Cover Photograph: DPI, Hoban.

Teaching Science in the Elementary School, Third Edition

Copyright © 1979 by John W. Renner and Don G. Stafford

Library of Congress Cataloging in Publication Data

Renner, John Wilson, 1924–
  Teaching science in the elementary school.

  Includes bibliographical references and index.
  1.   Science—Study and teaching (Elementary)
I.   Stafford, Don G., joint author.   II.   Ragan, William
Burk, 1896–   III.   Title.
LB1585.R4 1979   372.3′5′004   78–26580
ISBN 0–06–045381–8

To our friend, colleague, and coauthor,
Vivian Jensen Coulter

Contents

Preface

The educational climate into which the third edition of this book appears is considerably different than that existing at the times of either previous editions. People are talking about the "basics" in education, and emphasizng that the "basics" are what should be taught. That attitude immediately raises the question as to what "basics" elementary school science should be directed toward. The Council for Basic Education states its position this way:

> Science should teach more than facts and mechanical skills. It should help develop children's abilities to think critically, to seek and use evidence before jumping to conclusions, and to begin developing some of the other more complex intellectual skills.[1]

In other words, developing children's ability to think represents the "basics" for science education. The first two editions of this book focused on using science to develop the thinking abilities of children. This third edition also stresses the development of the ability to think as the paramount responsibility of science education.

In order for science to fulfill its basic responsibility to elementary schools, teachers must operate first, from a frame of reference that tells them what science is, and second, from a frame of reference that describes how children learn. The authors subscribe to a frame of reference that defines science as a process of finding out. Our fellow Oklahoman, Dr. Duane Roller, has said: "Science is the quest for knowledge, not the knowledge itself"[2] Subscribing to that frame of reference leads the classroom teacher to view science as the *children* doing investigations, interpreting data, making predictions and constructing models. True, facts and principles will result from the quest for knowledge, but they do not represent science. Science is represented by the process of the quest. Without the quest there is no science. This book is written on the premise that science *is* the quest for knowledge.

[1] Howard J. Hausman, *Choosing a Science Program for the Elementary School,* Washington, D.C.: Council for Basic Education, 1976, p. 1.
[2] Duane Roller, "Has Science a Climate?" *Sunday Oklahoman,* Oklahoma City, Oklahoma, February 22, 1970, p. 23.

How can a quest for knowledge be carried out with children? First of all the teacher must decide what type of content the children *can* investigate. The work of Jean Piaget has proved to be invaluable in making that decision, and this book utilizes the findings of that educational giant. In his book *To Understand is to Invent*,[3] Piaget gave the beginning of a teaching procedure that can be used to involve children in a quest for knowledge. With the introduction of the *learning cycle*—exploration, invention, and discovery, however, Dr. Robert Karplus, Professor of Physics at the University of California, Berkeley, and Director of the Science Curriculum Improvement Study gave teachers real direction on how to organize their work to lead children on a quest.

Because it represents a quest, the learning cycle is a teaching method that is compatible with the frame of reference with which this book regards science. Furthermore, to truly implement the learning cycle, children must explore concepts at their intellectual level. Therefore, the learning cycle depends upon the Piaget's model of intelligence. When students finish this book, they should have a teaching method (the learning cycle) which can be implemented using any system of science teaching materials because (1) a frame of reference for science exists (a quest for knowledge); and (2) that teacher will know how to select content for any grade level (using Piaget's model of intelligence).

We are grateful to all of the publishers and authors who have permitted us to reproduce their materials. A special "thank you" is extended to the Glencoe Publishing Company and its President, Mr. Jack Witmer, for permitting us the extensive use of materials from the *Learning Science Program*.[4]

We would also like to acknowledge the contributions of the late William B. Ragan, a former David Ross Boyd Professor of Education at the University of Oklahoma, who was a coauthor on the two previous editions of this book.

You will note that throughout the book you are occasionally asked to respond in writing to a special situation. Please do this. The only opportunity authors have to teach by inquiry from the printed page is for the reader to get involved by responding to particular situations. Have a pleasant, profitable set of inquiries.

John W. Renner
Don G. Stafford

---

[3] Jean Piaget, *To Understand is to Invent*, New York: Grossman, 1973.
[4] This program is a seven-book elementary school science program. The titles of the books, starting with kindergarten, are *Images, Things, Change, Systems, Variation, Action*, and *Models* by John W. Renner, Don G. Stafford, and Vivian Jensen Coulter.

Teaching Science in the Elementary School

Part 1
GATHERING DATA

The classroom teacher works with children and the disciplines—in this case science—and uses the disciplines to lead children to achieve educational purposes. When developing an understanding of the instructional process, therefore, the teacher first needs data about those three factors. This section of the book leads the reader to gather the data needed about the discipline of science, educational purpose, and how children learn.

Chapter 1
The Dimensions of Science

As a teacher you assume the responsibility of leading children to those learnings that will enable them to become intelligent, happy, productive people. The tools the society and the school have provided you to accomplish that task are curricula. You must, therefore, examine every element of the curricula from the frame of reference of its usefulness in assisting you to discharge your responsibilities.

Science is certainly no exception to the foregoing. But before any discipline within the curricula can be so clinically evaluated, the evaluator must understand what that discipline really is. Then, and only then, can a person make judgments about that discipline's usefulness in a classroom. Attempts are not made, for example, to teach computer design in the first grade because such subject matter is not suitable or usable at that educational level. But what from the several disciplines can be used to educate children at various educational levels? Or more particularly, what can science contribute to the education of children? Before that question can be answered, another must be asked and answered. What is science? Is it the facts and generalizations about the physical world and all of the entities in it? Is it knowing what gravity and DNA are? Is it being able to apply mathematics to a series of data from an experiment and arriving at some conclusion? Or is science the solving of a problem to arrive at an answer? Is science answers or is it questions? Or is it both?

Since this is a book about teaching science, a clear understanding of what we call science is essential.

WHAT IS SCIENCE?

The question is simple and clear. Now let us seek an answer. First, perhaps you would like to think about the question and state an answer.

GATHERING DATA

The next logical step seems to be, ask someone who should know. Of course, you would want to ask someone who is involved in the practice of science or one who has studied science and scientists. Here are five statements about science and scientists. Each is a piece of information about science. You might wish to add some other statements to this collection. Read each statement carefully. Decide which are the key words in the statement. Discuss each statement and your interpretation of it with others in the class.

1. "The object of all science is to coordinate our experiences and bring them into a logical system."—Scientist, Albert Einstein[1]
2. "The task of science is both to extend the range of our experience and reduce it to order."—Scientist, Niels Bohr[2]
3. "Science is the quest for knowledge, not the knowledge."—Historian of Science, Duane Roller[3]
4. "Fundamentally, science is an intellectual enterprise, an attempt to understand the world in a particular way. The development of science is a story of expanding intellectual horizons."—Author, Theodore Ashford[4]
5. "The scientist does not study nature because it is useful; he studies it because he delights in it because it is beautiful—of

---

[1] Verne H. Booth, *Physical Science*, New York: Macmillan, 1962, p. 151.
[2] Ibid.
[3] H. Duane Roller, "Has Science a Climate?" *Sunday Oklahoman*, Oklahoma City, Oklahoma, 22 February, 1970, p. 23.
[4] Theodore Ashford, *From Atoms to Stars*, New York: Holt, Rinehart and Winston, 1960, p. 3.

course, I do not speak of that beauty which strikes the sense, the beauty of quality and appearances; not that I undervalue such beauty, far from it, but it has nothing to do with science; I mean that profounder beauty which comes from the harmonious order of the parts and which a pure intelligence can grasp— intellectual beauty is sufficient unto itself, and it is for the future good of humanity, that the scientist devotes himself to long and difficult labor."—Scientist, Henri Poincaré[5]

Now, look at the above statements as a collection of information about science. Are there certain ideas that are common to most of the statements? Is there a pattern or generalization that can be made about "What is science?" based on this collection of information?

Make a record of any patterns that you see in the collection of statements. See if others in your class agree. Next, try to draw the notions about science and scientists into a statement using your own words, that is, invent a definition of science that summarizes and draws into clear focus the notions presented in the collection of information (or statements). This definition will be your beginning idea of "What is science?" The activities in the remainder of this chapter will allow you to expand this idea.

The authors of this book did a similar assignment to that which was just given to you. Keep in mind that authors of books are people like yourselves. Be willing to challenge their views or opinions; retain a healthy skepticism about their ideas. Compare the authors' statements with your own. Such steps will allow you to bring your own ideas into better focus, and, by using a different frame of reference, perhaps expand your ideas.

GETTING THE IDEA

Here are some of the generalizations or patterns in the collection of statements: Do you agree with them?

1. Science has to do with direct experience (investigation, observation, or both), with natural phenomena and with the collection of information.

---

[5] Jules Henri Poincaré, *Foundation of Science*, New York: Science Press, 1929, p. 18.

2. Science has to do with the organization and interpretation of information collected by logical means.
3. Science has creative aspects since it attempts to explain and extend experience beyond the direct sensory level and to understand nature or all phases of the environment.
4. Science has a dual character. It is on the one hand *what scientists find out about nature;* it is on the other hand the quest for new information and understanding about nature.
5. *Science is an intellectual process.* In science, a person is using the intellect to collect information about nature, gained through the senses (experience). Science is also using the intellect to coordinate or interpret experience, and it is using the intellect to create explanations.
6. *Science has an aesthetic nature.* This aesthetic nature is derived from the beauty of logic, of order, and of the structure of relationship.

Did your interaction with these stated generalizations expand or change your idea about "What is science?" If so, restate your idea now. Perhaps the entire class might develop a statement now—or choose one of the six that best represents the class idea at this time.

EXPANDING THE IDEA

In this section you will experience more directly the idea of science. You will do this through participation in three activities or investigations. Each activity is designed to focus on certain aspects of science and to introduce vocabulary used in the language of science.

ACTIVITY ONE

Materials Needed

1 meter stick
2 glass marbles (1 small, 1 large), 1 steel ball
1 ruler with a groove

Begin the investigation by placing a book on a flat table. Then lean the grooved ruler on the edge of the book. The grooved ruler will serve as a launching ramp. Place the smaller glass marble at the top of the ramp, then let it roll down the ramp, across the table, and onto the floor as shown in Figure 1–1.

Observe the event and then carefully describe the path and motion of the ball. Record your description. Stack one book on top of another and repeat the observation. Repeat the activity with stacks of three, four, and five books or more. How does the motion of the marble vary or change? How does the shape of the path of the freely falling ball vary?

Figure 1-1   How does the height of the stack of books affect the speed of the ball when it is released? (Martin J. Lollar)

Repeat the activity with the large marble and the steel ball. Compare the motion and path of the three balls. Describe any differences that you observe. What similarities do you observe? Make a record of your observations.

Your descriptions of the event which you observed are called *information* or *data* (or facts). The general descriptions of the events with the three balls are called qualitative data. A more useful kind of data are produced when you make accurate measurements. This is called quantitative data. Repeat the experiment and collect some quantitative data.

Place the edge of the ruler on one book as shown in Figure 1-2. (a) Measure how high the ball is from the table when it is in the position to be released. (b) Measure how far the end of the ruler is from the table edge. (c) Measure how far the ball lands from the table.

Repeat the event using two, three, four and five books. Keep the distance from the end of the ruler to the table edge the same for all trials. Put the data you collect in a table like Table 1-1.

When an observation is done under careful control it is called by a special name—experiment.[6] What you have just done is an experiment! You controlled how far the ball rolled on the table. The height of the table was the same, of course, for each trial. The type of ball you used was the same each time. Two parts of the experiment changed—

[6] Chemical Education Material Study, *Chemistry, An Experimental Science,* San Francisco: Freeman, 1963, p. 3.

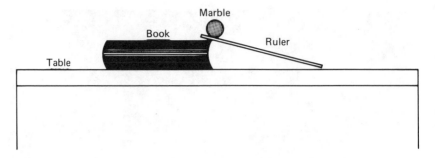

Figure 1–2 This figure shows you how to set up the experiment for Activity One.

the starting height of the ball and the distance from the table of the point at which the ball struck the floor. Factors in the experiment that could have assumed different values (distance of the ball from the floor, distance from ruler end to the edge of the table, distance the ball landed from the table, the table heights, and the ball size or material) are called *variables.*

In this experiment you held some of the variables constant. These are called *controlled variables.* You allowed only two variables to change—the starting height of the ball and the distance the ball landed from the table. You can now compare these two variables. Examine the data in your data table. What is the pattern relating the two variables? Next, graph the data. Place the measurements of the starting

Table 1–1

(A) HEIGHT OF THE BALL (CM) FROM THE TABLE WHEN RELEASED	(B) DISTANCE (CM) FROM THE END OF THE RULER TO THE EDGE OF THE TABLE	(C) DISTANCE (CM) BALL LANDS FROM THE TABLE

heights of the ball on one axis of your graph and the distance the ball landed from the table on the other. Use your graph to make a prediction. Select some books that give you a starting height of the ball different from the ones you used. Before you release the ball, use your graph to predict how far from the table the ball will strike the floor. Then test your prediction.

Repeat the experiment with the larger glass marble and then with the steel ball. What difference did size or weight make?

ACTIVITY TWO

Design experiments to let two balls roll off the table at the same time. Vary the speeds of the balls. Vary the sizes of the balls. Collect and interpret the data from the experiments. What variables will you control in each experiment? Describe any general patterns that you found.

ACTIVITY THREE: THE PENDULUM

Materials Needed

> 3 washers about 1 or 2 centimeters in diameter
> string of smooth cotton or nylon about 1 meter long
> watch or clock with a second hand

Tie one washer to the end of the string as in Figure 1–3. Hold the string at the opposite end and let the washer hang freely. Next, pull the washer to one side about 30 centimeters (1 foot) and release it. This system is called a *pendulum.*

Describe the motion of the pendulum. Observe the changes in direction and speed of the washer. The time required for the washer to move through one complete motion over and back is called the *period.*

Do an experiment to find out about the period of a pendulum. First, use a pendulum 20 centimeters long. Hold the string with one hand and pull the washer to the side 10 centimeters and release it. Count the number of complete swings in 10 seconds. Then calculate the time in seconds of the period of the pendulum. Repeat the measurement for pendulums 30, 40, 50, 60, 80 and 100 centimeters long. Put the data collected in a table like Figure 1–4.

Now use the data you collected to invent a relationship. Make a generalization relating the period of a pendulum to its length. Use your generalization to predict the length of a one-second pendulum. Check your prediction. Explore two other parts of the pendulum to answer these questions. How does the number of washers (the weight) affect the period? How does the distance the washers are pulled to the side (displaced) affect the period of the pendulum? What variables must you control in each experiment? In this activity you have begun to

Figure 1–3 Careful observations and measurements are important when you do science.

become acquainted with two additional very closely related ideas associated with doing science.

1. The search for patterns or generalizations in data.
2. The search for relationships between variables.

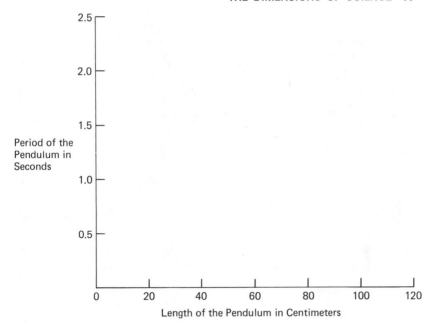

Figure 1–4

You have no doubt noticed that the question, "Why?", has not been asked yet. It is possible to do many investigations, find patterns and relationships, and make predictions based on observed patterns without knowing why the patterns or relationships exist. The simple question, "Why?", is perhaps the most difficult and yet the most satisfying aspect of science. To explain why a pattern or relationship exists between variables, a scientist uses *models* or theories. The next activity allows you to explore a very common model of the earth—the globe.

ACTIVITY: THE MODEL

Materials Needed

One globe

You are given the following information concerning patterns involving the earth, sun, moon, and stars. Your job—to produce a logical model of the earth. All of these patterns and data were available several centuries before Christ.

1. The sun and moon as viewed from the earth have a round shape.
2. If two people are located several hundred miles apart in an east-west direction, the person who is east of the other will see the sun rise first. Or more generally stated, persons east on the earth see the sun rise before those west of them do.

Figure 1–5   The globe is a model of the earth. (Martin J. Lollar)

3. As a person journeys northward, the north star will be located higher and higher in a regular manner above the horizon until it is directly overhead. If a person travels southward, the north star gets closer and closer to the horizon and finally disappears. For each 100 miles one travels north or south, the north star rises or falls approximately 15 degrees.

A model must explain the observed patterns. Now, suppose you have not already been told repeatedly that the earth is spherical; try to use logic to create a model. For example, you could try some shapes to see if they explain the patterns. Five possible shapes are shown in Figure 1–6 that could be proposed. Test each to see if they agree with the patterns of data. Answer, for each model, these questions.

1. Would the pattern of the north star rising higher when traveling north or lowering when traveling south be observed?
2. Would persons east on the earth see the sun rise first if the earth had this shape?
3. Which model best explains the observed patterns of the sun and north star?

Now that you have developed a model of the earth, use it to make some deductions. The north star rises approximately 15 degrees for each 100 miles traveled in a north-south direction. What is the

Figure 1–6   Which of these five models best fits the observed patterns?

approximate circumference of the earth? (Hint: A circle has 360 degrees).
What is the approximate diameter of the earth? (Refer to Figure 1–7.)

All of the above information was available to the Greeks by 300 B.C.
Therefore, it is not very reasonable to think that the scientific
community believed the earth was flat until 1492 A.D.

Use the earth model again. Use the globe to represent the model.
Locate Portugal on the globe. Suppose you wish to move to a position
east of you. Be sure you understand that by using the spherical model,
one could logically arrive at a position east of one's present position
by traveling west.

The earth model is a very concrete model. You can hold it in your
hands. Many models in science are much more abstract—the atom

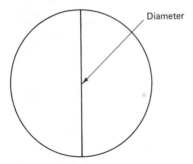

Figure 1–7 The circumference of the circle equals 3.14, or π, times the diameter, $C=3.14d$.

for example—but they are used in the same way: To explain patterns and to make and test logical deductions. Models help the scientist to reason. Some models are represented by sketches or objects, some by written statements, and some by mathematical equations. Once a model is proposed, it can be expanded and refined.

To explain the rising of the sun every 24 hours, the spherical earth model was expanded. The earth was assumed to turn or spin on an axis—like a ball—one rotation each day, or each 24 hours. Now, new questions can be asked.

Suppose three persons were standing on the surface of the earth at positions A, B, and C (see Figure 1–8). Compare the speed each would be traveling. How fast would the person at the middle of the earth (point B) be traveling? Why does the wind not sweep the person away? Are the movements of winds on the earth related to the movement of the earth?

Now take the time to summarize or review what you have done to answer the question, "What is Science?" First, you began by exploring

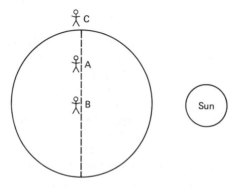

Figure 1–8 A model allows you to ask new and different questions.

statements or gathering data about science. Then you invented a beginning idea or statement that that was your understanding of science at that point. Next, you expanded your idea of science in the four activities or investigations. As you expanded your idea of science, hopefully some other ideas concerning a philosophy of science began to come into focus. We will introduce some of these concepts or ideas here for you. You can expand these ideas as you participate in science.

A BRIEF PHILOSOPHY OF SCIENCE

As a person examines what scientists say science is, and what a scientist does, a philosophy of science begins to emerge. The key word in the philosophy appears to be *order*. By their statements and their actions, scientists say,

Order alone is understandable.

Although there is fantastic variety in the universe, we must assume that underlying this diversity is order. The task of the scientist, then, is to search for the underlying order and to create logical explanations for that order. (Even where a collection of objects becomes disordered, they become disordered in a predictable way.)

A scientist seeks to understand nature, then, by discovering the existing order. There appear to be three ideas that are keys to understanding the order of the universe, as shown in Figure 1–9.

· **Balance.** Nature is always seeking a state of balance—electrical and magnetic forces, gravitational forces, and ecosystems demonstrate balance. When a person learns how one part of nature is balanced with another, understanding results.

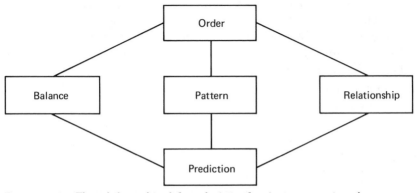

Figure 1–9 The philosophical foundation of science contains these five key ideas.

· **Pattern.** There are repeating cycles in pendulums and planets, in weather and tides, in elements and energy, in people, and plants. To discern a pattern in nature enhances understanding.

· **Relationship.** Weather is related to the rotation of the earth. The tides are related to the positions of the earth, sun, and moon. Throughout nature, one part appears related to others. When a person discovers a relationship, that person's understanding of nature is increased.

As you continue to explore science notice how often the foregoing ideas occur. In each of the three ideas resides the notion of predicability. If you know how factors are balanced, you can predict what will happen if one part is changed. If you know a pattern or cycle, you can predict changes or positions in the cycles. If you know about relationships among variables, you can predict one variable if the others are given.

PROCESSES OF SCIENCE

Recall now the definition of science by Duane Roller, "Science is the quest for knowledge, not the knowledge." How does this definition fit with the idea that "order alone is intelligible?" The answer is simply that "the quest" and "order" have a hand-in-glove relationship. Order in the form of generalizations, models to explain, and organizational schemes, such as classification and graphs, is the philosophy which provides meaningful direction to the quest—the search for order.

The quest is, therefore, the vital part of the hand-glove relationship. Without the quest, order alone is static or lifeless. The focus in science teaching, then, should be on the "quest" or "search." That is, the vital aspect of science is a process which is directed toward making natural phenomena intelligible. Stated very simply, *science is a process!*

The processes of science are those activities which scientists engage in the practice of science. You were involved in most if not all of the processes used by scientists when you did Activities One, Two, and Three. The processes you used were:

Observing
Measuring
Interpreting (or making sense of data)
Experimenting
Predicting
Model Building

These processes are essential for doing science and will be expanded in Chapter 6.

Observing and *measuring* are essential to the collection of information, or data collection. Without data, there is nothing to interpret.

Interpretation of data is essential to the search for patterns and relations. During interpretation, new ideas are invented.

Experimenting is essential to the collection of data through controlled observations and to the testing of patterns or relationships (ideas) gained through interpretation.

Predicting is essential to the testing of proposed ideas, such as generalizations, patterns, or relationships among variables. Prediction is the practical aspect of science. It is also the path used by scientists to gain confidence in their ideas. For example, if a prediction based on a pattern (generalization) or a model gives good results, the scientist increases in confidence and becomes more certain of having an understanding of that aspect of nature about which the prediction was made.

Model building is the most creative aspect of science. In model building, the scientist "sees" with the eye of mind what aspects or qualities of nature might exist so as to produce the pattern or relationships observed. Models of nature are essential because they allow one part of nature to be related to another. Models also allow scientists to ask questions that have no meaning without the model.

To engage in the full spectrum of science, a person must use all six of the above essential processes. A person can do legitimate science, however, without using all six processes. For example, Tycho Brahe, a renowned astronomer who can be found in many books on the history of science, focused on just one of the six processes of science—observing. Brahe spent several decades making observations and careful measurements of the position of Mars. Thus, when children in kindergarten and first grade focus on data collection, they are engaging in legitimate science. Another famous scientist, Johannes Kepler, focused on another part of the essential processes. He interpreted the data collected by Brahe. His interpretations led him to several famous ideas or generalizations about the motions of objects in the heavens. These ideas (patterns and generalizations) are known as Kepler's laws.

The great Isaac Newton explained the patterns (laws of nature) by creating a model to explain them: Gravity, the attraction of one object for another, is a model (or theory). Gravity can be used to explain why objects fall to the earth. The concept of gravity can be expanded to include the moon, the sun, and all other objects in the universe. Many aspects of nature can be related through the concept of gravity. When a teacher is developing or engaging in scientific activities with children, it is not imperative that each activity include all six essential processes.

PRODUCTS OF SCIENCE

The products of science are not television, radio, rockets, airplanes, refrigeration units, automobiles, and so forth. These objects are products of engineering. The products of science are the ideas used to help a person understand nature. These products include laws (generalizations or patterns describing part of nature) and explanations of nature using models or theories. The same processes used in achieving the products of science can be used to develop the products of engineering. Scientists explore what exists in nature, and engineers, using the findings of scientists, create things that did not previously exist in nature.

WHAT IS SCIENCE?

Although there are six essential processes in doing science, these processes are not necessarily used singly. They can be used in combination. Therefore, science can be described as taking place in the above six phases. The Chemical Education Material Study Group described the phases of doing science in this way:

> The scientist *accumulates information, organizes information and seeks regularities, wonders why regularities exist and attempts to explain them,* and *communicates ideas to others.*

We believe that the phases of doing science can be stated in three steps; this is our science model. The steps are: *Gathering Data, Getting the Idea,* and *Expanding the Idea.* This model allows a person to use all of the six processes or only those required for the immediate problem. Briefly, here is what each phase involves.

· Gathering Data. During this phase a person collects information about a particular aspect of nature. This phase could be called exploration. The data or information collected are organized into groups, serial orders, tables, histograms, or graphs. Appendix A explains each of these types of organization of data.

· Getting the Idea. This phase involves data interpretation. Seeing a relationship or generalization is "Getting the Idea." Summarizing a collection of intuitive ideas by inventing a concept or model is also included in this phase.

· Expanding the Idea. This phase involves testing patterns or models by prediction. It also involves searching for (discovering) ways in which a new concept or model is related to others. Experiments can be used to search for possible relationships.

The three step model described above is not only a model for doing science, it is also a model for teaching science. How this model can be used for teaching science will be a recurrent topic in the remainder of this book.

CASE STUDIES

To further expand your knowledge of what science is, we have included three case studies in Appendix A of this book. These case studies describe in considerable detail how three persons recognized by the scientific community as outstanding scientists participated in the quest for knowledge. These are not meant to be biographical sketches. They are intended to broaden, reinforce, and bring into focus the concept of doing science.

As you read the case studies, label the activities of the scientist using the three step model. In what part (or parts) of the process of doing science was the scientist Gathering Data? In what part was the scientist Expanding the Idea? Compare your labels with other students. Discuss any differences. Also, remember that no model is perfect—not even this one! A model is useful if it helps you to organize your ideas, or if it allows you to explain something or to ask questions that could not be asked without the model. We suggest that you stop at this point, turn to page 305 and read one, two, or all three case studies.

This chapter has been devoted to the development of a science model. This model, which emphasizes the quest or search for knowledge or understanding, is a process model. Chapter 2 relates this model of science to a model of educational purpose.

Chapter 2
Science and the Ability to Think

Americans today live in a very complex society. In addition to facing the basic problems of food, clothing, and shelter, they face the complex problems of environmental pollution and energy shortage. If these extremely complex problems are not solved, future generations of Americans will face an ever-decreasing standard of living and quality of life. But these are complex problems and do not have simple solutions. For example, as we impose stricter environmental standards, both employment and energy consumption can be affected. Other aspects of our society are also related in a like manner and these relationships must be analyzed and evaluated before changes are made.

Americans have an additional responsibility that citizens of some other countries do not have: Each citizen has the responsibility of government. Each citizen, through voice, vote, and actions is responsible for seeking solutions to the problems facing this country. This is not an easy task.

If American citizens are to participate effectively in solving present and future problems, the ability to think logically is imperative! And, of course, the institution which must accept the primary responsibility for accomplishing this task is the school. The primary responsibility of the schools in teaching logical thinking is not a new idea; it was suggested about two decades ago by the Educational Policies Commission of the National Education Association.[1] Large scale implementation of programs which aim specifically at the development of the ability to think logically is long overdue.

How does a person or school program aim toward the goal of logical thinking? The Education Policies Commission narrowed the target area somewhat when it said:

> The cultivated powers of the free mind have always been basic in achieving freedom. The powers of the free mind are many. In addition to the rational powers, there are those which relate to the aesthetic, the moral, and the religious. There is a unique, central role for the rational powers of an individual, however, for upon them depends his ability to achieve his personal goals and to fulfill his obligation to society.
>
> These powers involve the processes of recalling and imagining, classifying and generalizing, comparing and evaluation, analyzing and synthesizing, and deducing and inferring. These processes enable one to apply logic and the available evidence to his ideas, attitudes, and actions, and to better pursue whatever goals he may have.
>
> This is not to say that the rational powers are all of life or all of the mind, but they are the essence of the ability to think.[2]

To develop the ability to think, therefore, schools must aim directly at the target of rational power development!

THE ROLE OF SCHOOLS AND TEACHERS

Have teachers in the past not striven to develop the ability to think? If a person judges by the instructions which are given elementary school children, would that person perhaps conclude that "thinking" is a desirable activity in the classroom? One frequently hears such instructions as: "Now, think before you answer," or "Don't just give me the first answer that comes to your mind; think about the question for a time." The fact is, however, that teachers simply request logical thinking as if it is an innate ability rather than something to be developed.

The development of the ability to think will not be accomplished unless, and until, the school focuses on it. To date the success of any educational system in developing the individual's rational powers has been something less than spectacular. Here, then, are the specific guidelines which must guide our daily classroom teaching. The devel-

[1] Educational Policies Commission, *The Central Purpose of American Education*, Washington, D.C.: NEA, 1961.
[2] Ibid., p. 5.

opment of the individual rational powers within our pupils represents the specific objective toward which our teaching must be pointed. But how does a teacher use this specific objective?

Stating that anything our educational system achieves must be accomplished through the curriculum is almost prosaic. But, also, there can be little doubt as to the reality of the statement—curricula represent the tools with which the teacher has to work. These tools must be employed in a manner (methodology) which leads the learner to achieve the purpose for which the school has been established. Let us recognize, then, that the central role of the school is to develop in children the ability to think, and that curricula must be selected which will allow that responsibility to be discharged. In addition, methods of employing the proper curriculum must be used which will permit it to make its optimum contribution to the development of thinking ability. If we also accept the premise that the ability to think is defined by the rational powers, we then have specific criteria to guide us in selecting curricula, instructional techniques, and teaching materials.

When units of study are chosen, learning aids are secured, and classroom procedures are decided on, the rational powers represent an important and valuable standard against which to measure the potential effectiveness of these three educational components. Teaching materials and techniques that stuff the mind of the learner without giving him the opportunity to develop some of his rational powers are nearly valueless. Sometimes, the use of purely information-centered materials can be justified because they provide the learner with information which is "nice to know," or make an enjoyable experience possible. Many of the currently available motion pictures provide the learner with nice-to-know information and are fun to watch. School time spent on using such teaching materials can be justified because they provide a change of pace in a school day and can frequently be used as a culminating experience for a unit of study which has concentrated upon developing rationality. A teaching device, such as film, can pull together in a few minutes all of the information about a discipline which the learner will have acquired in a few weeks or months of investigation. The actual investigation provided the learner with the opportunity to develop his rational powers and gather a great deal of factual information; the film could easily review and summarize the findings of the investigation for him.

We must not, however, delude ourselves into thinking that providing factual-centered learning experiences about investigation substitutes for investigation itself. Our central responsibility is to lead the learners to develop their rational powers, and only actual investigatory experiences can do that. There is little doubt that 90 percent of the time of the school has frequently been spent upon the development of

10 percent of the rational powers (recall), whereas 10 percent of the time (if any time is spent at all) is devoted to the development of the other 90 percent of the rational powers. This type of activity in our schools cannot and will not produce citizens who have developed freedom of the mind. Possessing the ability to recall is important—extremely important—but recall cannot substitute for the other rational powers when a free mind is needed.

Saying that the central purpose of the school the development of the ability to think) represents the sole purpose, or that purpose to which the greatest priority is given, is to misunderstand the use of the term "central." The development of the learner's rational power is basic, or central, to the achievement of any other purposes which the school, society, or both may wish the learner to achieve. Regardless of what we wish the learner to achieve—selection of a vocation, deciding upon leisure-time activities, or understanding ones own civic responsibilities—that achievement will take place only to the degree to which the learner has developed his or her rational powers. The development of the ability to think, then, represents the unifying purpose (the common thread) which ties together all learning experiences provided by our educational establishment. If every teacher in every class in this country made the development of the ability to think central to teaching, the goals of modern education would be achieved and, because of the information that the learner would gather (in a meaningful way), the educational conservative would find less fault with our schools.

Since rational power development is the pathway that leads to logical thinking ability, perhaps we should explore in some depth what each rational power contributes to logical thinking. When a teacher understands how each rational power is utilized, then activities that focus on rational power development can be provided. The teacher is also then able to evaluate activities for their potential in developing rational power.

A large portion of the remainder of this chapter is devoted to activities and discussion of each of the ten rational powers. Do the activities—all of them if possible. If you do, you will be much better prepared to understand the value of science, properly taught, in the elementary school curriculum. Hopefully, you will also develop the idea that activities to develop rational powers do not have to be complex. Nor do they have to involve expensive or complicated materials.

THE RATIONAL POWERS

Some of the rational powers of the mind are relatively easy to separate from others for the purpose of discussion. Others of the rational powers are so intimately related and dependent upon one another that their separation is almost impossible. Also, there appear to be some patterns of use of some rational powers. Five of the rational powers appear to form a chainlike sequence in the logical thinking process. Those rational powers—and the sequence—are recalling, comparing, inferring, generalizing, and deducing. These rational powers will be discussed first.

The other rational powers do not appear to follow a single, linked relationship. They seem to be woven into the process of logical thinking to perform their special function when and as needed. These rational powers are classifying, analyzing, synthesizing, evaluating, and imagining. A discussion of those rational powers will be presented later.

Recalling

Perhaps the most fundamental and probably the most abused rational power is recall. To recall is to retrieve ideas that have been stored in the mind and bring them into conscious awareness. Without recall, no thinking is possible. And, as a matter of fact, recall functions as the base of all logical thinking and in the production of information. The description of objects and events depends on the ability to recall properly ideas used to describe and compare.

There are two reasons in the educational process for retrieving ideas. One reason is to pass the idea on to someone else—back to the teacher in many cases. The other is to use the idea—to enhance it or to relate it to other ideas, or to gain new ideas through it.

If the primary use of recall in the education process is to retrieve ideas to pass on to someone else, then recall is used much like obtaining something from a warehouse in which ideas are stored in bins. *This is cheap recall.* If the primary use of recall is to selectively retrieve ideas for use in thinking, then recall is used as a dynamic reservoir of ideas. *This is enriched recall.* To enrich recall, it must be used with other rational powers. In the educational process, recall is *least likely* to be enhanced through memorizing separate pieces of information to be repeated on cue. Recall is *most likely* to be enhanced by relating ideas about a subject to other ideas. The first use of recall focuses on cheap or simple recall. Have you ever been asked to fill in blanks to show how much you "learned?" That is what you will be doing in this activity.

ACTIVITY: CHEAP RECALL
Turn to page 26 and study Figure 2–1 for 2 minutes. Try to memorize as many details as you can. Then turn back to this page and answer the following questions.

    1. Did the person in picture one have on a helmet, a cap, or a hat?
    2. What was the person holding?

3. What kind of cycle was it?
4. Were there other cycles in the picture?
5. Was the person in the picture smiling?

If the mind were a muscle, this kind of exercise might be of some value. But since the mind is not a muscle, an enriched type of recall is needed. The following activity provides this type of enrichment.

ACTIVITY: ENRICHED RECALL
You have probably observed the sun rising many times already. (If not, you have missed a great experience. Do it!) Describe the sun as you remember it just as it rises above the horizon. How does the sun change in appearance and position as it rises higher into the sky?

Describe the appearance and position of the moon when it rises. How are the sun and moon alike as they rise? How are they different?

Stop here and compare the use of the rational power "recalling" in this example with the first. What did you have to recall to describe the appearance and positions of the sun and moon? How was recall essential to participation in this activity? Record your answers.

Comparing

The last recall activity (*Enriched Recall*) involved another rational power, comparing. Recalling and comparing form a linked pair of rational powers. They are perhaps the simplest and yet one of the most useful combinations. This combination allows new information to be produced and initiates the activity of processing information.

Next to recall, comparing is the rational power most often used. It is fundamental in producing information about an object or an event. If a person is limited only to recall, that person can do no productive thinking. But a person can extend learning from what the person already knows by matching similarities and differences. We describe objects, events, situations, and ideas by comparing them to other objects, events, situations, and ideas. We observe and describe changes in systems by comparing. We observe variation by comparing. In order for an educational program to promote the ability to think it must be rich in comparing experiences. Questions such as, "How are the objects or systems alike?" and, "How have the systems changed?" are valuable tools. Educational programs which focus entirely on enhancing recall are not contributing to their students' ability to think. But an educational program which links recall and comparison has at least started in the right direction.

Figure 2–1 See how many details of this picture you can memorize in two minutes. (Martin J. Lollar)

You are no doubt familiar with *standard units* for comparing objects, systems, or events. There are units of weight, volume, distance, time, and many others you can name. The heaviness of one object can be determined by comparing that object with the gram or kilogram weight. The length or width of an object can be described by comparing it with the meter. Colors, odors, hardness, texture, and all other properties are given by comparing with some standards. Using the rational power of comparing is a productive means of generating data— which is the working material of all other logical thought processes. There is another way in which we use comparing almost on a moment-by-moment basis. *We use it to tell when changes occur!* The next activity uses comparison in this way.

ACTIVITY: CHANGE
Examine the left picture in Figure 2–2. Has a change occurred in the room in the past 15 minutes? Can you tell?
    Now look at the picture on the right taken 15 minutes later. What changes have occurred? How can you tell?

ACTIVITY: STEEL AND WATER
In this activity you will observe a system. This system is shown in Figure 2–3. First, wet a piece of steel wool about the size of a marble.

Figure 2–2 These pictures were made of the same classroom. What changes do you observe? (Martin J. Lollar)

Push the wet steel into a test tube (a narrow jar such as the type in which olives or cherries are packed in can be used instead of a test tube). Invert the test tube in a glass one third full of water (see Figure 2–3). The air in the test tube should keep the water out.

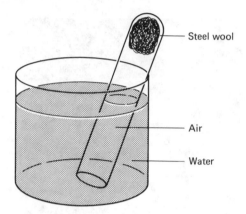

Steel wool

Air

Water

Figure 2–3   Is interaction taking place in this system? What is your evidence?

Make a sketch of the system as soon as you have it set up. Then leave the system for 24 hours. Make another sketch of the system and compare it with the first sketch. What changes have taken place? Wait another 24 hours and again compare. Describe the changes.

What evidence is there that an interaction is taken place in the system? An interaction occurs when one object does something to another. If there is an interaction taking place, what is happening?

Next, break the activity you just completed into parts. Which parts of the activity were recalling? Which parts of the activity were comparing? What else did you need to do to answer the questions about an interaction?

Inferring

In the two preceding activities you made comparisons, but you also used another rational power during each activity. That rational power was inferring. Inferring is the rational power used immediately after information is collected or confronted. This rational power has to do with the first seed of an idea regarding a pattern or trend; it is the rational power which initiates limited explanations which can later become more general and abstract. Inferring is the explanation of a single action or event in a larger collection of actions and events.

Suppose you place a piece of cheese on a mousetrap near a hole in the wall. The next morning the cheese is gone. You might explain this by saying, "A mouse probably took it." This is a probable explanation of what happened. It is, of course, not the only logical explanation. Another person might have removed it. You did not see the action take place but the explanation "a mouse took it" is reasonable. Notice that the setting under which the activity took place influences the inference. If the cheese had been placed in a tall jar, it would probably be unlikely that you would infer that a mouse took the cheese. Of course, you could place more cheese on the trap and observe to see if a mouse came to take it.

Since logical inference is the first small leap of the mind toward explaining data, it is, or should be, widely used; it should be an integral part of almost every educational activity. The next six activities involve the rational power of inferring. As a teacher, you should allow your students many opportunities to use the power of inferring every day. These activities will suggest to you how simply this can be done. You probably will not use these particular activities to teach inferring, but many hundreds of others come as a natural part of many lessons.

ACTIVITY: READING A PICTURE
Observe Figure 2–4 carefully. What inferences could you make about the persons in the picture?

Figure 2–4   What inferences can you make from this picture?

ACTIVITY: READING AN AERIAL PHOTOGRAPH
Look at Figure 2–5. What inferences can you make?

ACTIVITY: READING A HAND
Have someone select a person to stand behind the door in a closet and hold only one hand and arm outside. Examine the hand. What inferences can you make about the person from the person's hand?

ACTIVITY: READING TRACKS LEFT BY BALLS
To do this activity you will first need to collect some data using these materials: 1 sheet of pencil carbon paper, 2 or 3 steel balls such as ball bearings, and 3 or 4 sheets of white paper.

Place the pencil carbon paper over a sheet of white paper with the carbon side next to the paper. Lay the two sheets of paper on a table with the carbon paper on top. Roll the steel ball across the carbon paper, then examine the track of carbon on the white sheet. Repeat this several times. See if you can determine the direction the ball travels across the sheet of paper from the appearance of the track.

Use different size steel balls. See what difference that makes.

Roll two steel balls at the same time and let them collide. Examine this track.

Figure 2–5 What do you think happened here?

Now look at the three tracks shown in Figures 2–6, 2–7, and 2–8 on pages 32–34. Explain each track using inferences.

ACTIVITY: READING AN EVENT IN A CLOUD CHAMBER
Figure 2–9 is a picture of a cloud chamber. A piece of radioactive material, such as radium, is enclosed in the chamber, which is filled with nitrogen gas and water vapor. What can you infer from the vapor trails in the chamber?

ACTIVITY: READING HISTOGRAMS
Inferences can be made from organized data. The histograms below show the amounts of food eaten by three persons, A, B, and C, at an evening meal (see Figure 2–10).
What inferences can you make from the amounts of each food eaten by persons A, B, and C?

Generalizing

Generalizing is an important rational power and generalizations are born from inferences. While an inference is limited in scope and generally applies to a specific action or event, a generalization takes into account a broader range of events and actions. As a very simple example, suppose a person has observed that a baseball bat, a log, and a table leg will burn. The person might infer that the objects burn because they are round and made of wood. Tests of other round objects, some of wood and others of glass and metal, would allow the person to conclude that indeed other round wooden objects do burn but round objects made of other materials do not.

If wooden objects with shapes other than round are investigated, they too are found to burn. The rational power of generalizing can now be used. The person can make the generalization "all wooden objects burn." Notice that the generalization takes in the class of all objects made of wood, even those of shapes and kinds of wood that the investigator has not used. The generalization can be tested. That is, other objects made of wood can be tested to see if they actually do burn. But there still exists the possibility that an object made of wood might exist somewhere that will not burn. Testing can verify or increase the confidence in a generalization but does not prove it "true" even if the tests are positive.

Hypothesizing is a term that is sometimes used for generalizing. In fact, it is quite difficult to determine where hypothesizing ends and generalizing begins. Some people have the idea, and we cannot refute it, that they are essentially the same thing. Others say that a generalization is a product of hypothesizing. In any case, there is an extremely close relationship between the two. Very often an investigator will

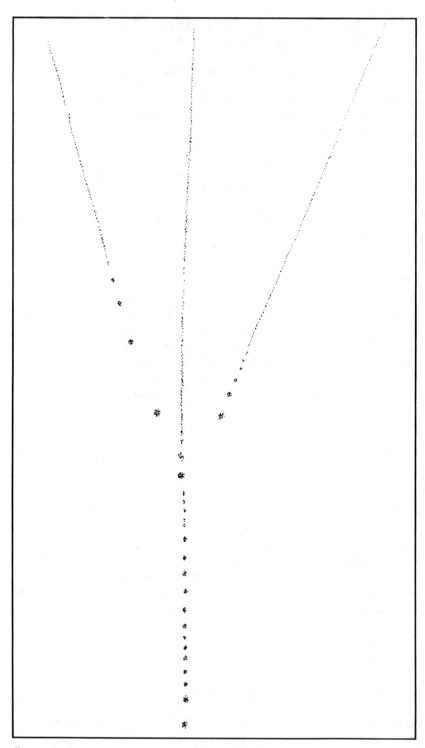

Figure 2–6

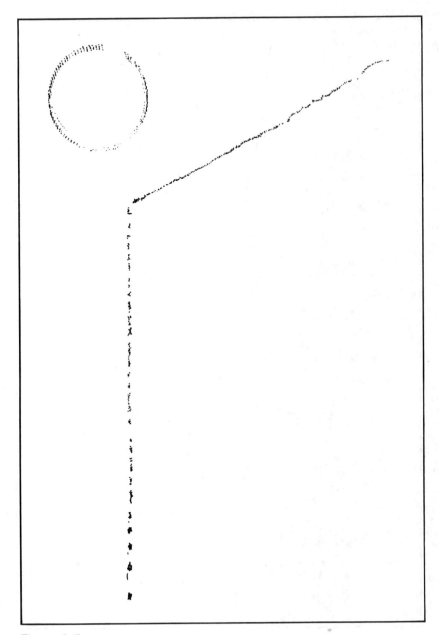

Figure 2–7

propose several possible patterns or generalizations that could exist. These tentative generalizations guide further experimentation and are usually referred to as hypotheses. Hypothesizing is not listed as a rational power: we will, therefore, use the term generalizing when describing the ability to hypothesize.

In the following activity, you will collect some information, make

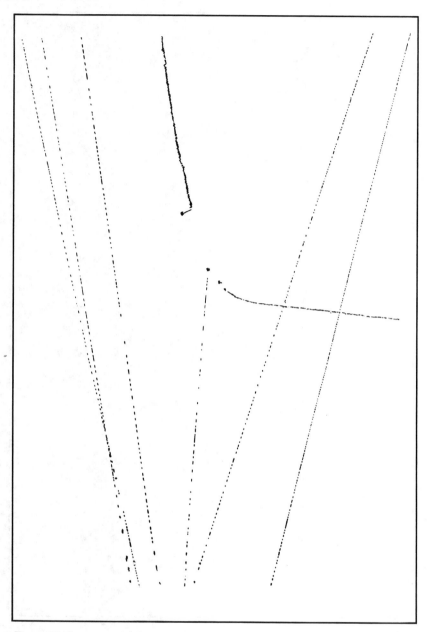

Figure 2–8

inferences, and then generalize. Notice the pattern of use of the rational powers.

ACTIVITY: A MAP
Look at a large map of the United States and locate ten or twelve large rivers. Next make a sketch of the United States showing the rivers.

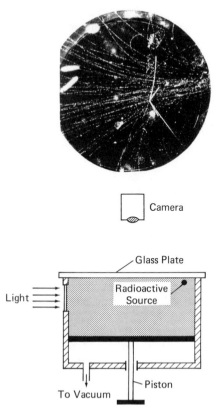

Figure 2-9 SOURCE: John W. Renner and Harry B. Packard, *Investigations in Physics,* Lyons and Carnahan, Chicago, 1974, p. 586.

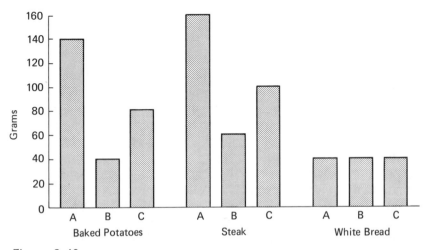

Figure 2-10

Consult a reference, such as an encyclopedia, to find the direction the water flows in two or three of the rivers you selected. What inferences can you make about the movement of water in the rivers in your sample?

Find the direction of water flow in several different rivers. Then make a generalization about the direction of flow of rivers in the United States. Then test it. How will you test your generalization?

If someone locates a river in the Eastern half of the United States that you have not included in your sample or group, predict in which general direction the water will flow. How good was your generalization?

ACTIVITY: CIRCLES
A generalization can be stated in words, such as "all forces come in pairs." Generalizations can also be stated using symbols, such as $\frac{V}{P} = k$. This is called an equation. Try to state the generalization in this activity with circles, using an equation.

Measure the circumference, the distance around, and the diameter (the distance across) of several circular objects. You may use the objects listed in Figure 2–11 or others about the same size. Make all measurements in centimeters.

Divide the circumference of each circle by its diameter. Place the number you get as a dividend in the third column. What pattern do you see? Make a generalization that you believe will be valid about circles. State the generalization as a mathematical equation.

Suppose you see a large storage tank such as those in which oil is stored. You measure the circumference of the tank but you cannot measure its diameter. The circumference of the tank is 6000 centimeters. Use your generalization to determine the diameter of the tank. Using a generalization to find a particular or specific value is kown as *deduction,* another of the rational powers.

Deducing

Deducing is reversing the direction of one's thinking and using a generalization to predict or deduce a specific outcome or value. *Inductive* thinking or reasoning is reasoning from the specific (one value or idea) to a general rule. Using the rule that has been derived from inductive reasoning to find a specific value or idea is deduction. Most mathematics courses emphasize deduction.

There are many generalizations in all areas of knowledge. A generalization about nature which has wide acceptance and application is sometimes called a law. Sometimes generalizations from which deductions are made are called principles. The following activity will require you to use at least the five rational powers already discussed.

Object	Diameter	Circumference	C/D (This means divide the circumference by the diameter.)
Coffee Can			
Automobile Steering Wheel			
Drinking Glass			
Plate			
Saucer			
Ring			
Barrel			
Small Can			
Bicycle Tire			

Figure 2–11   What general pattern is evident from the data about circles?

ACTIVITY: HEARTBEAT RATE

Table 2–1 lists the heart rates of several *adult* animals. First, make an estimate of the weight of each animal and enter this in the table. Now examine the data in the table. Compare the weights and heartbeat rates of the animals. Then record any inferences that you make.

Table 2–1   TABLE OF HEARTBEAT RATES

ANIMAL	WEIGHT	HEARTBEATS PER MINUTE
Dog		100
Pig		70
Cow		50
Cat		180
Mouse		610
Whale		15
Horse		45
Squirrel		390

State a pattern or generalization relating heartbeat rate to the weight of an animal. Find some information about one or more animals that are not in the table. How well do their weights and heart rates follow the generalization you made?

Make a graph of the heartbeat rate of each animal in Table 2–1 and others you have found and the weight in grams of the animals (see Figure 2–12). Refer to Appendix 2 if you need to know how to make a graph.

A person can of course make inferences, generalizations, and deductions about data someone else has collected and organized, but following the sequence through many activities is very important for children in elementary school. Graphs and tables are very useful techniques for organizing information. Explain the pattern shown by the graph you made relating heart beat to weight.

Deduce from the graph (generalization) the number of times a human's heart should beat each minute. How good is your deduction compared to accepted values for the human heartbeat rate? According to the pattern (generalization) about heartbeat rates, what do you deduce about the heartbeat rate of adult male and adult female humans? The ability to collect information, state generalizations, and make predictions based on generalizations represents an important and significant portion of logical thinking.

The next five rational powers introduced do not necessarily fit into a sequential pattern in their use. Also, they can be used in many places either alone or in conjunction with other rational powers.

Classifying

When a person makes a systematic arrangement of objects, events, or ideas into groups or categories according to some established criteria,

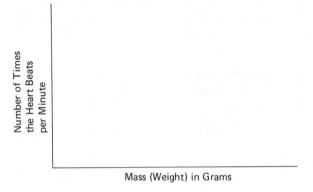

Figure 2–12   Make a graph from the data in Table 2–1. Label your graph like this.

that activity is called classifying. The rational power of classifying is one which often makes using the other rational powers easier. A collection of pieces of information or objects is much easier to use if the parts which are alike have been separated or organized into groups. Also, storage and retrieval of information through recall is made more efficient through classification.

A classification scheme is a kind of multiple generalization. Thus deductions can be made from it. For example, if a person knows the criteria used in the classification of animals and is told a particular animal is an insect, a certain set of properties about the animal is automatically given.

The simplest classification is simple grouping: that is, placing sets of objects, events, and ideas into two or more groups. Humans are grouped as male and female. Elements are grouped as metals and nonmetals. Foods can be grouped as meats, vegetables, fruits, and beverages. Money can be grouped into coins and bills. Of course, the group can be subdivided into subgroups based on criteria that are established. As criteria and subgroups are established, a classification scheme evolves. There are usually several ways to classify a collection of objects. There is nothing sacred about any one classification scheme, even the one used by biologists to classify plants and animals.

If the rational power of classification is to be developed and utilized to its fullest, activities which encourage and employ classification must be used. Children should classify the same collection of objects in different ways using different criteria. The following activities should suggest to you how frequently we use classification every day.

ACTIVITY: CLASSIFICATION OF COINS
Work in a group of three or four persons. Pool the coins from your pocket or purse. Then decide on the criteria you will use to classify the coins. After you classify the coins using one scheme, think of another and use it.

ACTIVITY: GENERAL CLASSIFICATION IN USE
Think about a grocery store. Then try to reconstruct the classification scheme used by the store. What are the major groups? What subgroups can be placed under these major groups? Continue each part of the scheme until you can list individual items such as fresh corn on the cob.

Repeat the activity for a variety store, a clothing store, a library, and a school. Compare your classification scheme to those developed by others in the class.

Analyzing

To analyze is to separate and examine components. A sample of matter is analyzed to determine what substances are present and in what amounts. A speech or article is analyzed to determine the major points and the relative amounts of emphasis on each point. A curriculum is analyzed to determine what educational elements are present and the relative importance of each element. A social situation can be analyzed to find what pressures or influences are present and what is their effect on those present. To some extent, analysis also involves the idea of grouping or classifying, but the grouping is usually for the purpose of establishing relationships between or among categories.

Teachers frequently analyze tests to determine what types of questions are asked. Tests often reveal the real purpose of a teacher or a program. For example, if a test contains many cheap recall type questions, the teacher is interested in stocking the mind with information that can be recalled to present to someone. On the other hand, open-ended, or divergent questions, or questions which allow the student to use rational powers, indicate an orientation by the teacher toward developing the ability to think.

Analyzing should be used in curriculum development to plan activities. Suppose a teacher wishes to help a child develop a particular concept or skill. The teacher should analyze the skill or concept to determine what components it contains. This is called task analysis. Learning the skill of swimming might be resolved into such components as shown in Figure 2–13.

The following activity is designed to introduce you to the use of analysis in curriculum planning.

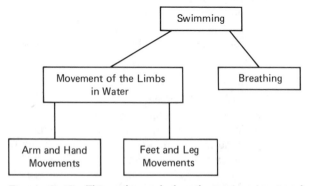

Figure 2–13   This scheme helps the swimming teacher decide where to start and how the components should be fitted together into a logical sequence.

ACTIVITY: PLANNING A LEARNING ACTIVITY
Suppose you wish to teach children to measure the length of objects using the metric system. Begin by separating the skill into components. Then decide what relationship each component has to others and fit them into a scheme. You may use Figure 2–14 to help you think of a starting place. Which part of the plan will you implement first?

> Analyzing is a rational power that is almost totally neglected in most elementary school programs. Think of an activity that would allow a child to use this rational power. Ask others for their ideas so that you can develop a larger reservoir of ideas to use in teaching analyzing.

Imagining

Suppose someone is telling you about a person they met on a weekend vacation. As the person is discussed, a mental image of the person forms in your mind. This forming of a mental image of something (or someone in this case) not actually present is called imagining. Often the mental image formed is quite different from the person you see later.

Imagination is linked with another rational power, *synthesizing,* to produce the most creative aspects of thinking—art, poetry, literature, music, architecture and design, and model building in science. Of course, the creativity is not in viewing, listening, or feeling. The creativity is in the doing! To use and develop the rational power of creativity, a person must be involved in writing poetry, music or literature, building models to explain nature, designing a garment or a building, or another related activity.

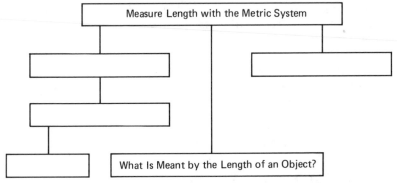

Figure 2–14   Analyzing is an important part of teaching.

Synthesizing

When you are putting parts together to form a meaningful whole you are using the rational power of synthesizing. This is what the designer does to create a new garment. This is what the architect does in creating a building design. This is what the scientist does to create a model to explain some aspect of nature.

Many of the drugs to combat disease, the fabrics from which clothes are made, and the materials from which furniture is made have actually been created, since they do not occur naturally, by persons who imagined the parts and put them together in a logical whole. Also, models such as the sketches so often shown of atoms are created through imagination and synthesis. The following activities are simple but important types of synthesis. They also illustrate the broad area of the application of the natural power of synthesis.

ACTIVITY: DAILY ACTIVITY MODEL
Examples of imagination and synthesis most commonly encountered are organizing ideas or plans. Imagine your average school or working day as a cycle of activities. Think about each activity and what part of the 24-hour cycle it is. Next, make a circle and fit the parts (your activities) into it in wedge shaped pieces. How large will each wedge of the circle be?

When this activity is accomplished, you will have synthesized a model of your daily activities. You could, of course, make the model more detailed by showing how the pieces of each wedge are distributed and when each activity occurs.

ACTIVITY: PLANNING AN EXPERIMENT
When a pattern or generalization has been stated, the generalization is usually tested by doing an experiment. But an experiment must be designed. First the experimental idea must be imagined and then the actions or parts of the experiment must be fitted together. In other words, a whole is synthesized from its parts. The person planning the experiment must take into account the variables and decide which will be held constant or controlled. Planning and implementing experiments requires the use of both imagination and synthesis.

You have, no doubt, heard television advertisements concerning dishwashing liquids, each claiming their product is the best. Usually a dishwashing liquid is judged on the basis of how much grease or oil it will remove. Discuss how you could design an experiment to test several of the top brands of dishwashing liquid.

ACTIVITY: A FRIEND MODEL
What are the intellectual and social qualities you admire most in a person? What traits must a person have to allow you to feel comfortable

in that person's company? What factors about a person's appearance make you want to share experiences with that person? Take the parts and synthesize a friend model!

The last rational power to be discussed is one that you should use in all aspects of the educational program. You should *evaluate* your curriculum, the children you teach, and yourself.

Evaluating

Evaluation is a type of comparison. It is comparison to some predetermined value or to certain performance criteria. When you took your examination to obtain your driver's license, your performance on certain predetermined tasks was compared to a minimum-performance model. Steering, parking, backing, signaling, and braking were all a part of the criteria.

ACTIVITY: PERFORMANCE CRITERIA
Tell how each of the following might be evaluated. What criteria would you use?

1. A person who seeks employment as a stenographer.
2. Someone who wants to play a violin in an orchestra.
3. A football player.
4. Toothpaste.
5. Razor blades.
6. Tires.
7. Clothing.

A relatively common type of evaluation in education is based on behavioral objectives. The teacher or curriculum developer determines what behavior will indicate that the desired learning has taken place. Then the performance criteria are established. A teacher evaluates student achievement on the stated objective. For example, suppose the goal or objective is the following.

Objective The student will be able to measure the length of objects with a meter stick.

Acceptable performance level The student will make measurements correct to the nearest centimeter eight times out of ten trials.

Many educators believe that stating all learning outcomes behaviorally is too restrictive. What do you think about this? How will you decide?

In science, evaluation is in almost continuous use. Measurements are evaluated to determine if they meet the required degree of accuracy or precision. Generalizations are evaluated to determine whether deductions or predictions made are valid. Models are evaluated to see how well they explain.

If you believe, as we do, that the development of the ability to think should be central in American education, then you should evaluate all curriculum activities to determine their potential for rational power development. Alter the activities in a lesson if necessary to allow rational power use. Almost all curriculum areas provide opportunities for rational power development. How you, the teacher, use the opportunities available will determine the extent of your success. Of course, some curriculum areas are richer in opportunities to develop the entire spectrum of rational powers.

SCIENCE AND THE RATIONAL POWERS

In Chapter 1 you explored the dual nature of science. You found that on the one hand, science is a dynamic reservoir of "best yet" explanations of natural phenomena. On the other hand, science is the process of exploring and explaining natural phenomena. If the primary goal of teaching science is to help children become acquainted with what scientists have found out about nature (products of science), then teaching techniques which transmit information are the ones to use. The pupils would read about science, listen to lectures and view films about science, and perhaps view some demonstrations. At best, pupils will become involved in the use of two rational powers, recalling and comparing. There certainly would be little need to involve analyzing, deducing, inferring, generalizing, classifying, synthesizing, evaluation or imagining.

As you can see, science taught with the principal emphasis on transmitting information has little value in developing the full spectrum of rational powers required in logical thinking. In fact, if a course is taught in which students only read about science, or watch demonstrations, or view films, or listen to the teacher, we would not call it science at all. Perhaps it would be interesting information but it would not be science. Of course, science deals with content about natural phenomena. But the mental activities involved in searching for patterns and explanations are not only an essential aspect of science: they are, educationally speaking, the most important aspect. If a person learns about science, that person has an interesting body of knowledge to recall. If a person learns to do science, that person has learned to produce new knowledge. The person has *learned how to learn!*

When a person *does* science, that person involves the rational powers of *recalling and comparing* to produce data or information. The data are *classified*. Then the rational power of *inferring* is used to seek patterns or *generalizations*. *Deductions* (predictions) are made based on the generalizations. An experiment is *imagined* to test the predictions. The experiment and the results are *analyzed* and *evaluated*. An explanation of the patterns is *synthesized*.

As you can see, if children learn science by becoming involved in the process, the full spectrum of rational powers is in continuous use. This method of teaching science is called "inquiry teaching." You will learn much more about teaching by inquiry in Chapter 4. When it is taught by inquiry, science is an excellent vehicle for developing the rational powers. The children get opportunities to use the rational powers separately and in combination as they are used naturally in problem solving.

Teaching science as a form of investigation demands that all of the children in the classroom make individual inquiries. They must be placed in a situation where they will have to observe some type of experimental situation and interpret their observations as they see them. In short, the learners must be allowed to inquire in their own unique ways. When an individual conducts an inquiry, it is usually done so as to find out something that individual does not know. This is exactly the manner in which the word "inquiry" must be interpreted when it is applied to learning. The inquiries of elementary school children are not expected to discover something new to the world—only something new to the child. As you might suspect, the teacher has an important and unique role in an inquiry-centered learning situation. That role will be considered in Chapter 5. For the present it is sufficient to say that if the discipline of science is to be used to develop the rational powers of children, it must be taught by a method that fosters inquiry (the structure of the discipline of science).

THE OBJECTIVES OF ELEMENTARY SCHOOL SCIENCE

From what has been said in Chapter 1 and in this chapter, three objectives of elementary school science can be synthesized.[3] Since science is a natural vehicle to use to develop the learner's powers, the first objective of elementary school science can be stated as: *To develop in the learner a command of the rational powers*. From what has been said about the relationship between inquiry and rational-power development, you have probably concluded that using inquiry fosters rational-power development and that the systematic use of the rational powers

---

[3] Donald G. Stafford *et al.*, "Wings for a Dinosaur," *BIOS*, October 1970, pp. 114–119.

is inquiry. The second purpose of elementary school science, therefore, is: *To develop in the student the ability and confidence to inquire.* But the vehicle of science must use subject matter to accomplish these objectives. Thinking and learning do not happen in a vacuum; we think with facts, notions, and ideas. In selecting the curriculum that will allow the learner to develop his ability to think, the notion that learning takes place in terms of those things with which we are already familiar must be kept in mind. This immediately tells us that the content of science selected for study should be related in some way to the learner's environment and those factors which affect that environment. There are, of course, times during the pupil's education when he must, in order to develop an understanding of the environment, become acquainted with ideas not directly obtainable from his immediate, direct experiences. These ideas or concepts help the pupil develop a structure into which new information can be stored and interpreted and from which information can be retrieved. Karplus summarizes these content notions from the teaching frame of reference.

> Two aspects of the teaching program should be distinguished from one another: The experiential (student experience with a wide variety of phenomena . . .) and the conceptual (introduction of the student to the approach which modern scientists find useful in thinking about phenomena they study).[4]

A thorough acquaintance with the learner's own environment will give the learner a much better experienial background for stretching the imagination, later in the educational program, up to the far reaches of the universe and down to the realm of the atom. The third principal objective, then, which can be listed for elementary school science is: *To develop an understanding of the changing nature of the environment in terms of matter, life, energy, and their interaction.*

Many other objectives for elementary science teaching could be listed. Examples of these are: To develop scientific literacy; to develop scientific attitude and open-mindedness; and to develop skill in the use of the methods and processes of science. These are perfectly good, sound objectives. If, however, you study the three general objectives just described, you will discover that these objectives will be accomplished if the three general objectives are achieved.

So far in our discussion of elementary school science, we have considered the discipline of science and the purpose for which the institution in which it will be taught—the school—exists. We have seen that science in its most refined form is an intellectual process and

---

[4] Robert Karplus, "Three Guidelines for Elementary School Science," *SCIS Newsletter,* no. 20, Spring 1971, University of California at Berkeley.

that the schools must concentrate on developing the rational powers of the free mind (intellectual ability). Science, we have demonstrated, is a natural and logical curriculum vehicle to use in leading the learner to develop the ability to think, and, in addition, the inquiry experiences provided can lead the learner to understand a great deal about the learner's environment.

There is, however, still one element of the content-teaching-learning enterprise which has not been considered. That element is the child! Are the learning experiences that the study of science can provide, even though they will lead a learner to develop rational powers, proper experiences for young children to have? (Remember, we are concerned here with children from kindergarten through the sixth grade.) In other words, are science and children "right" for each other? To be able to answer that question, we must briefly refresh ourselves on the fundamental characteristics of children. Those characteristics will be explored in the next chapter.

Chapter 3
Children Learning Science

What goes on within children's minds when they learn a scientific principle? Actually, that question can be asked in a more general way: What goes on within children's minds when they learn anything? No one has ever observed the activities, changes, or both taking place in the nervous system while learning is going on. What is believed about learning, therefore, comes from theories that have been constructed about it. These theories are usually the result of the experiences the theorizer has had plus the theorizer's own personal feelings.

When a theory is used to guide actions and activities—such as a curriculum in a school—those actions and activities are said to be *theory-based*. That simply means that all the actions and activities have been constructed on the belief that the theory is true. If, of course, the actions and activities produce results that do not support the theory, then using the theory as a basis for designing actions and activities must be reconsidered. In other words the *theory-base* for what is going on must be reexamined.

You know, for example, that when you drop an object it falls. You probably also know that the reason for this is said to be gravity. No one has ever *seen* gravity; it is a theory. An airplane pilot knows that the theory of gravity must be relied on if the airplane being flown is to be returned safely to earth. That pilot's activities, therefore, are carried out on the theory-base that gravity exists.

Suppose you released a ball from your hand and instead of falling down, it traveled sideways—that is, parallel to the surface of the earth. Would that discrepant event prove that the world can no longer operate on the theory-base that gravity makes objects fall downwards? Maybe. But much more data would be needed before that drastic step could be taken. What the gravitational theory-base provided was a way to look at the event (a frame of reference) of the ball going sideways. That would cause us to say that the event we are observing should not be happening. In other words, a theory-base not only allows its user to construct actions and activities to implement it but it also provides a frame of reference to allow that user to evaluate the results of the implementation.

When childrens' learning is considered there is more than one theory that can be used. This book is, in general, based upon a *cognitive* theory-base for learning. That theory-base is concerned with the *mental processes* involved in knowing; these processes include perception, imagery, reasoning, and so on. Specifically, this book is based upon the theory of the Swiss psychologist-epistemologist Jean Piaget. He and his associates have been studying the development of cognitive processes in children (and publishing their findings) since the 1920s, and have accumulated the greatest amount of data that exists in that field. Keep in mind that Piaget's theory is basically cognitive and is essentially a model of intelligence. In fact, Piaget has stated[1] that the basic aim of his work has been "to explain the development of intelligence and to comprehend how from elementary forms of cognition superior levels of intelligence and scientific thinking came about. . . ." Frequently the theory of Piaget has been said to be a model of *Intellectual development,* which it is. Do not confuse the intelligence that concerns Piaget with that which is measured by an I.Q. test. Piaget has in mind intelligence that directs our interaction with our surroundings and those persons and things in it. He is concerned with the development of the entire intellect.

PART 1—BUILDING MENTAL STRUCTURES

A Model of Intelligence

In the last chapter you found that the central purpose of the school is to teach children to think, that is—to use their rational powers. But in

---

[1] Jean Piaget, Foreword to: Hans G. Furth, *Piaget & Knowledge: Theoretical Foundations,* Englewood Cliffs, N.J.: Prentice-Hall, 1969, p. vii.

order to think, the learner must think about something. If, for example, children are to learn how to use the rational power of comparison, they must have two or more objects, events, or situations to compare. But while comparing, not only will children learn something about the rational power of comparison, they will also have learned something about whatever is being compared. Data from the environment[2] will have been gathered by the learner.

Suppose you asked a six-year-old to compare two automobiles. The child would probably compare their sizes, colors, and other properties which are obvious to a child of that age. A sixteen-year-old may talk to you about tire size, speed, engine size and other properties the six-year-old had not mentioned. Suppose you had next asked a mechanic to compare the same two automobiles; you would probably get a completely new set of comparisons.

Each of the three persons observed the same two automobiles: why would they compare different properties? The obvious answer is that the three persons were concerned about, or attended to, different properties. But different properties were seen because each of these persons had different mental abilities, procedures, and/or systems to use in processing the data received from the environment. The notion of how data from the environment are processed is central to the theory of Piaget.

From birth each of us develops mental processes to use in dealing with incoming data from the environment. Piaget calls these mental data-processing procedures *mental structures,* which get more and more complex as we grow older. In other words, as children grow older they can process more and more complex data from the environment. That explains why the child, the adolescent, and the adult would probably give different and increasingly complex comparisons when observing two automobiles.

Mental-structure building probably begins at birth, but the early structures built are very simple. When a baby looks at a toy and picks it up, that baby can now do that with any object that he or she can grasp and lift. A system for looking-grasping-and-picking-up has been established. This system is, of course, a small mental structure, which Piaget calls a *scheme.* The quality of the early developing schemes are undoubtedly dependent upon the quality of the nervous system we inherited from our parents. Notice, however, that the scheme of the baby included the stimulus (looking) and all of the other processes

---

[2] The term "environment" is used as an umbrella term in this chapter to mean whatever the learner is involved with at a particular moment. Thus an infant's input data might come from a rattle while a third grader's data might come from a frog. Both are represented here by the term "environment."

that led to the complete act. A scheme, according to Piaget,[3] is "whatever is repeatable and/or generalizable." As a child grows older and older more and more schemes are constructed, which eventually become integrated with each other and form structures because a "'scheme' is a generic unit of structure."[4] That is, the basic unit of the structure is the scheme.

As more and more cognitive mental structures are built, more and more data from the environment can be incorporated into them. The process of incorporating data into existing structures is known as *assimilation*. The teacher must keep in mind that only the learners themselves can assimilate incoming data from the environment; no one can do it for them. The learner must experience the hardness of a brick, watch mealworms go through a life cycle, or observe a lens form an image. Then and only then does assimilation take place. *Giving a child information does not lead to assimilation.*

No doubt any data are changed by the structures which assimilate them, just as food, for example, is changed when it is digested by the body. Now if the incoming data are changed by a learner's structures, the understanding of those data may be different from the environment which delivered them, and possibly erroneous. Not infrequently, however, the learner is aware that what has been assimilated is not being understood. Perhaps a helpful way to think about such an event is that a *mismatch* has occurred between the cognitive structures of the learner and what has been assimilated. The learner is now in a state of *disequilibrium*.

Just as structures can change the input from the environment, the input can also cause structures to change. The disequilibrium caused by the mismatch of input and mental structures can cause new schemes to be built, structures to be modified, combined, or both, or new structures to be constructed. This entire process of the adjustment or change of mental structures is called *accommodation* and is brought about by the existence of disequilibrium. But when structures have been adjusted to accommodate the new inputs (or intrusions) from the environment, the learner has once again reached a stage of equilibrium.

Describe a situation in which you made an assimilation and found yourself in disequilibrium. What did you do to put yourself back in equilibrium?

---

[3] Jean Piaget, "Genetic Epistemology," *Columbia Forum,* Fall, 1969, p. 5.
[4] John L. Phillips, Jr., *The Origin of Intellect: Piaget's Theory,* 2nd ed., San Francisco: Freeman, 1975, p. 12.

The procedure, therefore, by which mental structures are revised is the process of equilibration (see Figure 3–1). The revised mental structures make possible assimilations that were not possible before. Therefore, the child can now accomplish learning that could not have been accomplished before the new and/or revised structures were present. This entire *process* is diagrammed in Figure 3–1. But remember that the new learning depends upon accommodation which is the result of disequilibrium, but disequilibrium is caused by assimilation. In the truest sense, therefore, without assimilation there is no accommodation and no new learning. Remember also, however, that the impetus which promotes accommodation is disequilibrium.

Teachers must be aware that the key to the entire process of bringing about disequilibrium is assimilation, which must be done by the child—no one can do this except the learner. (Piaget has frequently[5] used *self-regulation* as a descriptor of equilibrium.) When the theory-base of Piaget is used to develop a view of the responsibilities of a teacher involved in promoting learning, the first of those responsibilities is to involve the learner in an assimilation that will cause disequilibrium. Do not attach to disequilibrium a meaning that *in any way* reflects something undesirable. *Disequilibrium does not mean frustration.* In fact, a good portion of the responsibility of a teacher using the theory-base of Piaget revolves around insuring that

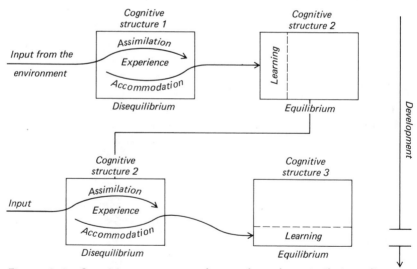

Figure 3–1   Cognitive structures change through assimilation, disequilibrium, and accommodation.

[5] Piaget, Foreword to: *Piaget & Knowledge,* op. cit., p. vi.

disequilibrium *does not* degenerate to frustration. That point will be reconsidered in Chapter 7.

Assimilation and accommodation cause a change in the mental structures of the learner. That change represents an *adaptation* of the learner to the inputs received from the environment. But adaptation is accomplished only "when there is equilibrium between accommodation and assimilation."[6] The learner has found, according to Piaget, an "accord of thought with things."[7] A learner making an adaptation and putting thought in accord with things—inputs from the environment—is certainly at least a part of learning.

But no thought exists in our cognitive structures by itself. Every adaptation which results from assimilation and accommodation is always related to all other adaptations—which resulted in structures—made earlier. In other words the new structure is placed among all the other structures in some type of mental-structure *organization*. An obvious definition for organization is the relationships that exists between a new mental structure and previous mental structures. Piaget defines organization as the "accord of thought with itself."[8]

Explain why organization and adaptation are complementary processes.

Earlier the point was made that the impetus that promotes mental structure construction and reconstruction is disequilibrium. But disequilibrium was *caused* by assimilation and *causes* accommodation. In other words, in Piaget's theory, equilibrium is dynamic—not static. It is consistently being caused or causing. In addition, as disequilibrium diminishes, the newly constructed and/or reconstructed structures become more and more stable, and we begin to see inconsistencies and gaps in them that were not seen before. These gaps and inconsistencies are perhaps what lead us to say "yes, but . . . ." after we believe a new concept has been mastered. The "yes, but . . . ." response can cause a new assimilation which can produce a new disequilibrium. Phillips explains the entire process in this way:

> Each equilibrium state, therefore, carries with it the seeds of its own destruction, for the child's activities are thenceforth directed toward reducing those inconsistencies and closing the gaps.[9]

---

[6] Jean Piaget, *The Origins of Intelligence in Children*, New York: Norton, 1963, p. 7.
[7] Ibid., p. 8.
[8] Ibid., p. 8.
[9] Phillips, *The Origins of Intellect*, op. cit., p. 16.

Piaget refers to assimilation, accommodation, adaptation, and organization as the functional *invariants* of intelligence.[10] By that he means that regardless of the age of the learner the process is the same. It begins with assimilation and stops with organization and adaptation. Now the material with which the human organism functions and the sophistication with which functioning goes on no doubt change as a learner gets older. But the process of functioning itself is an invariant.

Although mental structures are also part of Piaget's model of intelligence, they are not invariant; they are consistently changing. Those changes probably begin the instant we are born and continue throughout our entire lives. To us, mental structures—to our knowledge Piaget has not said this—represent learning. Professor Piaget has said that "a structure is a system of transformations."[11] Now when we ask children to "learn something" they have been asked to transform the inputs from the environment into their own mental structures. That event will happen only if each child has a system which can make the required transformations. Suppose children are to be taught how to weigh a liquid. They must understand that the beaker must be weighed empty, then with the liquid in it, and the two values subtracted. Unless the child can make all of the transformations required in this act, the child cannot understand that at the end of the process, the weight of the liquid is known. Being able to make transformations on the data received from the environment represents learning to us; knowing how to describe the mathematics involved in a first-class lever does not. The type of mental structures available to learners must be understood by a teacher and age is certainly one influencing factor. We shall return to that point later. Figure 3–2 shows the relationship between struc-

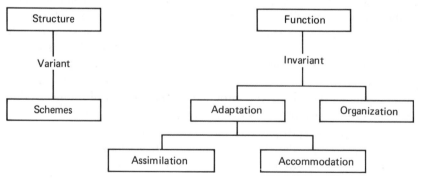

Figure 3–2   One variant and one invariant in Piaget's model of intelligence.

[10] Piaget, *The Origin of Intelligence in Children,* op. cit., pp. 3–8.
[11] Jean Piaget, *Structuralism,* New York: Harper & Row, 1970, p. 5.

tures and schemes and among accommodation, assimilation, organization, and adaptation.

A child is shown two balls of modeling clay and told to pick them up and handle them in any way the child wishes. After a period of examining the clay balls, the child agrees there is just *as much* clay in one ball as in the other. Notice the child agrees that the quantities of clay, *not* necessarily the weights, are the same. Next the person conducting the experiment flattens one of the balls into a pancake shape. The child is now asked if there is more clay in the ball, more clay in the pancake, or if the amounts of clay are the same in each. Our data[12] show that until they reach the age of from six to seven years, children believe there are different amounts of clay in the two balls.

Recently 1108 students in grades 10–12 were shown two identical glass cylinders filled to the same heights with water (see Figure 3–3). They were next given two solid metal cylinders having exactly the same shape and size but having different weights. They were told that the two metal cylinders were going to be put into the partially filled glass cylinders, that the metal cylinders would sink, and that this would result in the levels of the water rising. They were then asked, before the cylinders were submerged, whether one of the metal cylinders

Figure 3–3 The conservation of volume task tells you a great deal about the reasoning abilities of adolescents.

[12] Those data are shown in Table 3–1 and will be fully explained later.

would push the water level up more and which cylinder would do this, or if the metal cylinders would push the water levels up equally. A total of 484 of the 1108 students (44 percent) stated that one metal cylinder would push the water level up more than the other.

The examples just given demonstrate the third factor in Piaget's model of intelligence—content. Phillips defines content as "observable stimuli and responses"[13] and Flavell states that "content refers to the external behavior that tells us functioning has occurred."[14] In the clay-balls instance, young children state that there is more clay in the pancake. This occurrence tells the interviewer that the situation has been assimilated and how the child's content directs the child to behave. Do not be misled to believe that the child was not asked the proper questions or did not understand what he or she was expected to do. Neither redirecting the question nor making the questions "smaller" will change the child's response. The response the child gave was dictated by content, and to change the response the entire functioning, structure-building process must be activated and disequilibrium must be brought about. In other words, the content portion of Piaget's intelligence model is a variant and is inextricable from the structure and function portion. We have found it extremely useful to think about content as the way the child believes the world works.

In Piaget's model of intelligence, therefore, there are three principal subsets—content, structure, and function. Figure 3–4 presents a diagrammatic explanation of the intelligence model. Bear in mind that the diagram was not prepared by Piaget but is our interpretation of the relationship among the elements in his model of intelligence. Reading the diagram from top to bottom explains the overall model. In implementing the model with learners, however, you must remember that actual learning starts with assimilation.

Actions and Operations

Knowledge is not a copy of reality. To know an object, to know an event, is not simply to look at it and make a mental copy or image of it. To know an object is to act upon it. To know is to modify, to transform the object, and to understand the way the object is constructed. An operation is thus the essence of knowledge; it is an interiorized action. . . .[15]

[13] Phillips, *The Origins of Intellect,* op. cit., p. 8.
[14] John H. Flavell, *The Developmental Psychology of Jean Piaget,* Princeton, N.J.: Van Nostrand, 1963, p. 18.
[15] Jean Piaget, "Development and Learning," *The Journal of Research in Science Teaching* (3): 176–186, 1964.

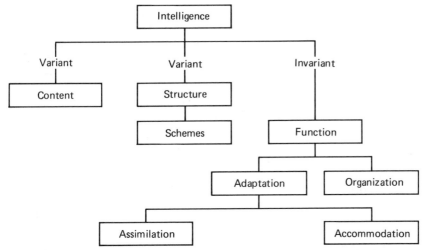

Figure 3–4   A diagrammatic interpretation of Piaget's model of intelligence.

The foregoing quotation tells us a great deal about what Piaget believes is actually necessary to promote assimilation and to begin the entire process of intellectual development. The learner must engage in actions, operations, or both. Notice in the quotation the statement is made that to know an object or event, the learner must act upon it; there are, however, different ways of acting. Very young children simply hit, grab, squeeze, and do all manner of physical things in interacting with an object. In other words, their actions are entirely overt. Next comes a time when "the young child simply runs off reality sequences in his head just as he might do in overt action."[16] The child has made a "step-by-step mental replica of concrete actions and events."[17] In other words, the child who is capable of *actions* with objects and events is interacting with them or is running off mental "reality sequences" with them. That child is really trying to reproduce reality. All of this, of course, is assimilated into the existing structures and schemes and changing them.

Eventually, if the child has had enough experiences to effect enough mental-structure changes, a dramatic event occurs. Piaget explains it in this way.

When he (the child in the example) was . . . a small child—he was seated on the ground in his garden and he was counting pebbles. Now to count these pebbles he put them in a row and he counted them one,

[16] Flavell, *The Developmental Psychology of Jean Piaget,* op. cit., p. 158.
[17] Ibid., p. 158.

two, three, up to ten. Then he finished counting them and started to count them in the other direction. He began by the end and once again he found ten. He found this marvelous that there were ten in one direction and ten in the other direction. So he put them in a circle and counted them that way and found ten once again. Then he counted them in the other direction and found ten once more. So he put them in some other arrangement and kept counting them and kept finding ten. There was the discovery that he made.

Now what indeed did he discover? He did not discover a property of pebbles; he discovered a property of the action—which he introduced among the pebbles. The subsequent deduction will consist of interiorizing these actions and then combining them without needing any pebbles.[18]

The child in the example had made that dramatic move from a step-by-step mental replica of reality to mentally transforming and modifying what reality is. This child had begun to do what Piaget calls *mental operations*. The primary difference between actions and mental operations is that actions mentally reproduce reality, while operations do something with that reproduction.

Consider the example cited earlier of the child and the two balls of clay. The child who believes that there is more clay in the pancake is simply making a mental replica of the diameter of the pancake when compared to the diameter of the ball. That child cannot reverse the thinking process to include the data that the pancake is also much thinner than the ball. All that child can do is make a mental replica of the reality of both objects. The child that does mental operations can mentally reverse the clay pancake image to the clay ball image. That learner can indeed transform the data received from the environment; the action of producing a pancake from the ball has been interiorized. Piaget describes a mental operation as "an interiorized action. But in addition, it is a reversible action; that is, it can take place in both directions, for instance, adding or subtracting, joining or separating."[19] Think of a mental operation this way: it is mentally doing something with the data received from the environment.

A seed is planted in a cup and another is taped to the outside. When the plant appears the child who planted it does not see the connection between the seed in the cup and the plant. Defend whether this is evidence of an action or a mental operation.

---

[18] Piaget, "Development and Learning," op. cit., p. 179.
[19] Ibid., p. 177.

PART 2—LEVELS OF INTELLECTUAL DEVELOPMENT

In 1920 Piaget accepted a position in the Binet Laboratory in Paris. His assignment was to develop standardized French versions of certain English reasoning tests. While carrying out that responsibility he made two major findings which led him into the detailed study of intelligence. He found that children of about the same age frequently gave the same *wrong* answers to a particular question. In addition, "there were different kinds of common wrong answers at different ages."[20] These findings led him to believe that the thought of younger children was *qualitatively* different than that of older children. In other words, younger children actually believe that the world works differently than do older children.

These findings led Piaget to reject a quantitative definition of intelligence, which is what the number of correct responses on an I.Q. test tells. According to Piaget's theory, a young child may be just as bright as an older one, but the *quality* of the type of thought the two groups are capable of is distinctly different. Adults often believe that older children are brighter than younger children because the thought type of older children more closely approximates adult thought. That notion is built around the assumption that children are miniature adults. The Piaget model rejects this idea and states that each age group has its own quality of thought. The mental structures of humans, according to the Piaget model of intellectual development, pass through *stages* or *phases* in moving through life. The structures in each stage have certain properties that differ from those of the structures existing in other stages.

Many years of the exacting study of children of all ages have gone into the stages-of-intellectual-development model of Piaget. Phillips explains Piaget's method for gathering his data like this:

> He observes the child's surroundings and his behavior, formulates an hypothesis concerning the structure that underlies and includes them both, and then tests that hypothesis by altering the surroundings slightly —by rearranging the materials, by posing the problem in a different way, or by even overtly suggesting to the subject a response different from the one predicted by the theory.[21]

Piaget's data about the reasoning patterns of humans begins at birth and extend into the third decade of life. Obviously, the data gathered from birth and for several years thereafter are based only on his observations.

[20] Herbert Ginsburg and Sylvia Opper, *Piaget's Theory of Intellectual Development,* Englewood Cliffs, N.J.: Prentice-Hall, 1969, p. 3.
[21] Phillips, *The Origins of Intellect,* op. cit., p. 3.

Perhaps, for our purposes, Piaget's procedure for gathering data could be described as giving the child a task to perform which involves materials and reasoning, letting the child perform the task, and then asking the child what he or she did and why he or she did it that way. What is important for you as a teacher is that Piaget's model of intellectual development comes from direct association with learners of all ages. You are going to be directly associated with learners, and it is important that any model you use to guide you in selecting and employing content and materials be relevant to children.

The data which Piaget and his co-workers have gathered have led to the formulation of a model of intellectual development which includes four unique levels. The quality of thought in each of these levels (stages, phases, periods) is distinctly different from the quality of thought in each of the other levels. In other words, the mental structures and content of each level are unique. Do not interpret that statement to mean that all children in a particular level think *exactly* alike, but the thought of children in the same level has common properties.

The First Level

The first stage of intellectual development in Piaget's model begins at birth and continues until the child is approximately two-and-a-half years old. Piaget has called this period the *sensorimotor stage*. During this stage the child learns that objects are permanent—that just because an object disappears from sight does not mean that it no longer exists. Acquiring the characteristics of object permanence explains, for example, why a child approximately a year old will cry when his mother leaves. This separation anxiety, however, does not occur earlier because until that point "out of sight, out of mind" adequately describes the child. During the sensorimotor period, language begins to develop[22] (a development that is far too complex to explore fully in this book). Basically, however, the child learns how to attach sounds to the objects, symbols, and experiences he or she has had. But this inventing of appropriate sounds for something depends, as does later learning, on the child's having an experience with that something.

During the sensorimotor period the first signs begin to emerge that intellect is developed and is not spontaneous. Now, certainly, the way a child in the sensorimotor stage goes about learning is quite different from the way learning occurs in an adult. But throughout all the stages of Piaget's model the fact becomes obvious that later learning cannot occur unless early learning has been accomplished. This means that for culturally deprived children who have not had the benefit of a rich

---

[22] Ibid., pp. 25–60. Phillips presents a thorough picture of the sensorimotor child.

environment which will assist them in developing the beginnings of a language system, the school may need to provide many experiences that go far beyond the conventional reading readiness programs before traditional "school" activities can begin. There is little likelihood that you will be working with children in the sensorimotor stage. You need, however, to be aware that this is the stage in which intellectual development begins to emerge; and unless certain goals are accomplished in this stage by the child, later learnings must wait. Perhaps we, as teachers, need to spend more time determining what the learner is ready to learn and less time being concerned with the specific content being covered.

Much confusion has developed about the ages at which children move from stage to stage within the intellectual development model. Piaget has repeatedly said that the ages he has suggested are only approximations, and has gone so far as to say that to "divide developmental continuity into stages recognizable by some set of external criteria is not the most profitable of occupations. . . ."[23] The external criterion most often used is chronological age, and using it can be misleading.

There is only one stage in Piaget's model whose starting point can be precisely stated—the sensorimotor stage. As noted earlier, it begins at birth and ends around two-and-a-half years of age. A two-and-a-half-year-old child will begin to enter the *preoperational stage*, and his exit from that type of thinking *begins* around seven years of age. In other words, in the model, exact, precise ages at which a learner will progress from stage to stage cannot be stated. Piaget states that "although the order of succession is constant, the chronological ages of these stages varies a great deal."[24] As you read the remainder of this discussion about Piaget's model of intellectual development, keep in mind that a child does not move completely from one stage to another at one time. The evidence available suggests that a learner can easily be in the sensorimotor phase on some traits and preoperational on others. Rather than thinking about a child as moving from one stage to another, think of the child as moving into a particular stage on certain traits. As development progresses, the child moves deeper and deeper into one stage on some traits and begins to move into the next higher stage on other traits. There is not, in other words, a chronological line children pass which indicates that they have moved completely from one stage to another, as an individual is permitted to vote when reaching 18 years of age.

[23] Jean Piaget, *Psychology of Intelligence,* Paterson, N.J.: Littlefield, Adams, 1963, p. 139.
[24] Piaget, "Development and Learning," op. cit., p. 178.

In this paragraph the notion of "trait" is referred to. What is a trait? Based only on what you know so far, describe what you feel are the "traits" referred to.

The Second Level

Think back to the discussion regarding the difference between "action" and "operation." The name of the second stage in the Piagetian model is wonderfully descriptive of what the mental activities of children occupying that stage are like. The name of this second stage is *pre-operational.* Children of this age are confined to assimilating mental replicas of the environment and to running off reality sequences in their heads. However, doing something with those reality sequence— that is, performing mental operations—cannot be accomplished by the preoperational child. Perhaps the best description of preoperational thought is that it is *perception bound.*[25] Preoperational children see, decide, and report; these children think, but thinking about what they think is beyond their intellectual ability.

A complete description of all the intellectual characteristics of the preoperational child is far beyond the scope of this book. If, after studying what is here, you wish to further investigate the characteristics of preoperational children, we suggest that you consult the book written by John L. Phillips, Jr., which has been referred to throughout this chapter, or *The Psychology of Intelligence,* the book in which Piaget explains his intellectual model and the characteristics of the stages within the model. For the purposes of using the Piagetian model in selecting and utilizing content and instructional methodology, seven basic characteristics of the preoperational child warrant examination:

1. Egocentrism
2. Irreversibility
3. Centering
4. States in a transformation
5. Transductive reasoning
6. The semiotic (symbolic) function
7. Conservation reasoning

Egocentrism is one of the preoperational child's most prominent traits; the world is seen from only one point of view—the child's. The

[25] The authors wish they could take credit for inventing this phrase, but cannot. They first heard it used by Dr. Celia Stendler Lavatelli in the film *Piaget's Theory: Conservation,* produced by John Davidson Films, San Francisco.

world revolves around the child who is completely unaware of being a prisoner of only one way of viewing it. In other words, the preoperational child cannot see another's point of view and coordinate it with that of his own and that of others. The opinion given by perception—reality sequence—is what these children believe and they feel no responsibility to justify a belief nor look for contradictions in it. Preoperational learners have developed a certain language pattern which is used to communicate with others, *but* they do not have the ability nor see the need to adapt that language pattern to the needs of the listener.

The second trait of the preoperational child which has great importance from the curriculum-methodology frame of reference is that of *irreversibility.* In order for a human to begin to do intellectual operations, the ability to reverse one's thinking must be possible. Irreversibility of thought is beautifully illustrated by this dialogue with an eight-year-old boy:

> Have you got a brother?
> Yes.
> And your brother, has he got a brother?
> No.
> Are you sure?
> Yes.
> And has your sister got a brother?
> No.
> You have a sister?
> Yes.
> And she has a brother?
> Yes.
> How many?
> No, she hasn't got any.
> Is your brother also your sister's brother?
> No.
> And has your brother got a sister?
> No.[26]

The dialogue with the child continues until he finally recognizes that he is his brother's brother. This dialogue with a four-year-old girl also nicely illustrates the irreversibility concept.

> Have you got a sister?
> Yes.
> And has she got a sister?
> No, she hasn't got a sister. I am my sister.[27]

[26] Jean Piaget, *Judgment and Reasoning in the Child,* Paterson, N.J.: Littlefield, Adams, 1964, p. 86.
[27] Ibid., p. 85.

Reversibility means that a thought is capable of being returned to its starting point. For example: $8 + 6 = 14$, and $14 - 6 = 8$. The thought started with 8 and returned to 8. Preoperational children cannot reverse their thinking. Consider what that says to those planning a mathematics program for early primary grades. Much of our society has a real hang-up on mathematics. Perhaps understanding many of the mathematics concepts presently found in the early elementary education requires mental reversibility. Since the children cannot use reversibility they cannot develop the understanding demanded. They have no choice, therefore, but to use rote memory if they wish to survive the trivia contests (tests). Could it be that such an experience creates "hang-ups" about mathematics which individuals never conquer?

Isolating the irreversible trait in a young child's thinking is not difficult and is informative. The procedure using clay described earlier will enable you to do it. The materials you will need are simple—two equal quantities of modeling clay or plasticene (we found that using different-colored pieces facilitates communication with the child).

> Form the pieces of clay into two balls and explain to the child that you want to start the experiment with one ball just the same size as the other. In other words one ball should contain just as much clay as the other. Allow your subject to work with the two balls until the child believes they contain the same amounts of clay. Now, deform one of the balls; a good way to do this is to roll one of the balls into a long, cylindrical shape or a pancake.
>
> Next, ask the child (a five-year-old child will probably be best to work with) if there is more clay in the ball, more in the roll, or if there is the same amount in each (be sure to give the child all three choices), and ask the child why the answer given is the one the child believes is correct.
>
> Record the child's answer.

A child who has not developed the thinking trait of reversibility will tell you that there are different amounts in the two clay shapes. Our experience has been that most preoperational children will select the cylinder (or pancake) shape as the one containing more clay.

The preoperational subject is not able to make the thinking reversal from the cylinder-shaped object that now exists back to the clay sphere that did exist. That child cannot do the analyzing and synthesizing that would permit him or her to reconstruct the sphere mentally, although the child knows that the sphere existed. This can be proved by asking the child to restore the roll of clay to its original shape; a sphere will be produced and you will now be told there is the same amount of clay in each. A child of this age thinks, but that thought is so irreversible that the child cannot think about his or her thinking.

Why does the preoperational learner usually focus attention on the cylinder-shaped object rather than on the ball? This event is explained by utilizing another trait in the preoperational model—*centering*. When the one clay ball was deformed the child's attention was probably fixed on the detail of length, and rigid, perception-bound mental structures prevented anything else about the transformed object from being seen. Educational experiences provided for young children must avoid using materials, activities, or both that encourage the centering trait. If, for example, colors are used, they should all be attractive and appealing. Teachers must not be surprised when children focus their attention on one aspect of an object, event, or situation; they are only acting as preoperational learners can be expected to act.

Centering is a characteristic of preoperational children, and those working with them should expect to find it. Does a child's inability to reverse his thinking cause that child to center or does the child's centering trait cause irreversibility? Who knows? Besides, is it important? Both traits exist—and which comes first is really not relevant because they are obviously not mutually exclusive.

The extreme perception-boundness of a preoperational child is well illustrated by the trait known as *states in a transformation.* Figure 3–5 represents a wooden rod that is standing vertically (position 1) and is then released (positions 2, 3, and 4). The rod eventually comes to rest at position 5. Obviously, the rod was in a state of rest when it was held in position 1 and is again in a rest position in position 5. If a series of pictures is taken of the falling object, it would be seen to pass through many other states, as represented by position 2, 3, and 4. In other words, the series of states in the event resulted in a transformation from the stick standing erect to its horizontal position.

If preoperational children are shown the experiment, after having

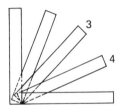

Figure 3–5 The ability of children to see states in a transformation can be assessed with the falling rod experiment.

been informed that they will be asked to draw a diagram of it, they will not draw what is shown in Figure 3–5, nor will they indicate in any way what successive states the stick went through in being transformed from position 1 to position 5. Our experience in asking children to do this task has been that they draw only positions 1 and 5. They see only the beginning and final states and do not see the transformation. This particular preoperational trait (which also shows irreversibility and centering) is particularly important when young children are studying science and doing experiments, as, for example, a plant-growing experiment. There is little need in trying to get them to see the importance of the several states in the transformation; they cannot do it. They will perceive the first and final states and nothing else. The process that allowed the final state to be a function of the intermediate states cannot be used by preoperational children. That state seems to call into doubt the insistence that young children do detailed *experiments;* they will see the beginning and the end, but as long as they are preoperational, they will not learn anything about the process of experimentation.

In his book entitled *Play, Dreams, and Imitation in Childhood* (translated by C. Guttegno and F. M. Hodgson), Piaget relates the following incident that occurred when his daughter Jacqueline was just past two years old:

Figure 3–6 Administering conservation reasoning tasks to a child can tell you much about the child.

J. wanted for her doll a dress that was upstairs; she said "Dress," and when her mother refused to get it, "Daddy get dress." As I also refused, she wanted to go herself "to mummy's room." After several repetitions of this she was told that it was too cold there. There was a long silence, and then: "Not too cold" "Where?" "In the room." "Why isn't it too cold?" "Get dress."[28]

As far as Jacqueline was concerned there was no difference in the logic between a warm room making securing the dress possible and getting the dress making the room warm. Jacqueline was reasoning from particular to particular and not from general to particular (deduction) or particular to general (induction). Piaget has called the particular-to-particular reasoning *transduction*. This type of reasoning begins to appear in the child with the beginning of language and generally lasts until about four years of age, but is sometimes found late in the preoperational period.

In our study of children, we have often used Piaget's classification tasks. One of these is showing a child a great number of wooden beads, all of one color, (we usually use red) and a few of another color (say, blue). Ask the child if there are more wooden beads or red beads. A truly preoperational child will tell you there are more red beads and when asked why, we often get the response: "Because they are prettier"—a perfect transductive response. As a teacher, do not be surprised if you encounter such transduction in kindergarten and first-grade children. If you do, be patient; usually it disappears with the increased experiences a school environment can provide over what the preschool environment supplied.

Marguerite Packnett, a kindergarten and first grade teacher at Wilson School, Norman, Oklahoma reported this incident to us. A child was watching snow falling and remarked that tomorrow would be Christmas. Ms. Packnett asked why that was true and the child replied that snow comes at Christmas time. Explain why the child's reasoning was transductive.

At the end of the sensori-motor period . . . there appears a function that is fundamental to the development of later behavior patterns. It consists in the ability to represent something by means of a "signifier" . . . which serves only a representative purpose . . . we generally refer to this function that gives rise to representation as "symbolic." However, since linguists distinguish between "symbols" and "signs," we

[28] Jean Piaget, *Play, Dreams, and Imitation in Childhood*, New York: Norton, 1951, pp. 230–231. (Original French edition published in 1945.)

would do better to adopt their term "semiotic function" to designate those activities having to do with . . . signifiers as a whole.[29]

The above quotation describes an important difference between the sensorimotor child and the preoperational child. Carefully consider the phrase "which serves only as a representational purpose"; that is what is meant by a "signifier"; it represents what is going to happen. Thus when the preoperational child hears the bell of the ice cream truck, that signifies to that child that ice cream is available. To the sensorimotor child, however, the sound of the bell and his taste of ice cream are not mentally separated. The assimilation of the sound of the bell also means taste of the ice cream. A sensorimotor child sees a sibling put on his coat and thinks the sibling is going to school. In other words the overt sign—the signifier—is not differentiated from what the sign means.

A preoperational child can think about signifiers and distinguish them from the objects, events, or situations they signify. That ability allows the teacher to utilize some definite characteristics in working with preoperational children. There are "at least five of these . . . whose appearance is almost simultaneous. . . ."[30] Each of these five is described, from the simplest to the most complex, in the following discussion:

1. Deferred imitation: This is the ability of a child to observe an event, object, or situation and later imitate what was observed. Children who have observed how a rabbit wrinkles his nose and later try to do it when asked are using this preoperational characteristic. The establishment of habits uses a good bit of deferred imitation.
2. Symbolic play: This trait is most adequately described by the preoperational child's game of pretending; that game is not found in the sensorimotor level. Using this trait allows a teacher to have a play-store in the classroom, for example.
3. Drawing: Here the child is able to represent his experiences graphically. Many times the symbols used are not clear to an adult, but the child can explain them. Piaget believes that this trait is an "intermediate stage between play and mental image."[31] If you doubt the importance of mental images to thinking, try to imagine thinking without them. (That, too, is a mental image!)

---

[29] Jean Piaget and Barbel Inhelder, *The Psychology of the Child*, New York: Basic Books, 1969, p. 51. For those wishing to pursue the topic of the symbolic function in depth, this reference is highly recommended.
[30] Ibid., p. 53.
[31] Ibid., p. 54.

4. Mental image: This is, of course, what must be available to children before they can describe anything they have experienced. Whenever a teacher says "Tell me what happened" or "Tell me what you saw" the ability to use the mental-image trait is assumed.

5. Verbal evocation: The increasing ability of children to use language makes it possible for them to describe the events that have already happened.

When children describe or comment on something that recently happened, they are using at least the mental images and verbal evocation traits. Obviously the five semiotic functions are interconnected.

Why is the semiotic function of young children important enough for their teachers to know? In answering that question a principle for using the Piagetian model in the classroom is evolved. If children are to develop increasingly complex mental structures and content (undergo intellectual development) they must have maximum opportunities to assimilate their environment. Through the complementary processes of assimilation and accommodation, mental structures and content change. *But* assimilation must at least begin by using those structures available to the learner. Preoperational chidren *can* use symbolic play, drawing, and all the other semiotic functions. Instruction must utilize those traits if accommodation is to take place. Reversing their thinking and using inductive and deductive reasoning cannot be used by preoperational children. Learning which depends upon these traits cannot take place because there is no structure to use in assimilation. You already know that if assimilation does not take place mental structures are not changed and learning has not taken place.

The teaching principle which can be deduced from Piaget's model says that teaching at any level of intellectual development must utilize the mental structures unique to that particular level. If teachers insist that children "know" something and mental structures are not present which can be used or can be adjusted to assimilate what is being pushed at them, the children have only one choice—they memorize. When the trivia contest is over, what has been memorized is promptly forgotten. This point will be returned to as the last two levels in Piaget's model are examined.

> Describe a classroom activity that would use each of the five semiotic function traits.

Identifying whether or not the preoperational thinker can see the relationship between states and transformations is a simple task; you do the falling stick experiment with the children and then ask them to tell you what happened. Identifying egocentrism, irreversibility, centering, and transduction, however, is not as easy as using the falling stick experiment.

There is, however, a procedure that can be used to identify the traits of preoperational children. You have already met one of the techniques used—that is, the clay balls activity. That activity can be described as illustrating the inability of a preoperational child to hold mentally the image of an object and see that distorting the object does not change the amount of material it contains. "Mentally holding" the original image of an object is called *conservation reasoning*, and preoperational children do not conserve—that is, they make decisions about the distortion of the object on the basis of what they perceive. This rigid, perception-boundness, however is due to their irreversible thinking, tendency to center, extreme egocentrism, not seeing a transformation among several states, and transductive reasoning. In other words, isolating a child who does not use conservation reasoning will allow you to describe his stage of intellectual development in terms of the preoperational traits already described and the trait of conservation reasoning. According to Piaget: "The clearest indication of the existence of a preoperational period . . . is the absence of notion of conservation until about the age of seven or eight."[32]

Conservation, then, is an overt manifestation of whether or not a child is a preoperational thinker. As was said earlier, this stage of development begins at about two-and-a-half years of age. In describing the beginning of a child's ability to conserve, Piaget has also provided information about the end of the preoperational period.

> There always comes a time (between 6 and one-half years and 7 years 8 months) when a child's attitude changes: he no longer needs to reflect, he decides, he even looks surprised when the question is asked, he is certain of the conservation.[33]

The beginning of the ability to conserve and the beginnings of the child's entry into the third stage in the Piagetian model—*concrete operations*—occur, then, in the late first or second grade. For purposes of designing a first grade curriculum for most of the year, the teacher can consider that the children are preoperational.

You have seen one activity (the clay balls experiment) that will reveal the child's ability to conserve. That activity tells you whether

---

[32] Ibid., p. 97.
[33] Jean Piaget, *The Psychology of Intelligence*, Paterson, N.J.: Littlefield, Adams, 1963, p. 140.

or not the learner conserves solid amount. We have found the clay balls task and five other Piagetian tasks to be very useful in identifying preoperational thought. These other tasks are the conservation of number, liquid amount, area, length, and weight. The descriptions for all of these tasks follow. As you read them, keep in mind the definition of "conservation," which may be stated thus: Children who conserve can hold a concept regarding an object in their cognitive structures at the same time that a second object, like the first, is distorted, and can see that the distorted object is still like the nondistorted object in many specific ways.

CONSERVATION OF NUMBER TASK[34]
Have the children line up six black checkers in one row and six red checkers in another row, as shown in Figure 3–7. Ask the child if he or she agrees that there are as many red checkers as there are black checkers. After the child agrees, stack the red checkers, one on top of the other, and leave the black checkers as they were; the checkers will now appear as in Figure 3–8. After the checkers have been rearranged, ask if there are more red checkers, more black checkers, or if the numbers of black and red checkers are the same. If the child reports that the numbers are the same, number is conserved. Be sure to ask why the child believes as he or she does not only on this task but also on all of the others. Getting the child to explain his or her answer will tell you a great deal about the state of the child's intellectual development.

CONSERVATION OF LIQUID TASK
Pour the same amount of water into two containers of equal size (see Figure 3–9). For convenience, you may wish to color the water in one container red. Ask if the child agrees that the containers are the same size and that they contain the same amount of liquid; if the child wishes to adjust the levels, let this be done. After agreement has been reached that the amounts are equal, have the child pour the clear liquid into a taller, thinner container (see Figure 3–10) and ask if there is

Figure 3–7

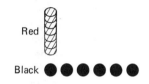

Figure 3–8

[34] The utilization of these tasks is illustrated in the film *Piaget's Theories: Conservation*, produced and distributed by John Davidson Films, San Francisco. The directions for these tasks have been tried by several hundred elementary school teachers and we appreciate their suggestions and contributions.

Figure 3–9   Figure 3–10

more colored water, more clear water, or if the amounts are equal.
A report that the amounts are equal shows that the child conserves
liquid; a report that there is more water in one of the containers
demonstrates a lack of liquid-conservation ability.

CONSERVATION OF SOLID AMOUNT TASK
This task has already been referred to. Prepare two pieces of clay, each
containing the same amount, and roll them into balls of equal size
(see Figure 3–11). For convenience, you may wish to use two colors of
clay, blue and red, for example. Ask the child if there is the same
amount of blue clay as red clay; let any adjustments in the balls he made
to convince the child the balls are of equal size. Next, deform the
piece of red clay by rolling it into what you may want to call a "snake"
(see Figure 3–12). Ask the learner if there is more clay in the ball,
in the snake, or if there is the same amount in each. Recognizing
that the amount of the solid remains constant indicates solid-amount
conservation ability.

CONSERVATION OF AREA TASK
Begin this task by showing the child two pieces of green construction
paper of *exactly* the same size. Explain that the pieces of paper represent
two fields of grass and that they must be exactly the same size. Give
the child the opportunity to examine the two pieces of paper and to
make adjustments on them if necessary. The child must be convinced
that the two fields are exactly the same size. Be sure to ask the child to
explain to you why one field contains as much grass as the other.
That act of explaining convinces the child that he or she must think
about the papers as grass (a preoperational child can do this; think
about the semiotic function) and will indicate that the child understands
the "sameness" concept in this task.

Next show the child some wooden cubes (about 2.5 centimeters
on a side). Explain that you are going to pretend that each of these
cubes is a barn. Give the child the opportunity to examine the "barns"
until the child is convinced they are all of the same size. Place a
barn on each field (see Figure 3–13) and ask the child whether, on each

Figure 3–11   Figure 3–12

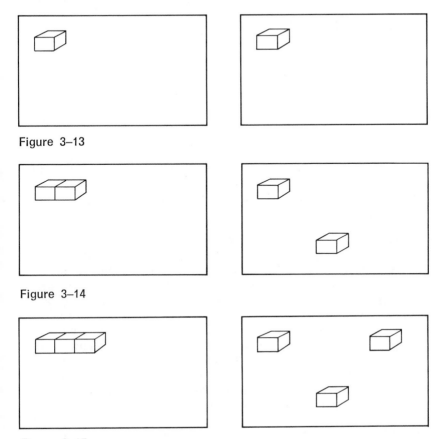

Figure 3–13

Figure 3–14

Figure 3–15

field, there is still the same amount of grass that has not been covered, or whether one field or the other has more grass. After adding barns to each field and having the child tell you which has more uncovered grass, *always* ask why the child believes the answer given is true. Record the child's answer. Now place one more barn on each of the fields, but on one field of paper place the barns very close together and on the other separate them (see Figure 3–14). Again ask the child if there is still the same amount of uncovered grass on each field and why. Use a third barn as shown in Figure 3–15 and again ask questions about the amount of uncovered grass.

Not infrequently the only justification a child gives for the grass area being the same on both fields is because the number of barns on each field is the same. These data suggest that the child is conserving number and not area. To determine whether or not this is what the child is doing, follow the procedure shown in Figure 3–16; here one of the barns has been placed on top of another. Ask the child the question

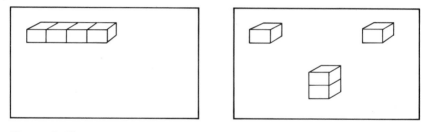

Figure 3–16

as before. The child who responds to the arrangements in Figures 3–13, 3–14, and 3–15 by stating that the amounts of uncovered grass are equal and unequal in Figure 3–16 has demonstrated the ability to conserve area.

CONSERVATION OF LENGTH TASK

This task requires a wooden dowel 12 inches long and four dowels of the same diameter each 3 inches long. The exact lengths of the dowels are not important, but the combined lengths of the four smaller dowels must equal the length of the long dowel. Two identical toy cars are also helpful. Place the long dowel and the shorter pieces parallel, so that the combined length of the pieces just equals the length of the long piece (see Figure 3–17). Be sure the child agrees that the line of pieces is exactly the length of the long piece; let adjustments be made if necessary. Inform the child that the dowels represent roads and there is going to be a race. Place identical toy cars (say, a red car and a blue car) at the same ends of the roads and then pose this question: "If the cars travel the same speed, which car, the red one or the blue one, will reach the end of the road first? Or will they reach the ends of the roads at the same time?" If the child does not ultimately agree that the cars will reach the ends of the roads at the same time, abandon the task.

Next, move two pieces of the four-piece road as shown in Figure 3–18 and ask the question about the race. If the child states that the cars will reach the ends of the roads at the same time, he conserves length.

CONSERVATION OF WEIGHT TASK

Give the child two balls containing equal *weights* of clay; two colors of clay, such as red and green, facilitate communication in this task (see Figure 3–19). Add and subtract clay from each of the balls until the child agrees that the balls *weigh* exactly the same. Next, take the two balls of clay from the child and flatten one of them into a pancake or distort it in some other way. Don't let the child lift the two clay objects after this distortion. Next, ask the learner if the green clay weighs more, the red clay weighs more, or if the weights are still the same. Failing to recognize that the weights of the red and green clay objects are still equal shows that the child does not conserve weight.

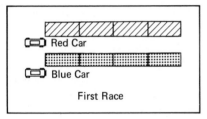

Figure 3–17

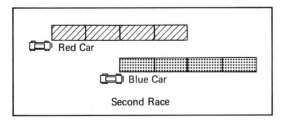

Figure 3–18

Arrangement A   red ⊘   ○ green
   Cross-sectional view   Cross-sectional view

Arrangement B   red ⊘   ○ green
   Cross-sectional view   Top view

   ⊂═════════⊃ green
   Cross-sectional view

Figure 3–19

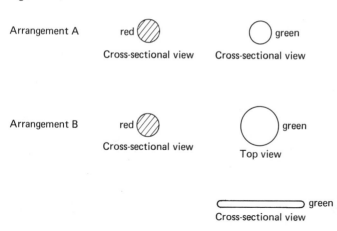

Administer the tasks to three children and record your results. A five-year-old, a seven-year-old, and a nine-year-old will probably give you an age range that will allow you to see preoperational thought and thought moving into the concrete operational stage. After the child has given you his reasons for believing as he does on each task, be sure to give him the opportunity to explain his reasoning to you.

The conservation tasks you have just read are neither meaningful nor functional until you employ them with children. You are probably thinking that the tasks are so simple that anyone can do them. All that thought proves is that you are not preoperational!

Your results will increase in meaning if you combine them with those of your colleagues. The combination of data will also show you that age alone does not determine when a preoperational learner leaves that stage. Additionally, the data combination will show you that just because a child conserves on one task does not necessarily determine what other tasks will be satisfactorily completed. Our experience with the task suggests that the first conservation usually made is of number, and the second and third conservations are of liquid and solid amount.

The data shown in Table 3–1 are informative when a frame of reference for studying them is considered. The 252 children represented in that table are a random sample of children from the Norman, Okla-

Table 3–1

				CONSERVATION OF			
AGE—MONTHS	SAMPLE SIZE	NUM-BER	SOLID AMOUNT	LIQUID AMOUNT	LENGTH	AREA	WEIGHT
60–64	12	3	2	2	—	1	1
65–68	12	7	2	—	2	2	3
69–72	12	6	3	4	1	2	1
73–76	12	8	7	7	3	6	3
77–80	12	8	5	5	3	2	6
81–84	12	9	5	5	—	3	5
85–88	12	11	11	9	6	9	10
89–92	12	11	9	11	9	8	11
93–96	12	9	9	8	7	6	8
97–100	12	12	12	11	9	8	11
101–104	12	12	11	8	5	7	8
105–108	12	11	9	9	7	8	10
109–112	12	11	10	10	7	7	6
113–116	12	11	11	10	7	7	7
117–120	12	12	12	10	7	6	9
121–124	12	9	12	11	7	8	9
125–128	12	11	11	10	9	7	11
129–132	12	12	11	11	12	10	10
133–136	12	12	12	12	8	7	12
137–140	12	12	10	10	10	10	12
141–144	12	12	12	12	12	12	12

SOURCE: John W. Renner, Judith Brock, Sue Heath, Mildred Laughlin, and Jo Stevens, "Piaget *Is* Practical," *Science and Children*, October 1971, p. 23. These data were gathered by a group of experienced test administrators, all of whom cannot be acknowledged. The authors are especially grateful however, to Jo Stevens, Judith Brock, Mildred Laughlin, and Sue Heath, elementary teaching colleagues.

homa, school system. Those doing the evaluations used identical task directions and objects, and standardized their questioning techniques.

If you adopt the policy of interpretation that all twelve children of any particular age must complete a specific task satisfactorily before the group can be regarded as exercising conservation reasoning in that task, conservation reasoning appears rather late for some tasks. In evaluating data from the responses of children to a type of task just slightly different from conservation reasoning, Piaget used the following procedure: "We have followed the accepted custom of considering a test successfully passed when 75 percent of the children of the same age have answered correctly."[35] This means that in Table 3–1 conservation reasoning is achieved when nine children (in the 12-child sample) in any cell respond satisfactorily. (The number in each cell of Table 3–1 are those responding correctly.) In each column, however, the number should not fall substantially below nine once it has been achieved. We have taken the position that eight is not seriously below nine but that seven is. We fully recognize that our interpretation is arbitrary. If you disagree, please make your own interpretation and operate with it on what follows.

If Piaget's "75 percent" rule-of-thumb is adopted, the data in Table 3–1 take on a meaning that tells those concerned with curriculum a great deal. Conservation of number, for example, is not achieved until 84 months of age (seven years). What does that tell you about using numerical experiences with children in science experiments? Conservation of length is not achieved until 136 months (11 years 4 months). Where do you usually find the teaching of systems of measurement?

Whatever the outcome throughout the conservation tasks, the children are being evaluated on their ability to reverse their thinking, decenter their attention, cease using transductive reasoning, and overcome all of the other characteristics of a preoperational thinker. A child who does not reverse his thinking does poorly in science experiments; he can only observe and report what he saw. All of the conservation tasks indicate a child's ability to carry out reversals of thinking; those reversals get more difficult as the complexity of the tasks increases.

Explain the mental reversals in each conservation task, and how difficult an experiment each successful conservation allows a child to perform.

---

[35] Piaget, *Judgment and Reasoning in the Child*, op. cit., p. 100.

The conservation tasks can be used not only to measure the presence or absence of the trait of conservation reasoning but also the other traits which appear during the preoperational period. The semiotic function, of course, was present at the end of the sensorimotor period and is, therefore, present during the entire preoperational period.

The conservation concept is a potent tool in the hands of a teacher who knows how to use it. That teacher can identify preoperational and concrete operational learners and immediately know something about their thinking processes. The type of curricula which can be used with this type of thinker can then be identified. There is no use, for example, in asking a preoperational thinker to become involved in an educational activity that requires thinking reversals—preoperational thinkers cannot do them. They can observe, perceive, and report their perceptions. They need educational experiences that use the mental structures and schemes available—the semiotic function, for example.

The Third Level

You have probably learned more about the preoperational child than you wanted to know! There is a reason for treating the preoperational period of intellectual development as thoroughly as has been done— understanding of preoperations makes understanding the third stage of intellectual development, *concrete operations,* much easier. The *gross* way in which to think about concrete operational children is that they are what preoperational thinkers are not; that is, they can decenter, do mental reversals, begin to reason inductively and deductively and not transductively, use conservation reasoning, and see the relationship between states in a transformation; and their egocentric structures begin to thaw out—they can begin to see objects as other people do. You have seen, however (Table 3–1), that conservation ability does not develop in all areas at one time. Children, then, do not move from the preoperational to the concrete operational stage all at once. Rather, they begin to leave the preoperational stage and *enter into* the concrete operational stage. They continue this movement for some time and move deeper and deeper into concrete operations.

Just as the name preoperational thought is descriptive of that stage, the name *concrete operational* thought is also descriptive. During this stage "the first operations appear, but I call these concrete operations because *they operate on objects and not yet on verbally expressed hypotheses.*"[36] In other words, the student cannot learn unless he or she deals with reality—actual objects, actual events, actual situations

[36] Piaget, "Development and Learning," op. cit., p. 177. (Italics added.)

are mandatory. In many elementary science programs, for example, children are asked to "learn" about the atom. Now to understand the atom and what it means, you must understand data which support the existence of the atom. No one has ever seen an atom; it is an abstraction.

Concrete operational learners cannot assimilate abstractions. What they do assimilate is data from reality; they can accommodate to and build mental structures from such data. Concepts that are built from concrete experiences—reality experiences—are *concrete concepts*. Research has shown[37] that concrete operational learners can develop understanding of concrete concepts, but that they *cannot* develop understanding of concepts based upon abstractions. Understanding what that research-finding means is vital to teachers.

All school subject-matter must be evaluated from the frame of reference of concrete and abstract. If the material the children are to learn can be derived from reality—actual objects, events or situations, or both—children in the concrete operational stage can assimilate it. If the material is not from reality, no mental-structure change will result from the child interacting with it. *Do not believe* that concepts will be learned if children are given only the data from some concrete event; object or situation, or both. They must become involved in gathering the data, evaluating what data they have been given, discussing the sources which produced the data, or in some way have an actual concrete experience with the particular data that are to lead the students to the concept that is to be learned. The most beneficial experience is, of course, gathering the data themselves; vicarious experiences do not have the efficacy that an actual experience has. We believe there is much content in many elementary school science programs that is not concrete, that needs to be eliminated. We shall return to this topic later.

Piaget originally stated that children begin to move into the concrete operational stage between six and seven years of age. The data in Table 3–1 tend to corroborate this generalization. The original investigation carried out by Piaget and his colleagues led them to state that children began to move out of the concrete stages of thought "at about 11 or 12 years. . . ."[38] In 1972, however, Piaget wrote an article[39] in which he stated that the students used in the original investigation were taken from "the better schools in Geneva." He further stated that

---

[37] John W. Renner, Don G. Stafford, Anton E. Lawson, Joe W. McKinnon, F. Elizabeth Friot, and Donald H. Kellogg, *Research, Teaching, and Learning with the Piaget Model*, Norman, OK: University of Oklahoma Press, 1976, ch. 9.
[38] Piaget, *Psychology of Intelligence*, op. cit., p. 148.
[39] Jean Piaget, "Intellectual Evolution from Adolescence to Adulthood," *Human Development* 15 (1): 1–12, 1972.

he felt that the ages of eleven to twelve years, as being the time during which children began to leave concrete thought, were derived from data taken from "a somewhat privileged population." He proposed that the point at which the exit from concrete thought begins is "between 15 and 20 years and *not* 11 and 15 years."

Our own research data tend to corroborate Piaget's statement that concrete thought is still present in many students at an age older than 15 years. Recently[40] 811 students in grades 10 through 12 and between the ages of 13.75 years and 18.58 years completed tasks whose results revealed the type of thought in this group. Concrete thought was found 57 percent of the time. Data[41] also show that approximately 50 percent of entering college freshmen also utilize concrete thought most of the time. Such data vividly demonstrate that teachers must thoroughly understand concrete thought. It usually begins in the late first or early second grade and persists with the majority of students through high school.

The presence of concrete reasoning means that actual experience with those concepts which are to be learned is the *only* way *understanding* develops. To be sure, students capable of concrete reasoning can memorize the definition of an atom, or of how to divide fractions, and perform—and perform or act is what they do—with such memorized content in the classroom. But when that content is to be used in another context in the classroom, or outside the classroom, performances do not take place. Many reasons are given by the general public for this lack of success. Generally, these reasons come down to "The schools are not bearing down enough!" All sorts of remedies are employed to try to "make the kids learn." The "back-to-the-basics" folks want the learners to do more and more of the same kind of activity that did not result in learning the first time the children attempted it. By some magic, the second time is to produce results. Frequently test scores do go up on a second time around, but there is no lasting effect from these increased test scores. The second time through the content the children could memorize a little more. That, too, will soon be forgotten. But the learners did not assimilate any more because the early learnings necessary to build the structures to make assimilation possible have not been accomplished. The "back-to-the-basics" advocates do not realize that the real basic is school activities that build mental structures which will allow more and more assimilation as children move through the schools.

[40] John W. Renner, Dianna K. Prickett, and Michael J. Renner, *Evaluating Intellectual Development Using Written Responses to Selected Science Problems,* Norman, OK: University of Oklahoma, 1977, pp. 24–27.
[41] Renner, et al., *Research, Teaching, and Learning With the Piaget Model,* op. cit., ch. 7.

> Earlier in this chapter the statement was made that you would understand why so much time was spent on the preoperational stage of thinking. Stop reading at this point, pick up your pencil and organize your thoughts about why understanding the preoperational stage is so important, and record those thoughts.

The Fourth Level

Preoperational thinkers often indulge in the wildest kind of fantasy which often has no basis in fact. If the world does not suit them, they just imagine it to be different until they have the type of fanciful world they want. Concrete operational thinkers are concerned with the actual data they extract from objects, organizing those data, and doing mental operations with them. These learners do not formulate abstract hypotheses from their experiences; they confine their thinking to events in the real world. They can categorize, compare, seriate, and perform all various thinking acts that will lead to the extraction of information from objects and to rational power development if they are given experience with concrete objects. In short, children in the concrete operational stage of thinking do not take departures from reality, as do preoperational thinkers even though these departures have no lawful or logical basis.

At some time between 15 and 20 years of age, many persons find that they can do a type of thinking that is not completely dependent upon reality. These persons find that they can do a type of thinking that depends upon "the basis of simple assumptions which have no necessary relation to reality or . . . beliefs. . . ."[42] According to Piaget, such an individual "thinks beyond the present and forms theories about everything, delighting especially in considerations of that which is not."[43] The foregoing quotations describe a kind of thought that can best be named *abstract*. The persons using this thought do not need to have direct experience with reality, they can assume that it exists and use that assumption as though it were reality. Piaget states that a person performing abstract thinking has become capable of "hypothetico-deductive" thought which consists of " 'implications' and 'contradictions' established between propositions. . . ."[44] In other words, these persons can think about the consequences (implications) of their thinking.

[42] Piaget, *Psychology of Intelligence*, op. cit., p. 148.
[43] Ibid.
[44] Ibid., p. 149.

When one analyzes what is truly meant by hypothetico-deductive thinking and thinking with assumptions, another descriptive term that could be used for this stage of thought is "propositional reasoning." A proposition says: "*If* the assumption or deduction (about such and such) is true; *then* it follows that (such and such is also true); *therefore* (this or that action is dictated or suggested)." In other words, the thought of this level in the Piaget model has a particular *form*. Here again the title given this stage is descriptive, Piaget has called it *formal operational.*

Formal operational thought is the type of thought that is needed to see the relationships that exist among the elements of grammar; to see the relationship between the force, weights and distances in a first-class lever; and to visualize the distance between the planets in the solar system. Understanding the description of the DNA molecule—often presented in books for the upper elementary grades and junior high school—also requires formal thought. Whenever understanding an idea which has "no necessary relation to reality," the type of thought required is formal operational. The key word in distinguishing concrete operational thought from formal operational thought is *reality*. The concrete operational thinker can think *only* about reality—experiences the thinker is having or has recently had. The formal operational thinker "is concerned with reality, but reality is only a subset within a much larger set of possibilities."[45] That larger set of possibilities exists because those capable of formal operational reasoning can think on "the basis of single assumptions" and "delight in the consideration of that which is not." That description shows that formal thought is capable of departing from reality, "but those departures are lawful . . . ;"[46] they are based upon assumptions. Reasoning from assumptions—whether or not they are true is unimportant—is as legitimate to formal thought as reasoning from reality is to concrete thought.

Earlier the point was made that Piaget claimed that most learners enter the formal reasoning period between 15 and 20 years old. When children have *just begun* to enter the formal thought period—or have just begun to leave the concrete thought period—they will succeed with the conservation of volume task (see Appendix D). In the spring of 1974, we administered the conservation of volume task to 17 randomly-selected sixth graders from one school and 16 randomly-selected sixth graders from a second school in the same system.[47] Of that group, 29 were 12 years old and four were 13 years old. Only six—18 percent—

[45] Phillips, *The Origins of Intellect,* op. cit., p. 131.
[46] Ibid., p. 131.
[47] The school system was Norman, Oklahoma.

of those 33 students were successful with the conservation of volume task. These data show that students can *begin* to enter formal thought before 15 years of age, but that very few do.

Earlier we quoted data that demonstrated that among 811 students in grades 10 through 12, concrete thought was found 57 percent of the time. In that sample each student had the opportunity to demonstrate *complete* formal thought three times. In other words a total of 2433 (811 × 3) formal thought demonstrations was possible. A total of 1038 formal thought demonstrations was found (43 percent). The distribution of formal and concrete reasoning among the 811 students is shown in Table 3–2. In this table, the *complete* thought pattern of each student (a total of 811), rather than the three thought demon-

Table 3–2 THE PRESENCE OF CONCRETE AND FORMAL THOUGHT AMONG STUDENTS IN GRADES 10 THROUGH 12

| | SAMPLE: 412 MALES | | |
| | 399 FEMALES | | |
SCORE	10	11	12	TOTAL
4	0	3	2	5
5	11	19	5	35
6	18	26	14	58
7	32	34	19	85
8	34	53	27	114
9	34	40	29	103
10	26	54	40	120
11	20	57	33	110
12	8	43	28	79
13	7	26	20	53
14	5	11	16	32
15	1	8	8	17
	196	374	241	811

SCORES 4–8: Concrete Operational Reasoning
    Grade 10:   95 (48.5%)
    Grade 11: 135 (36.1%)
    Grade 12:   67 (27.8%)
        Total: 297 (36.6%)

SCORES 9–11: Transitional Reasoning
    Grade 10:   80 (40.8%)
    Grade 11: 151 (40.4%)
    Grade 12: 102 (42.3%)
        Total: 333 (41.1%)

SCORES 12–15: Formal Reasoning
    Grade 10:   21 (10.7%)
    Grade 11:   88 (23.5%)
    Grade 12:   72 (29.9%)
        Total: 181 (22.3%)

strations each student gave (2433), was used. In other words the data in Table 3–2 shows you the percentages of *students using concrete and formal reasoning.*

Quite apparently the thought content and structures of children change as they move from period to period within the Piagetian model. But what happens or can be made to happen that will encourage a child to begin to move out of one stage and into another? Piaget lists four factors[48] that contribute to movement from stage to stage— maturation, experience (physical and logical-mathematical), social transmission, and equilibration. He contends that any one of the first three factors is insufficient by itself to account for sufficient mental structure change to encourage a person to move from one period to the next.

You have already found out how equilibration leads to changes in mental structures; that discussion will not be repeated. But before examining the other three factors there is one important point you need to keep in mind. Mental structure change is the reason that persons move from stage to stage within the model. All structure change begins with assimilation. How then do maturation, experience, and social transmission contribute to a person's ability to assimilate?

The simplest definition of maturation is the process of maturing or growing. When relating growth to the increase of intelligence— mental structures—what has to grow and mature is the nervous system. The maturation of the nervous system gives each of us the opportunity to see, hear, feel—in short, experience—more and more objects, events, and situations within our environment. That, of course, leads to increased assimilation, disequilibrium, accommodation, and, consequently, changes in mental structures.

There are two types of experience that influence assimilation. The first is *physical* experience, which is simply the poking, breaking, lifting, and squeezing of objects, the putting of objects in water, the throwing of objects into the air, and engaging in all manner of activities that allows learners to assimilate data about their physical environment. Walking in the mud is as important as hearing pleasant sounds. There is, however, a second kind of experience that Piaget calls *logical-mathematical.* He believes that through this experience "knowledge is not drawn from the objects but it is drawn by the actions effected upon the objects . . . ."[49] Earlier, we had the example of the young child discovering that regardless of how stones were arranged, there always were ten. These experiences require mental operations and have to do with the logic and order of the environment. Discouraging children

[48] Piaget, "Development and Learning," op. cit., pp. 170–175.
[49] Ibid., p. 179.

from touching, feeling, and interacting with the environment in the classroom deprives them of needed physical experience that leads to mental structure change. Asking children not to use objects and to think only about numbers provides them an impoverished logical-mathematical experience.

Transmission means to pass along. Social transmission means to pass along what the society you are in is like, and the most common kind of social transmission in oral language—talking. But social transmission also occurs through the institutions of the society—schools, churches, museums—indeed, everywhere a child can interact with the society, social transmission and the concomitant mental structure change is taking place. The interaction concept is so important to us that we use social interaction as a synonym for social transmission.

Write a paragraph on what prohibiting children from talking, and having inadequate materials, do to the child's opportunities for moving upward through the stages in Piaget's model of intellectual development.

PART 3—INTERPRETATION

School experiences can accelerate the movement of children from the preoperational to the concrete operational stage,[50] and the movement of junior high school students[51] and college students[52] from the concrete to the formal operational stage. Whether or not such acceleration is desirable is questionable. (Piaget has called this "the American question.") We believe that whether or not acceleration is desirable depends upon what is meant by acceleration. Most assuredly young children can be trained to give satisfactory answers to the conservation tasks. We once trained a group of kindergarten children on the conservation of liquid task.[53] They became so proficient that regardless of the liquid or container used, they always gave the correct response. Next we used salt instead of a liquid. Now salt takes the shape of the container and pours just as a liquid does, yet when salt was used the children failed the task.

---

[50] Renner, et al., *Research, Teaching, and Learning With the Piaget Model*, op. cit., ch. 2.
[51] Ibid., ch. 5.
[52] Ibid., ch. 7.
[53] Our thanks to Maxine S. Edwards, a teacher in the Corpus Christi, Texas, school system, for her excellent work on this project.

That simple experiment demonstrates, we believe, how and when acceleration from stage to stage within the Piagetian model is desirable. In order to see its importance and to understand how and when acceleration is desirable, study Figure 3–20. The diagram in this figure indicates that the period of intellectual development which students occupy depends upon their content and structures. If learners are provided assimilatory experiences that lead to accommodation, those experiences will lead to structure and content changes. Repeated content and structure changes will lead students to begin to leave one intellectual development period and to enter another. Now if schools allow learners to interact with the disciplines they teach—art, language arts, mathematics, science, and so forth—through assimilation, there will result changes in the intellectual development period the students occupy. The intellectual level of the students will be raised and the material the schools wish to teach will be learned. (Much of the material schools want to teach today will be learned only if intellectual levels are raised.)

Figure 3–20 also demonstrates why those persons are incorrect who say that training students to pass the conservation or formal operational tasks represents intellectual development. The experiment with the kindergarten children which we just described demonstrates that training does not necessarily lead to mental structure change, and that when the vocabulary and techniques memorized during the training have been forgotten, the learners can no longer perform the task trained for or those other tasks the training was to prepare them for.

In summary, then, acceleration through the stages of thought is desirable if the criteria by which acceleration is judged—satisfactory completion of the conservation task, for example—are *proof of mental structure change*. If students satisfy the criteria for acceleration because of memorized information which came from training, the apparent acceleration is undesirable; in this case, acceleration has *not* occurred. Only those persons who do not understand that the basis for Piaget's model is the concept of mental structures will believe acceleration has occurred. Data from research support the hypothesis that teaching science as it is structured—the quest for knowledge—encourages the movement of students from one intellectual level to the next. That type of teaching, therefore, has led to increased assimilation and desirable acceleration. Piaget believes that "perhaps nothing stands in the way of further reduction of the average age (of entering a particular stage) in a more or less distant future."[54]

Not infrequently the notion is advanced that if students in the

---

[54] Barbel Inhelder and Jean Piaget, *The Growth of Logical Thinking*, New York: Basic Books, 1958, p. 337. Parenthetical phrase added by the present authors.

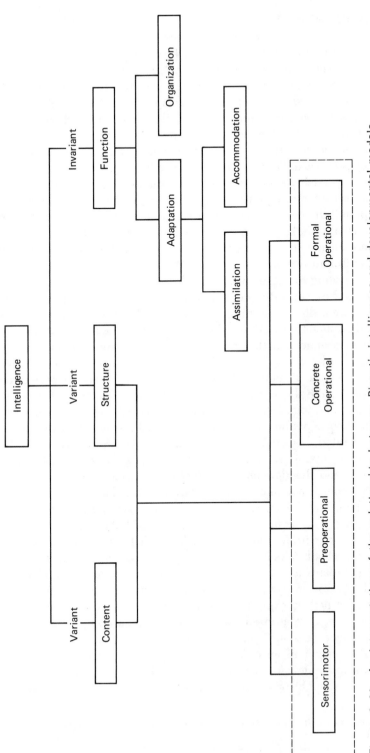

Figure 3–20 An interpretation of the relationship between Piaget's intelligence and developmental models.

concrete reasoning stage are to enter formal operational thinking, they must be given formal operational material to study. That makes them "stretch their minds," say proponents of this hypothesis, because, after all, one's "reach should exceed one's grasp." When the Piagetian model is used as a theory base for education, the foregoing position ceases to be logical, for with this theory, learning begins with assimilation, and if the mental structures present do not permit assimilation, learning cannot take place. Disequilibrium takes place when a mismatch occurs between what is to be assimilated and the existing mental structures. But in order for disequilibrium to occur, mental structures must exist that permit the person to recognize that a mismatch is present. Integral calculus or a Shakespearean play do not disequilibrate second graders because mental structures do not permit assimilation to the point that disequilibrium occurs.

According to Piagetian theory, then, formal subject matter cannot be learned by concrete operational learners because the mental structures present do not permit its assimilation. In order to begin to move from the concrete period into the formal period, mental structures must begin to change and that change requires accommodation, which is brought on by disequilibrium. That is, of course, a hypothesis which arises from the Piagetian theory. Our research[55] has supported that hypothesis. We did our research in high school biology, physics, and chemistry and found that students who reasoned concretely could learn concrete concepts but not formal concepts. Formal reasoning students demonstrated they could learn both concrete and formal concepts. Our research is supportive of Piaget's statement that "development explains learning, and this opinion is contrary to the widely held opinion that development is a sum of discrete learning experience."[56]

The answer, then, regarding whether or not students in the concrete stage will begin to move into the formal stage by insisting that they interact with formal content is "*no.*" That answer puts a responsibility on schools which tells them they must know what levels of reasoning students are using and whether the concepts the students are asked to learn are concrete or formal. A concrete concept is one that can be learned by experience alone. A formal concept, however, cannot be learned from experience because it is based upon assumptions or, as Piaget has said, "consideration of that which is not."

The weight of an object, for example, when thought of as how heavy something is, is a concrete concept; it can be experienced. When weight is thought of as the interaction between an object's mass and

---

[55] Renner, et al., *Research, Teaching, and Learning With the Piagetian Model,* op. cit., ch. 9.
[56] Piaget, "Development and Learning," op. cit., p. 176.

the earth's gravitational field, it is a formal concept because it it based upon the formal concepts of mass and the earth's gravitational field. Neither of these formal concepts can be experienced; to understand them depends upon certain assumptions. Gravity, however, is a concrete concept if it is thought of as the factor that makes objects fall downward. Downward is a formal concept when it depends upon the assumption that it is toward the center of the earth. If downward is thought of as being in the direction of the observer's feet, it is a concrete concept.

Find two concrete and two formal science concepts and explain why they are concrete or formal.

For many years the most common learning model used in schools has been stimulus-response (S-R). This model is, for example, the basis for programmed learning. B. F. Skinner has been the most vocal spokesman for this technique. The area of behavior modification, and most forms of training, both use S-R as their theory base. The S-R theory assumes that a learner will respond if the stimulus is adequate. In other words, the S-R theory confines its attention to inputs (stimuli) and outputs (responses) and "the direct relationship between them, ignoring the internal connection."[57] Piaget believes that ignoring the internal connections between the stimulus and the response is improper and has stated so.

> I think the stimulus-response schema, while I don't say it is false, is in any case entirely incapable of explaining cognitive learning. Why? Because when you think of a stimulus-response schema, you think usually that first of all there is a stimulus and then a response is set off by this stimulus. For my part, I am convinced that the response was there first . . . A stimulus is a stimulus only to the extent that it is significant, and it becomes significant only to the extent that there is a structure which permits its assimilation, a structure which can integrate this stimulus but which at the same time sets off the response.[58]

The foregoing quotation explains why, in preparing programmed-learning materials, care must be taken that each question asked does not involve too much material. The stimulus (the question) must be able to be assimilated into existing structures. If the learner has not had the opportunity to build new structures through assimilation (which programmed learning does not provide), the question must be an-

---

[57] Jean Piaget, *Science of Education and the Psychology of the Child*, New York: The Viking Press, 1971, p. 76.
[58] Piaget, "Development and Learning," op. cit., p. 182.

swered from the existing structures built by accommodations not necessarily related to the new stimulus. To lead a learner to respond to a stimulus (answer a question) from mental structures only remotely related to the stimulus requires the questioner to use a great deal of care. In other words, the S-R model is only a small part of Piaget's mental structure model.

We have found the work of Piaget to be extremely helpful. That work could, we believe, serve as a theory base for all education, something education in the United States does not now have. It contains, we believe, an inherent teaching method which will be examined in the next chapter. When a teacher has thoroughly accommodated the concepts of assimilation, accommodation, and mental structures, the materials of a discipline and how children are encouraged to interact with them will take on a new perspective.

Part II
GETTING THE IDEA

How can I find out? People have probably asked themselves that question since the capability for thought has existed. The role of teacher exists for the purpose of helping those in the role of students to find out. But leading people to find out does not include telling them what they do not know. This section of the book deals with how the teacher functions in leading people to find out what they do not know.

Chapter 4
The Elements of Inquiry

The term "inquiry" comes from the word "inquire," and a dictionary tells you that inquire means to ask about. That same dictionary would tell you that an inquiry is a request for information, and, therefore, that the inquirer who receives the information has done the learning.

When inquiry is applied to learning, one must immediately consider two separate roles in the classroom—the teacher and the learner. Traditionally the role of the teacher has been that of the question-asker and, therefore, of the inquirer. But the inquirer is the one who learns and the students are supposedly the ones in the classroom doing the learning. If the teacher is the inquirer, the wrong person is doing the learning. What do teachers who look upon themselves as the principal inquirers in the classroom learn? They learn whether or not their students have the information which has been given them by the teacher, textbook, motion picture, or whatever.

When the phrase inquiry-centered teaching is used, the manner in which the word inquiry was used in the last paragraph is *not* what is meant. In inquiry-centered teaching the students, *not* the teacher, ask questions that will deliver them information. The teacher does ask questions but these questions are not demands for specific information. Rather, these questions guide the students in carrying out activities which will provide the needed information. In other words, in an inquiry-centered classroom the specific requests for information are made of the materials and activities being used. The teacher's questions are intended to guide the students in the use of the materials. The specific responsibilities of the teacher will be discussed in Chapter 5.

But rather than attempting to find out about inquiry by reading about it, you will find out much more, and more rapidly, by experiencing it. An experiment follows. You *must* do the experiment. Only in that way can you begin to gain an understanding—a "feel"—of how inquiry learning is accomplished, and only if you understand inquiry learning can you develop an understanding of what inquiry-centered teaching is all about. Now, *do the following experiment*—please!

GATHERING DATA

TEACHING PROCEDURE A[1]—THE LEARNING CYCLE

GATHERING DATA

Experimenting You will need a wire, a dry cell, and a light bulb. The objects are shown in the picture. Make a system of the three objects (see Figure 4–1). What evidence do you find that the objects will interact? After you find evidence of interaction, draw a picture of how you connected the wire, the dry cell, and the light bulb.

First, use one wire to produce interaction. Then use two wires.

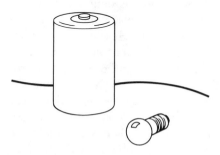

Figure 4–1

---

[1] This teaching procedure was adapted from John W. Renner, Don G. Stafford, and Vivian Jensen Coulter, *Models* (Book six from *The Learning Science Program*), Encino, CA: Benziger Bruce & Glencoe and New York: Macmillan, 1977, pp. 44–48. Parenthetical references to figures have been added.

Draw a picture of how the two wires, the dry cell, and the light bulb were connected when you saw evidence of interaction.

Compare the two pictures you have drawn. How are they alike? How are they different?

At how many *different* points did you have to touch the dry cell before you observed evidence of interaction? At how many places did you touch the light bulb before you saw evidence of interaction?

Predicting   Each of the six pictures on this page (Figure 4–2) shows a system made up of a wire, a dry cell, and a light bulb. The objects in the system are connected differently in each picture. Why does the system remain the same system?

Study the various ways in which the objects in the system are arranged. Predict which of the arrangements will produce evidence of interaction. Record your predictions in a table like the one shown (Figure 4–3). Each end of a dry cell is called a *pole*. Notice that one pole is marked "+" and the other is marked "−." The "+" stands for *positive,* and the "−" stands for *negative.*

You are predicting whether each of the arrangements of the objects in the system will give evidence of interaction. Write "yes" or "no" in your table to show whether or not you expect to see evidence of interaction.

Earlier, you answered questions about the number of places a dry cell and a light bulb had to be touched before you observed evidence of interaction. Refer back to the answers to those questions. If you wish to change any of your predictions, do it now.

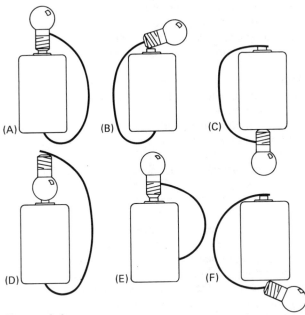

Figure 4–2

Picture	Prediction (yes or no)	Experiment (yes or no)
(A)		
(B)		
(C)		
(D)		
(E)		
(F)		

Figure 4–3

Experimenting From now on, do not change any of your predictions. You are going to do experiments with a wire, a dry cell, and a light bulb to test your predictions. Arrange the objects in the system just as they are shown in pictures (A), (B), (C), (D), (E), and (F). Record in your table whether or not you found evidence of interaction by writing "yes" or "no."

Do not be concerned if you predicted incorrectly for some arrangements of the objects. Figure out why you predicted incorrectly. Record what you decided about incorrect predictions.

GETTING THE IDEA
A wire, a dry cell, and a light bulb can be arranged in a system which does something. There is evidence of interaction.

With the lighting of the light bulb, energy is being used. The dry cell supplies the electrical energy. But in order to see evidence of interaction you had to arrange the wire, the dry cell, and the light bulb in a certain way.

The wire, the dry cell, and the light bulb were arranged in a special way. With this arrangement you observed evidence of interaction. Such an arrangement is called an
electrical circuit.

The light bulb will not light without the dry cell. The dry cell is the energy source in the circuit. The *interaction* of the wire, the dry cell, and the light bulb causes something to happen in the circuit. That interaction causes
electrical current
in the circuit.

Any evidence of electrical interaction requires current. When the starter on a car begins to hum, current is there. When a refrigerator, an electric razor, or a television set operates, current is present. Current is present when an electric light is turned on.

People sometimes refer to electric current as "juice." The word "juice" suggests a mental picture. Those who use the word are trying to make a model of electric current.

EXPANDING THE IDEA

Experimenting   You will need a dry cell, a light bulb, two brass clips, three pieces of wire, a holder for the dry cell, and a socket for the light bulb.

Put the objects together as shown in the photograph. As you will observe, the light bulb gives no evidence of interaction. Next, touch wire (A) and wire (B) together. What happens?

Put different kinds of objects between wire (A) and wire (B). Touch the two wires to the objects. Which objects cause the light bulb to light?

When the light bulb lights, the circuit is a *complete circuit.* Make a record of the kinds of materials you used in your circuit. Indicate which materials made a complete circuit.

Refer once again to the photographs . . . (Figure 4–4). When a system of electrical objects is arranged like the system in the first photograph, the arrangement is called an *open circuit.* The circuit is a *closed circuit* when something is put between wire (A) and wire (B) and the light bulb lights.

· An Analysis. Closely examine the foregoing activities. We have found that those activities usually require about five class periods. The activities are divided into three major divisions—*Gathering Data, Getting the Idea,* and *Expanding the Idea.* When those three major divisions of activities are considered together, they are the *learning cycle.* In Chapter 1 you found that the phases of the learning cycle constitute the structure of the discipline of science. When children engage in studying phenomena from the natural world, therefore, using the three phases of the learning cycle—gathering data, getting the idea, and expanding the idea—*they are studying science as the discipline is structured.* If you have any doubts or questions about the statement that the activities from *models* included here are science, go back and review the concepts introduced in Chapter 1.

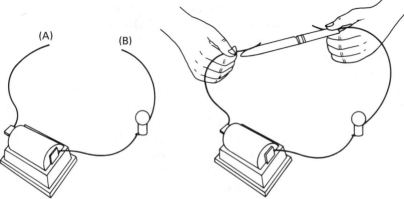

(A)   (B)

Figure 4–4

Using the structure-of-science model that you were introduced to in Chapter 1, write an explanation of why "Teaching
Procedure A," with which you just interacted, is an accurate
representation of science.

Gathering Data, Getting the Idea, and Expanding the Idea also
represent another cardinal idea in learning and teaching. Analyze what
happens in each phase of the learning cycle. In gathering data—we
are assuming you have completed the foregoing learning cycle—you
asked questions of the materials. For instance, what evidence do you
have that the objects interacted? Answers: The bulb was lighted. When
you lighted the bulb with one wire and then with two wires, you had
asked how the two arrangements of the materials were alike and different. You asked the materials at how many places the bulb and dry
cell had to be touched before the bulb lighted. You asked the materials all such questions during the "Gathering Data" phase of the
learning cycle.

How did you know what questions to ask the materials? In this
case a printed page provided the guidance you needed. That guidance
could just as easily have been supplied by a teacher. But notice that
the type of questions asked all related to the materials. The information to use in answering those questions came from the materials, and
not from some authority such as a teacher or a book. The answers came
from concrete experience; remember, the children for whom that learning cycle was written reason concretely.

You were earlier told that to inquire is to ask. In the last paragraph the point was emphasized that during the "Gathering Data"
portion of the learning cycle questions are asked of materials. When
data are gathered, then, is the inquiry complete? Not quite. When
gathering data, learners are assimilating; all the information that *can*
be acquired is being assimilated into their mental structures. Hopefully,
disequilibrium results.

The most successful inquiries are those in which the learners have
found out something definite; they are not left in a state of disequilibrium. The learners need something around which they can organize
all the information they have collected. They need an idea they can
use which tells them what all the information they have assimilated
means. In short, they need to be helped to adjust their mental structures by accommodating. At this point in the learning cycle the teacher
—or in your case the printed page—intervenes and provides the idea
or ideas needed.

The "Getting the Idea" phase of the learning cycle provides the idea that allows the learners to put all their information together. In this experiment the students need the ideas of electrical circuit and electrical current. Notice that there are no mysterious words or phrases, such as electrons, used in presenting the ideas the students need to accept when the new concept is introduced. Both of the new ideas are presented in terms of the concrete experiences the student already has had. (The students would have previously learned, using the learning cycle, the concepts of system, interaction, and evidence of interaction.) The students already had the two concepts of electrical circuit and electrical current; they had obtained them from the "things" with which they had experimented. Either a person or the printed page was necessary to introduce an idea so as to reduce the existing disequilibrium and—as Piaget said when describing adaptation (see Chapter 3)—put thought in accord with things. That is primarily an experience in accommodation.

But introducing the idea to the learners before they had had the experiences would not have been meaningful. Most certainly the phrases electrical circuit and electrical current could have been memorized but they would not have had the meaning that can be derived only from direct, concrete experience. That is why simply reading the concept(s) introduced in a learning cycle is not of educational value; the assimilation that makes the "Getting the Idea" phase of the learning cycle meaningful has not taken place.

So the students have now asked questions of the materials ("Gathering Data"), and have derived one or more organizing concepts from the answers the material has given. Is the inquiry then complete? Not quite. In science, one also asks the question of whether or not the results obtained can be replicated. Can the results be expanded to other problems? Can the results be obtained in another way? In other words, can the idea be expanded? That, of course, is the reason the third phase of the learning cycle ("Expanding the Idea") is important. Every new concept that is used to assist learners in putting thought in accord with things should be tested with three questions. These questions are:

1. What does this new idea tell me that I didn't know before?
2. Now that I have this new idea, what can I do that I could not have done before?
3. What questions can I ask using the new idea that I could not have asked before?

As a result of the experiments you did, the learners now understand the concepts of electrical circuit and electrical current, which they did not know before. They can now explain how to insert the bulb and battery in the circuit, which was a process of trial and error at the beginning. Also, they can now ask questions about what kinds of materials complete a circuit and what are the differences between a closed and an open circuit. All of the activity that goes on in answering the three questions just stated certainly helps the students to expand and apply the new idea they have just found ("Expanding the Idea"). Furthermore, the learners are also organizing the new idea they have just met with all the other ideas they have about electricity. This is, of course, the process Piaget calls organization and which he calls "putting thought in accord with itself." (If you are unsure what organization and adaptation in the Piaget model mean, please return to Chapter 3 and review these concepts.)

Explain the relationships between functioning (assimilation, accommodation, adaptation, and organization) and inquiry (gathering data, getting the idea, and expanding the idea).

GETTING THE IDEA

When a person has asked questions of materials, organized the information received, and discovered what else that new idea can be used for, the inquiry is complete. In other words, in order to teach by "the inquiry method" the complete cycle must be used. The following equation may help you apply the concept you have just learned:

inquiry = gathering data + getting the idea + expanding the idea

EXPANDING THE IDEA

What is the alternative to using the inquiry learning cycle in teaching science? Consider the following teaching procedure which is also designed to teach the concepts of electrical circuit and electrical current.

TEACHING PROCEDURE B[2]—EXPOSITION

LIGHTING A BULB
Let's do an experiment. The experiment will show us how a light bulb lights up. We can see how the electrons move from a dry cell to the bulb. The electrons cause the bulb to light. They flow through the bulb and back to the dry cell.

---

[2] John Gabriel Navarra and Joseph Zaffaroni, *Today's Basic Science, Grade 4,* New York: Harper & Row, 1963, pp. 190–192. Parenthetical references to figures have been added.

Experimenting You will need a wire, socket, dry cell, and flashlight bulb (Figure 4–5).

Place the flashlight bulb into the socket. Cut two pieces of wire. Scrape the insulation off each end of the wire. Connect the wires to the socket. Now connect the end of one wire to the negative terminal of the dry cell. Connect the end of the other wire to the inside post of the dry cell (Figure 4–6). What happens?

The electrons, or electric current, flow from the negative terminal of the dry cell. They move into the copper wire. The electrons can move into the wire because you scraped off the insulation. The electrons move along the wire to the screw on the socket. You took the insulation off the wire at this end, too.

Now the electrons move from the screw into the socket. From the socket, they go through the light bulb. The bulb lights up.

The electrons move from the bulb to the second screw on the socket. From this screw they flow into the wire again. They move back to the dry cell. They flow into the inside post, or positive terminal.

A COMPLETE CIRCUIT

Suppose you were to connect the wire only to the negative terminal and to the socket. Suppose you were to make no connection at the positive terminal. Would the light bulb still light? (Figure 4–7).

No, it would not. To get an electric current, you must always have a complete circuit. That is, you must provide a complete pathway for the electrons. You must make it possible for the electrons to flow from a negative terminal to a positive terminal.

The wires, screws, and bulbs are the path along which the electrons travel. Scientists call this path a *circuit*. The path, or circuit, is complete when the electrons can move from the outside post to the inside post of the dry cell. You must always have a complete circuit for things to work.

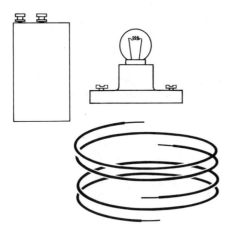

Figure 4–5

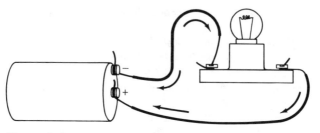

Figure 4–6

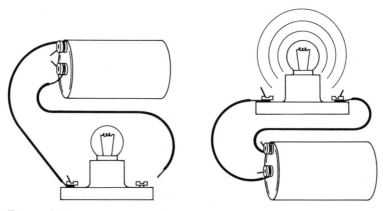

Figure 4–7

A SWITCH

A switch can be connected into a circuit. Shown on this page is a knife-blade switch (Figure 4–8). When the blade of the switch is pulled up, the circuit is not complete. Scientists say the circuit is open.

The electrons do not have a complete path when the circuit is open. They cannot move from the outside post to the inside post, or from the negative to the positive. There is no electric current. There is no flow of electrons.

Push the blade of the switch down. The circuit then is closed. The electrons can move from the negative terminal to the positive terminal.

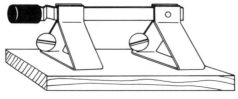

Figure 4–8

The circuit is said to be complete and closed. With a complete circuit, we have an electric current.

A switch provides a way of opening and closing a circuit. There are different kinds of switches. Among them, as we have seen, is a knife-blade switch. Another common switch is the pushbutton. Perhaps the switches in your home are toggle switches. A toggle switch is a small lever.

You can make a switch. All you need are two screws, a board, and a piece of tin.

MAKING A SWITCH
Bend the piece of tin into an L-shape at one end. Fasten this end to the wooden base with a screw (Figure 4-9). Put another screw into the wooden base. Extend the tin over this screw. Wire a circuit as shown.

Push down on the piece of tin. Make it touch the second screw. The circuit then is closed. The light bulb lights. Let the piece of tin spring up. It no longer touches the second screw (Figure 4-10). The circuit then is open.

• An Analysis. Closely examine the foregoing activities. They reflect a different purpose for teaching science than do the materials in Teaching Procedure A—The Learning Cycle. At the very beginning the activities in Teaching Procedure B—Exposition—tell the learners an experiment is to be done and then tell them why: "We can see how the electrons move from a dry cell to the bulb." In other words, the student is informed that the problem cannot be solved with observable results; its solution requires the introduction of an abstract concept—the electron. The learner is told that the assimilation which the experiment would permit would not be sufficient. The experiment is being done to see how something behaves which the learners cannot experience—an untenable situation for concrete-operational thinkers.

Experiments are very fruitful opportunities for learner assimilation, but of limited value if they do not permit maximum assimilation. According to Piaget,[3] "an experiment not carried out by the individual

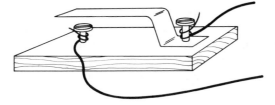

Figure 4-9

[3] Jean Piaget, *To Understand Is To Invent,* New York: Grossman, 1973, p. 20.

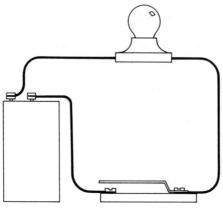

Figure 4–10

himself with all freedom of initiative is . . . not an experiment but mere drill with no educational value." When the learners are told why the experiment is to be done and what they will see, the "freedom of initiative" needed to make an exercise or experiment has been removed.

Questions are excellent vehicles to use in promoting both assimilation and accommodation. But in order for questions to so function, the learners must formulate answers, be introduced to new ideas, and generate their own explanations (with guidance, of course). In the materials in Teaching Procedure B—Exposition—study the section called "A Complete Circuit." The question is asked: "Would the light bulb still light?" The next sentence tells the learners "No, it would not." There is no need in that instance for learners to undergo any assimilation and accommodation. They do not need to use and/or change their mental structures in that situation; the answer is already provided.

Earlier we said that the materials under Teaching Procedure B were prepared to lead students toward a different objective than those in Teaching Procedure A. In the last paragraph you saw how the Teaching Procedure B materials minimized assimilation and accommodation. In Chapter 3 the case was made that when assimilation, disequilibrium, and accommodation are maximized, learning is maximized because mental structure change is maximized. Conversely, when assimilation, disequilibrium, and accommodation are minimized, learning is minimized. The teaching procedures used in the activities in Teaching Procedure B minimize assimilation, disequilibrium, and accommodation.

· **Science Learning Cycles.** The time has come to further expand your concept of inquiry. What follows are several learning cycles in the physical and biological sciences. You are encouraged to do as many

> Using the explanation of inquiry given in this chapter, explain why the activities in Teaching Procedure B are not inquiry-oriented.

> Go back to Chapter 1 and review what the structure of the discipline of science really is. Decide whether or not the activities given in Teaching Procedure B represent science. Write a paragraph defending your decision.

> Use what you have learned so far and write a "Getting the Idea" paragraph which explains inquiry to yourself. Have a friend read your paragraph, have the friend criticize it, and then rewrite it. You are introducing yourself to the concept of inquiry.

of them as possible. Each is, of course, a complete investigation. Much of the material that follows is not suitable content for elementary school children. The first investigation on measurement, for example, involves the use of a ratio. Nearly 100 percent of elementary children *cannot* use a ratio because it involves proportional reasoning—an element of formal thought. Some of the biological science investigations could be adapted for elementary school children, but as they appear here these investigations are intended for adults. Each single investigation, and the group taken together, have one primary purpose, to provide you experience with the learning cycle—that is, inquiry. Please keep adequate records of your investigations and write adequate "Getting the Idea" paragraphs when appropriate.

INVESTIGATION 1: MEASUREMENT

GATHERING DATA
You will be given a tape measure which has the length units of the metric system on one side and the length units of the English system on the opposite side. Study these two systems carefully. Measure the height of a door in metric units and English units. Measure five other objects (all longer than a meter) in both systems of measurement. Study the data you have collected and determine how centimeters

(cm) are related to inches. You must use *only* the data *you* collected to make that determination.

GETTING THE IDEA

There are two ideas you can gain from data you have just collected. The first idea involves the relationship between inches and centimeters. What is that relationship? Write a statement of that relationship. What evidence do you have that the relationship you have just stated is true?

The second idea you can get from the data you collected involves a process. You found a relationship between two measurements. What arithmetical process did you use to find that relationship? Write a statement that explains what you did to find the relationship.

EXPANDING THE IDEA

Make a measuring system using the length of your textbook as the basic unit. The centimeter, for example, is the basic metric length unit you used in "Gathering Data." Develop prefixes that mean less than one book length or more than one book length. For example, bugabook and suprabook.

A man who uses only the metric system is buying a table from a person who uses only the English system. The table is 32 inches wide and the door through which the table is to be taken is 75 centimeters wide. The man buying the table wants to know whether or not he should buy it. What would you tell him? Be as creative as you can in your answer.

INVESTIGATION 2: LIFE CYCLES

GATHERING DATA

You will need a flat, plastic (or glass) transparent container between 10 and 15 centimeters in diameter. The container should have a transparent cover. Fill the container with bran or crushed dry cereal and also place a piece of potato or apple about 1 centimeter square and 2 or 3 millimeters thick in the container. Next place four mealworms in the container and put the cover on the container. Place the container in a warm place in the classroom; neither darkness nor special light is required.

Observe the mealworms for a long period of time—as long as 2 months may be necessary. Make careful records of any changes you see in the mealworms. Pay close attention to the bran and the apple pieces. The apple pieces are the mealworms' moisture supply, but the apple pieces should not keep the inside of the container so damp that mold appears. If mold does appear, remove it and all the pieces of cereal affected. Replace the moldy cereal with dry, clean pieces. *Do not dump the contents of the container.* Keep making observations until you see whether or not something definite happens to the mealworms.

GETTING THE IDEA

Write a paragraph which forms a concept from the data you have collected. Have two classmates read your paragraph and see if it agrees with the concept to which they introduced themselves. Be sure to discuss with most of your classmates the results of your observations which led you to form your concept.

EXPANDING THE IDEA

In this investigation you are going to work with fruit flies (Drosophila). They require a special kind of food.[4] Place that food in about six small bottles; each bottle should be about one-third filled.

Place about one dozen fruit flies in each bottle used. During a period of several weeks, observe the changes in the fruit fly vial system and determine what happens. Do the flies remain unchanged? What new organisms appear? How are all the organisms related to each other and to the fruit fly? Your data should enable you to make some definite statements regarding the life of a fruit fly.

How do the data you collected here expand the idea you formed from your data about mealworms?

You can further expand your ideas about mealworms by doing experiments which will allow you to answer these questions:

1. Does the mealworm have eyes?
2. What processes does the mealworm go through in moving?

You will be given a paper plate, a small pile of bran, and a mealworm. Please ask for any additional materials you feel you need. The following general procedures may be helpful in guiding your work.

[4] A recipe for that food follows. This recipe prepares enough food for approximately twenty vials 8 centimeters tall and 3 centimeters in diameter when approximately 2 to 3 centimeters of food are placed in the bottom of the vial.

Solution 1
1 quart of hot water
10 grams of agar
2 teaspoons of Methyl Parasept
Solution 2
28 grams of yeast
10 ounces of cold water
mix these two ingredients until there are no lumps and then add
4 ounces of molasses
Solution 3
8 ounces (by volume) of cornmeal
16 ounces of cold water
mix until there are no lumps

Be sure that the agar in Solution 1 has *completely* dissolved; then add Solutions 2 and 3 and cook until the entire mixture is fairly thick. Place the food mixture in the vials loosely. Put on the lids and allow cooling to room temperature to take place.

1. Place the bran on one side of the plate and the mealworm on the other. Watch the worm and describe its actions.
2. Form an hypothesis as to whether or not the worm has eyes and design some short experiments to test that hypothesis.
3. Observe the motion of the mealworm and inspect it carefully. On the basis of these data, describe how the mealworm moves.

When you have collected enough information to satisfy yourself that you have discovered answers to the two questions asked, form the interpretation of these data into logical statements. Be sure to give adequate reasons for your beliefs.

If you could spend additional time with these mealworms, what additional activities, experiments, or both would you suggest?

INVESTIGATION 3: THE BURNING CANDLE

GATHERING DATA
This investigation should be made with two classmates. A flat container is needed in this investigation. The container should hold at least 300 milliliters of water. You will also need at least three different types of containers with which you can cover the burning candle in the experiment. One of these containers should be a cylindrical container which has a diameter of no more than 5 centimeters. All of the covering containers should have one end sealed (see Figure 4–11).

Stick a small piece of modeling clay on the bottom of the flat container. Now place a birthday-cake candle in the clay. Pour water into the container until it is about three-fourths full. Light the candle.

First use the cylindrical container. Hold it perpendicular to the surface of the water with the open end downward. Quickly move the cylinder down over the burning candle until the open end of the cylinder is at least beneath the surface of the water. You may permit the cylinder's open end to rest on the bottom of the container; the cylinder's open end must *not* touch the modeling clay. Practice several times so you can make the movement quickly. During your practice period have your classmates make observations. When you feel you have practiced enough, fill the container with water, dump the water out, and dry the container inside and out. You fill the container with water only to drive out all the smoke and candle-combustion products; the drying is insurance against cracking.

You are now ready to begin gathering data. Place the cylinder over the burning candle and observe what happens. The entire chain of events happens so rapidly you will probably need to do the experiment three or four times to be sure your observations are precise. Your observations here are exactly what you see happening. Be sure you remove all smoke and candle-combustion products from the container after each observation.

Measure such factors as how high the water rises in the cylinder

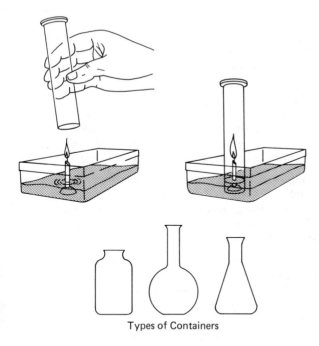

Types of Containers

Figure 4–11

and, if you have a stopwatch, how long the water continues to rise in the cylinder. Use two, three, four, or more candles. How does the number of candles used affect the results? Now use a different shape of container. What difference does that make in the results?

Many times, the question asked in this experiment is: "What makes the candle go out?" That is an easy question. Oxygen is required to keep a flame burning and the candle flame consumes oxygen until the oxygen decreases to a level which will no longer support burning. The question in this experiment is: "Why does the water rise in the container covering the candle?" The answer sometimes given to that question is that the oxygen was burned up and the water moved into the container to take its place because "nature abhors a vacuum." That answer is filled with errors and misinformation. First, a vacuum does not exist when the candle goes out; there are still many gases— including quite a bit of oxygen—remaining in the container covering the candle. Second, water does not move straight up without some assistance. Third, there is no "mysterious force" pulling the water into the container covering the candle. The answer often given, obviously, is inadequate; you need another. Do the experiment as many times as you need to gather enough data to help you get the idea for the concept involved in this experiment. Remember, when air is heated it expands and when it cools it contracts.

GETTING THE IDEA
What is the concept that explains why water is able to rise in the container covering the candle? Write a paragraph using the concept and explain why the water is able to rise.

EXPANDING THE IDEA
Four experiments follow. After you do each of them, you are to write a paragraph which explains how the concept which accounted for the water rising in the container covering the burning candle now explains what you see in each of the following experiments.

Experiment 1   A syringe and a piece of tubing are shown in Figure 4–12. Use the container which held water in your candle burning experiments. Nearly fill it with water and place the open end of the empty cylinder under the surface of the water. Hold the cylinder in that position. Use the syringe and the tubing to fill the cylinder with water.

Experiment 2   You will need three small bottles and three toy balloons. Fasten a toy balloon over the opening of one of the bottles and place the bottle in hot water. Place a second bottle in hot water for about 10 minutes, remove it, and quickly place a toy balloon over its opening. (Be careful you don't burn your fingers.) Place a balloon over the opening of the third bottle and let it stand at room temperature as a comparison. Compare the observations you make.

Experiment 3   For this experiment you will need a metal can with a tightly fitting cover that can be removed. Place a small amount of water in the can and, with the cover removed, heat the can until the water is boiling vigorously and steam is coming from the opening in the can. Remove the can from the heat and quickly cover it tightly (carefully, so you don't burn your fingers). Observe the can continuously for about 10 minutes.

Experiment 4   Remove the cover from a plastic squeeze bottle. Hold the opening under water. Squeeze the bottle vigorously. Now release your squeeze but keep the bottle's opening under water.

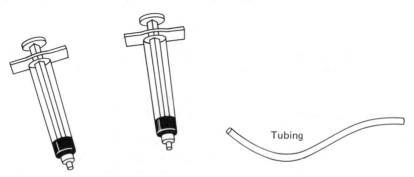

Tubing

Figure 4–12

INVESTIGATION 4: EATING AND BEING EATEN

GATHERING DATA

The animal you will meet in this investigation is called a *Daphnia;* you may have heard this animal referred to as a water flea. Study your *Daphnia* with a magnifying glass and draw a diagram of it. Identify its mouth and how it eats. Over a period of days, observe the *Daphnia* and determine how it reproduces. Next, place a few *Daphnia* in a container of clear, aged water for a day. What changes do you observe in the *Daphnia?* Place some algae in the container and observe the changes in the *Daphnia.* What do the data from this observation allow you to infer about the structure of the *Daphnia's* anatomy?

At the beginning of the investigation, place about three guppies in some clear, aged water and leave them for about 2 or 3 days. *Do not feed them.* Next, place the guppies with the *Daphnia.* What happens?

GETTING THE IDEA

Draw a diagram showing the relationship among algae, *Daphnia,* and guppies. Invent a name for that relationship. Use the symbol → to mean "is eaten by." For example, "steak → people" means steak is eaten by people.

EXPANDING THE IDEA

Select 30 living things—plants and animals—and draw a diagram showing who eats whom. Your diagram could quite properly show one living thing eating more than one other living thing and being eaten by more than one other living thing. What does your diagram make you think of? What would be a good name for your diagram?

INVESTIGATION 5: LENSES

GATHERING DATA

At the beginning of the period you will be given a convex lens and a white card. Study the lens carefully and find out all you can about it. Take it outside if necessary. Select several objects—do not use the sun—each of which is quite far away. Consider each object separately and focus its image on the card. Record the properties of each image and measure the distance between each image and the lens. Estimate the distance between each object and the lens. Make any other measurements which you feel will add to your understanding about what the convex lens is and how it functions. Now ask your instructor for a different lens and repeat your investigation.

Discuss your findings with your laboratory partners and clearly understand why you agree or disagree with them. After you have gathered all the information you need, return to the discussion area for a class summary of the findings about the convex lens.

GETTING THE IDEA
Make a chart of all the measurements you made on and with the lens.
You have just found the focal length of a lens. Write a paragraph
which describes what the focal length of a lens is.

EXPANDING THE IDEA
Fasten two convex lenses together with Scotch tape. Focus an image
from a distant object on the card with the two lenses taped together.
Now separate the lenses and focus an image with each of them. What
relationships can you see between the images formed individually by
the lenses and the image formed by the combination of two lenses?
Be sure you can prove your relationships.

Place an object just a few centimeters farther away from a lens
than its focal length. Place a white card on the opposite side. Focus an
image on the card. Describe that image. Take all the measurements
you can while the image is visible on the card (distances, size of
object, size of image, and so forth). Now see if you can find any other
point where there is an image. If you find a second image, describe it
and repeat the measurements you previously took. *Carefully* record
all your data. Study your data. What kinds of interpretations can you
make of your data? What kinds of generalizations about convex lenses
can you make? Be sure your data agree with your laboratory
partner's data or clearly understand why you disagree with your
partner. Check any data you feel should be checked.

INVESTIGATION 6: GROWING PLANTS

GATHERING DATA
Start the investigation with eight paper cups in which you can plant
bean seeds. *Do not soak the bean seeds before planting them.* Most any
type of bean will do, but we have had best results with bush beans.
Be sure you use the same kind of soil in each cup. Why is that
important? We have had best results with potting soil, which any
garden supply center will have. Plant *two* bean seeds in each cup, about
two centimeters deep. Why plant two seeds? Arrange your cups in
direct light and in a warm place.

The problem is to find out how much water will produce the best
results. Give each of three cups the following amounts of water.
(Be sure each cup has holes in it for drainage.) (1) What you believe
to be absolutely much too much. (2) What you feel is too much but not
as much as in (1). (3) What you believe is just the right amount.
(4) What you believe is not enough. Be sure you isolate all the other
variables you believe are involved and be sure they are controlled,
except the moisture. Continue your experiment until you have definite,
irrefutable results. Why were you asked to use three plants in each
moisture category?

For this investigation you need a good, healthy crop of rye grass,
some good, well-established clover plants, and some other type of

plant—we have found geranium plants to be satisfactory. Be sure to have two containers of each type of plant. Find an ideal place for the plants to grow in the same way. By ideal we mean room temperature, good lighting, and the proper amount of water—about 25 milliliters three times a week. Find a second place in the room where the temperature is satisfactory but that is in the dark. Place one of each kind of plant in the dark and one in the light. Observe and compare the pairs of plants daily. Be sure to keep records which provide you with adequate information. What do your data tell you over a period of weeks?

GETTING THE IDEA
Summarize what you have found into two concepts for growing the types of plants you have worked with.

EXPANDING THE IDEA
The concepts you just stated should enable you to decide what to do to get tall plants, really green plants, or tall green plants. You know now something about controlling the variables of light and water when experimenting with plants. Use what you know about those variables and experiment with two more. The new variables are the amount of fertilizer to use and the effect the type of soil has on plant growth.

Begin this experiment with three different types of plants (eight plants of each kind) already growing. The types we suggest are beans, peas, and clover. Be sure the plants are all growing in the same kind of soil, are in the same types of containers, and have been growing in the same environment. Why are the cautions listed in the last sentence important? Now divide the plants into four pairs of each kind. Select some chemical fertilizer, which can be purchased at any garden supply house. Give one pair just exactly what you feel is the correct amount of the chemical, a second pair just a little more, a third pair quite a bit less, and a fourth pair much too much. Why is it important to have one pair of each kind of plant receive just what you think is the proper amount? If no differences are noted at the end of a 10-day period, give all the plants a second application of the chemical. Collect all data carefully and draw some generalizations regarding plants and chemical fertilizers.

In this experiment you are to determine the affect that the type of soil has on seed and plant growth. We suggest you use at least two types of plant; for example, peas and beans. Secure three different types of soil from areas around you; sandy soil, loam, black soil, clay, and pure sand, for instance, are all suitable. In addition, use potting soil. Why is using potting soil important or even necessary? Plant three containers of each seed in each soil type. Why use three containers? Be sure the containers have proper drainage holes. Select a place in the room that has a fairly uniform temperature and adequate light. Keep the soil moist and make regular investigations over a period of several weeks. Be sure to include references to seed and plant growth in your report.

You have just participated in six science learning cycles. In each cycle data were gathered (exploration), the data were then reduced to one or two general ideas that summarized the focus of the investigation, and the concept was then applied in one or more situations. This procedure uses the three basic processes in learning—assimilation, disequilibrium, and accommodation; obviously the new thoughts developed also had to find accord with themselves (organization). Review assimilation, disequilibrium, accommodation, and organization in Chapter 3 if you have any doubt about the exact function of these concepts in learning.

In other words, the learning cycle is a teaching method inherent in the Piaget model of intellectual development. That "Piaget inherent method" not only takes into account how learning takes place but also closely adheres to the structure of the discipline of science. Review Chapter 1 if you now have any doubts about that statement. When the learning cycle is being experienced the learners are imagining, classifying, comparing, evaluating, and using all the rest of the rational powers. That is, the students are working toward the achievement of the rational powers of the free mind. Review Chapter 2 if you do not see the relationship between the "Piaget inherent method" and the central purpose of schools. The teacher next needs a procedure to use in selecting content for classroom use. That will be explored in Chapter 5.

So far this book has recommended that the learning which takes place in science should come entirely through the learning cycle. There is also a place for investigations and experiments which are done "just for the fun of doing them." They are free exploration experiments. The students can do them and the teacher may choose to complete the learning cycle. Sometimes, however, the students merely assimilate. Maybe the students accommodate by each one completing an individual learning cycle, but no data exist to test that statement. What follows are several such exploration experiments and investigations written at your level.

EXPLORATION 1[5]
Soak about 30 bush bean seeds in water for from 24 to 36 hours. Soaking beans is best done by placing several paper towels in the bottom of a container, covering them with more paper toweling, and then soaking the towels. Do not let the beans stand in water because they need air.

Split the bean seeds in half. Each half of the bean is called a

---

[5] This experiment was developed from the concept in *Communities Teacher's Guide*, "What Is a Seed? and "What Seed Parts Grow?" pp. 10–16, by the Science Curriculum Improvement Study, published by Rand McNally & Company, Chicago. Copyright 1971 by the Regents of the University of California.

> Select one science concept and prepare a learning cycle including any directions you would like the teacher to have.

cotyledon. Another structure is also found in the open seed. Separate the last structure from the cotyledons; do this for about 10 seeds. Next, plant the cotyledons in several containers and the unnamed structures in several others. Next, plant several cotyledons with the unidentified structure still attached. Also plant several containers of whole, soaked bean seeds. Paper or plastic cups which have drainage holes work nicely for this experiment. We recommend using potting soil. Watch the progress of the planted objects. Which seed parts grew? Which did not grow? What name could be invented for the unidentified structure found in the bean seeds? Why are both the cotyledons and the unidentified structure found in the bean seeds? Why are both the cotyledons and the unidentified structure necessary in the seed?

EXPLORATION 2
You will be given two eggs, each having a different color. These eggs may both be hard-boiled, one or the other of them may be, or they may both be uncooked. You are to find out the condition of the eggs you receive. You may use any three methods you wish to make your decision *except breaking the eggs*. You must return the eggs, unbroken, to the instructor. When you finish the experiment, be prepared to explain what your three methods were for determining the condition of the eggs, the data you received from those three methods, and why you made the inferences you did.

EXPLORATION 3
Complete the following steps:

1. Place a 1-kilogram weight on a small car. If necessary, place a piece of cardboard on the top of the car to provide a smooth surface for the weight to rest on. The surface should not have vertical ends. With a piece of string attached to the front of the car, start it with a jerk.
2. Repeat the procedure, but this time start the car very gradually until it has a pretty good speed. Now, by means of a string attached to the rear of the car, stop it very quickly. What happens to the weight?
3. Repeat the two previous procedures using 2- and 3-kilogram weights.
4. Interpret your data and make a tentative hypothesis as to what they mean.

Devise an experiment of your own to test the validity of the hypothesis you have drawn. After you have tested the validity of your hypothesis, what generalization can you draw?

EXPLORATION 4

This is a paper and pencil and library investigation. You need to accept that a plant grows from a seed. Next select the fruit of a plant such as an apple or a tomato. The fruit must contain seeds. Dissect the fruit and count the total number of seeds. Now go to a reference source and find out how many such pieces of fruit a plant will bear (in a lifetime in the case of the tomato or in one season in the case of the apple tree). Compute the total number of seeds the plant will bear in one season. That is called the *biotic potential* of that plant for a given season. Be sure you understand that term before going on.

Assume that each seed will produce the same number of fruits the next season. What is the biotic potential of a plant in 2 years? In 3 years? In 5 years? What has nature done to make sure the biotic potential of any plant does not reach 100 percent? How is this problem related to population growth and control?

Imagine this situation. In a large forest there are many rabbits. But in the same forest there are foxes, wolves, mountain lions, deer, and all other types of creatures. Some well-meaning persons decide that the foxes and wolves should be eliminated because they are eating the rabbits. A large fox-and-wolf drive is begun and these animals are eliminated. What will happen to the forest? Be sure to treat all the variables in your explanation. Mountain lions are natural predators on deer. Next, assume that the mountain lions are eradicated. Ultimately, what will happen to the deer? Invent a general concept that explains what these examples have been leading you to explore.

EXPLORATION 5

Water that contains hard minerals will not form lasting suds with soap until soap has combined with all the hard minerals. The reaction product usually forms a milky suspension in water.

The hardness of water may be tested by comparing the number of drops of a standard soap solution required to produce a suds lasting 30 seconds.

Prepare a standard soap solution by dissolving one level quarter-teaspoonful of granulated soap in 10 cc of distilled water. Place 5 cc (ml) of the water to be tested for hardness into a test tube covered with a rubber stopper. Then add the standard soap solution dropwise, closing the container and shaking after each drop until a lasting suds is produced. Determine the number of drops of standard soap solution required to produce lasting suds for samples of water taken from a variety of sources such as:

tap water	ditch water
distilled water	river water
farm pond water	well water
lake water	melted refrigerator frost
rainwater	

Organize your individual data in some way (or ways) and search for a relationship of pattern. These relationships or patterns will be further explored in class, where the data will be pooled.

How does a teacher go about selecting concepts to build learning cycles around? When an already-prepared program is being considered, what does a teacher look for in that program if the goal is inquiry-oriented teaching? How does the amount of time necessary to study a concept using the learning cycle compare with the time needed to cover that concept using exposition? What does a teacher do during class when using the learning cycle? These questions and others like them will be considered in Chapter 5.

Part III
EXPANDING THE IDEA

After a new idea has been found, the person having that idea can now ask many different kinds of questions. "What do I know now that I did not know before?" "What can I do now that I could not do before?" "What questions can I now ask that I could not ask before?" The foregoing three questions represent questions that can be asked after a new idea has been developed. These questions lead to the expansion of the idea to objects, events, and situations far beyond those used to establish the idea. The idea of inquiry that has just been established can now be expanded to include: (1) what the teacher does in the classroom, (2) the specific experiences the children need, (3) curricula that use inquiry and lead children to achieve the purposes of elementary school science, and (4) how that achievement is evaluated. This section of the book leads you to expand your ideas about inquiry.

Part III
DEFENDING THE IDEA

Chapter 5
Teacher Responsibilities in an Inquiry-Centered Classroom

The objectives of elementary school science were discussed in Chapter 2. These objectives are:

1. To develop in the learner the command of the rational powers.
2. To develop in the learner the ability and confidence to inquire.
3. To develop an understanding of the changing nature of the environment in terms of matter, life, energy, and their interaction.

In order to achieve the foregoing objectives, children must engage in the process of assimilation, experience disequilibrium, and make accommodations among their mental structures. These structures will then have undergone adaptation, or, in other words, the learner will have put thought in accord with things. But in order to put thought in accord with things, the learner must have things with which to interact. Now the things with which the learner interacts lead to mental-structure change and are, of course, the curriculum. *The first responsibility of the elementary school science teacher, therefore, is to select a curriculum which will lead to changes in mental structures.* How does a teacher do that?

TEACHER RESPONSIBILITIES BEFORE THE LEARNING CYCLE BEGINS

In order to experience mental-structure change, the learner must assimilate. But if a mismatch between a learner's structure and what is to be assimilated occurs, no assimilation—and, consequently, no disequilibrium and accommodation—occurs. In Chapter 3 the statement was made that formal subject matter *cannot* be learned by students in the concrete operational stage because the mental structures of concrete thought do not permit the assimilation of formal subject matter. That is a bold statement because it implies that judgments can be made which tell a teacher whether or not certain types of subject matter are concrete or formal. Also in Chapter 3 the criteria for judging whether a concept is concrete or formal were introduced.

If you are in the least bit doubtful about your ability to judge whether or not a concept is a concrete or a formal concept, return to Part 3—Interpretation, in Chapter 3, and do some assimilating and accommodating. If you are in a state of disequilibrium regarding concrete and formal concepts, the following examples should help you.

Suppose you wished to teach the concept of temperature. You could fill several beakers—or jars—with water, each having a different temperature, and have the learners measure the temperatures of the waters with a thermometer. Each student could then stick a finger in the water and tell that the warmer the water felt, the higher the reading on the thermometer. The experimenters would then have discovered that the higher the reading on a thermometer, the hotter the water would be. In other words, the temperature concept the students learned would be the reading of a thermometer. That is a concept of temperature that is entirely based upon first-hand experience. Taught in that way, temperature is a concrete concept.

There is a concept of temperature that reflects the molecular model of matter. That concept says that all molecules are constantly in motion and the more energy an object possesses, the faster the molecules move. Consequently, the hotter an object is, the faster its molecules are moving. Temperature, in other words, is a measure of molecular motion within an object. That model of temperature is derived from the kinetic theory of gases, but it can be extended to solids and liquids. When temperature is taught according to the latter concept, however, there is nothing that can be experienced. There is nothing concrete about the temperature concept. That concept is a formal concept because understanding it depends upon the students' building an abstract, mental model without benefit of experience. Such a concept cannot be assimilated by learners in the concrete operational stage because they do not have the mental structures necessary to transform the data.

In Chapter 3 the concepts of downward, weight, and gravity were examined, and whether those concepts were concrete or formal depended upon how they were taught—just as the temperature concept did. Can every concept in science, therefore, be made concrete or formal? Consider the concept of paper. If paper is thought of as something to write on, wrap packages with, use in sacks, print on, and many other such concrete uses, it is a concrete concept. But if paper is thought of primarily as a cellulose product that has a measurable thickness, a certain consistency, and other such abstract properties, it is a formal concept.

Think of the simplest concrete concept you can. Decide how it can be thought of in a concrete manner. Now decide how that concept could be thought of in a formal manner.

Next consider the concept of the atom. An atom is thought to be so small that 6.023×10^{23} atoms, for example, are found in one gram of hydrogen or 16 grams of oxygen. An atom, itself a particle, is said to be made up of many other particles. Among those particles are protons, electrons, and neutrons. Electrons have a negative electrical charge and protons have a positive electrical charge. Neutrons do not have an electrical charge; they are electrically neutral. The information about the atom just given did not come from *direct* observation of atoms, electrons, protons, and neutrons. Present beliefs about the atom and its particles are based on evidence which would not be available *if* those particles did not exist. In other words, the evidence is the product of abstract thought. Suppose, for example, that evidence were found to support the position that electrons did not exist. There would then result an entirely different model of matter than the one we now use. But such a model could be built. It would not conform to all of the generalizations to which we now subscribed about the structure of matter, but it would be a model which is compatible with the known evidence. Notice that all of the foregoing would have taken place without any direct, concrete experience with the atom or its components. The entire concept of the atom is an abstraction.

The temperature discussion and the activity you carried out demonstrate an extremely important idea in teaching. Some concepts are concrete or formal depending upon the way they are taught, and a concrete concept can be made formal. The discussion of the atom, however, demonstrates that there are some concepts which are completely formal and cannot be made concrete. An atom is an example of such a concept. The particle and wave theories of light are examples of other formal concepts which cannot be made concrete, as are the DNA molecule and genetic inheritance.

The relationship between the intellectual level of concepts and the intellectual level of students was investigated by Lawson and Renner.[1] In order to have a population which contained adequate numbers of students in the concrete and formal operational stages of thinking, grades 10, 11, and 12 were used. The courses from which the 133 participating students were selected were biology, chemistry, and physics. The concrete and formal concepts taught in each course were isolated. Examinations were then constructed which measured whether or not the students in each course understood those concepts. Using the Piagetian interview technique, the intellectual level of each of the students was determined. The investigators found that the levels of intellectual development could be subdivided into seven groups (see Figure 5–1). Next, the mean achievement score on both concrete and formal concept questions in biology, physics, and chemistry, respectively, was computed for each of the seven groups. Combining the scores of the disciplines within each of the seven groups enabled a bar graph to be drawn which displayed the relationship between success on concrete and formal concepts and levels of intellectual development. That graph is shown in Figure 5–1, and it clearly shows that students in the concrete operational stage have *no* success demonstrating that they understand formal concepts. Furthermore, only limited success is had with formal concepts by those students who have begun to leave the concrete thought stage but have not as yet entered the formal stage; we called that group "postconcrete." The success with formal concepts increases as students move more and more deeply into the formal thought period. The data shown in Figure 5–1 clearly demonstrate that students in the concrete operational stage do not develop understanding of formal operational concepts.

Not infrequently teachers believe that when a concept to be taught becomes too abstract, all that is necessary to help the students learn is a concrete model. Models of atoms and molecules, what happens in an electron tube, and how osmosis in the intestines takes place are examples of models often used to assist students in the concrete operational stage "learn" formal concepts. Teachers forget that the model, not the concept, is what is concrete. The students still must have the mental

[1] Anton E. Lawson and John W. Renner, "Relationships of Science Subject Matter and Developmental Levels of Learners," *Journal of Research in Science Teaching,* 12 (4): 347–357, 1975.

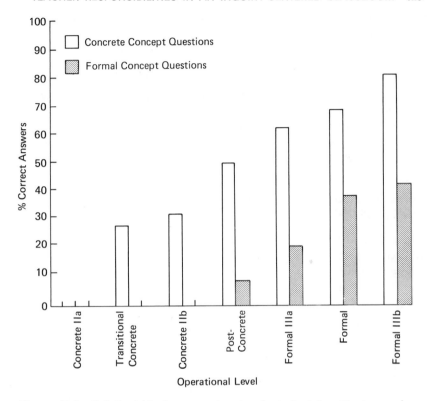

Figure 5–1   Relationship between levels of student functioning and success on concrete and formal concept questions. The data indicate that students do not experience any success with formal concepts until they have left the concrete thought stage and have entered that transitional period (postconcrete) leading to entry into the formal thought period. Even then, success is limited.

SOURCE: John W. Renner, "Significant Physics Content and Intellectual Development," *American Journal of Physics* 44(3): 218–222, 1976; based on research done by Anton E. Lawson and John W. Renner.

structures necessary to transform the data the model gives them, which was the problem before using the model—these structures were lacking. Using the model does not provide the mental structures necessary for the transformation of data. What do the students do? If they value survival in school, they have no choice but to use meaningless recall to memorize the model and hope they can survive the next test. That, of course, convinces the teacher that the concept is being understood, but when the students cannot use the concept in another context, the teacher explains that event by saying "they forget rapidly" or "they didn't study hard enough." Rarely does such a teacher attribute the lack of ability to use a concept presented through a model to the fact that the model, not the concept, was learned. After all, "they did a good job on the test." There is one type of model students can profit from; that type of model will be examined in Chapter 8.

The first responsibility of the teacher to implement the learning cycle, therefore, must be discharged before meeting the class for the first time. That is, the curriculum to be used must be selected. That selection must be based upon the facts that: (1) concrete learners *cannot* learn formal concepts; and (2) for all practical purposes, all the students in elementary school beyond the first grade are in the concrete operational stage of thinking.

TEACHER RESPONSIBILITIES IN THE "GATHERING DATA" PHASE OF THE LEARNING CYCLE

The curriculum has been selected. The teacher has discharged the first responsibility of teaching—something to investigate has been provided. There are existing programs—both textbook and nontextbook—which can be used in implementing the learning cycle. These programs will be discussed in Chapter 8. In addition to content being usable by learners in the concrete operational stage, there are two other criteria that content should satisfy; you have seen these before.

1. The content must be useful to lead the learners to develop their rational powers—it must lend itself to investigation.
2. The learners should gain an increased understanding of, and appreciation for, their environment as a result of having the learning experiences provided.

There is one additional criterion which a curriculum should satisfy. If science is being taught, the procedures being used should not be thought to constitute something else by an observer. In other words, the science studied in the classroom must be recognizable as science by a scientist; that is, the integrity of the discipline of science must be maintained. You will remember that in Chapter 1 science was found to be the quest for knowledge, not the knowledge itself.

What is the first classroom responsibility of the teacher? Keep in mind that during this phase of the learning cycle the students are to gather data about the concept to be learned. In order to do this the investigation must be begun, and our experience has taught us that the best way to begin an investigation is to provide the learners with materials to investigate. During the "Gathering Data" phase of the learning cycle, therefore, the first responsibility of the teacher is to make certain that materials are available to conduct an investigation. If you want the children to determine whether or not different types of plants need different amounts of water, you need several different types of plants. If, for example, you wish children to investigate whether or not plants need light, you need plants, a dark place to put some of them, and a place in the light for others. Regardless of the situation the teacher and pupils decide to investigate, the teacher has the responsibility for securing the necessary materials—this does not rule out teachers requesting children to bring specific items to school or accepting voluntary pupil-contributed materials. If chalkboard, chalk, and "good books" are substituted for actual experience with materials, however, you are asking children to construct mental models without experience. Thinkers in the concrete operational stage cannot do that. *To keep an investigation going the teacher must supply the child with proper and sufficient materials.*

The investigation is now under way; data are being gathered. What does the teacher do next? The second major classroom responsibility of the teacher is to keep the investigation going. Now if we assume the materials problem is taken care of, the best tool available

Figure 5–2 The materials used in science teaching often are those which are easily obtainable.

to the teacher to keep work under way is social transmission. You will remember that in Chapter 3 social transmission was one of the factors Piaget states as necessary to achieve movement from one intellectual development stage to another.

The first type of social transmission that can occur in a classroom is students talking to students. Now students talking to other students can cause noise. For some reason, and no one seems to know why, the attitude has developed that the quiet classroom is the classroom in which learning is progressing most rapidly. Perhaps this attitude that a classroom should be quiet developed in the educational past when books, charts, films, filmstrips, slides, and all other types of educational materials and proper learning activities were so scarce that if the learners were to find out anything, they had to *listen* to the teacher. If so, that attitude lost meaning with the invention of the printing press. Another notion about the quiet classroom that is sometimes advanced is that children being quiet in the presence of a teacher shows respect. It may—but it may also show fear. In any case, there are occasions when administrators, school board members, and even parents judge the effectiveness of a teacher by how quiet that teacher can keep the classroom. These persons seem to think that a quiet atmosphere is conducive and even essential to productive thinking; such is not the case.

We are not advocating a noisy classroom. What we are suggesting is that noise being made by a group of pupils involved in the planning

Figure 5–3 The teacher can help the children gather data.

of an experiment, carrying out that plan, or interpreting the results produced by an experiment is inquiry-centered noise, essential to the process of inquiry and to excellent social transmission. We would agree that unnecessary noise (yelling, foot stamping, desk pushing, and so forth) is not necessary or desirable to the progress of the learning experience, and can be very disturbing; in fact, such behavior is im-polite to other children in the class and to other classes within the school. Such behavior cannot be permitted, and, if it is, the teacher is allowing the children to develop irresponsible attitudes with respect to one person's responsibilities to another.

How can a teacher judge when the noise of social interaction be-comes excessive? You cannot be given an answer to that question be-cause no two school buildings are alike and no two teachers have the same tolerance level for noise. Ask yourself if the noise is *productive* noise and if in that particular building it will disturb anyone. If the answer to the first criterion is "No"—that is, the noise is not produc-tive—then you, as the teacher, should get the attention of the class and find out why. If the level of productive noise is disturbing other classes, you and the children need to determine an effective way to control it. Noise, as such, is not the hallmark of a good or poor investi-gation being carried on in the classroom—the deciding criterion is what is causing the noise or the lack of it.

When children are engaging in social transmission, they are re-flecting a classroom quality that must be present if the learning cycle is to be effective. That classroom quality is establishment by the teacher of an environment that tells students they are welcome to use materials, ask questions, talk among themselves, and act in a natural—but re-sponsible—manner. The establishment of a warm, friendly, accepting, responsible environment in the classroom is a major responsibility of the teacher. When that responsibility has been fulfilled, the teacher will find that the assimilation that occurs during the gathering-data phase of the learning cycle will have seriousness and productiveness not present without the environment just described. Furthermore, the in-creased depth of assimilation will facilitate the understanding of the concept presented in the next phase of the learning cycle.

All the while the children are engaging in social transmission among themselves, they are also engaging in social transmission with the teacher. That social transmission serves many different purposes and is essential to students' developing an understanding of the content as well as developing intellectually. Furthermore, student-teacher trans-mission is essential to keeping the investigation going. Some specific examples of student-teacher social transmission follow.

Suppose a class cannot get an investigation designed or gets one under way and becomes hopelessly "stuck." What responsibilities does the teacher have in such a situation? The Educational Policies Commission states that the teacher has the responsibility of "selecting problems which are within his (the child's) grasp, providing clues and cues to their solution, suggesting alternative ways to think about them."[2] That is another way of describing the teacher's responsibility of assisting in keeping the children moving in their investigation. That statement does not mean that children are not allowed to follow an incorrect hypothesis or assumption. In fact, there are many times when young investigators will teach themselves much more by following an incorrect assumption than they will by being kept on the precise course by the teacher. Children should be permitted to follow that plan of investigation which seems logical *to them*. If that investigative pattern is not a fruitful one, that fact will most likely be discovered, either because the data produced do not make sense, or the investigation itself cannot be pushed to completion using the operational plan with which it was begun. In either case, such a situation clearly demonstrates the need for informed, adult assistance. The teacher needs to step into the investigation at this point and review with the children how they reached the point in the investigation at which they have arrived. Often in such a review the children themselves will see where they began their search on an incorrect assumption or wrong information. If not, the teacher needs to suggest to them an alternate way of thinking about the original problem; a way that will ultimately lead them to a redesign of the investigation which they will be able to pursue to completion and which will provide them with usable data. An alternate way of thinking about a problem is not giving children an answer—it is simply a method of refocusing their attention on the problem being considered.

A group of children was studying the ideas of skeletal structure by assembling skeletons of various animals. Upon receiving their particular package of bones the children carefully inspected them, began to assemble the skeleton, and immediately became convinced that the skeleton was that of a rabbit (in fact, it was a cat skeleton). This assumption led the pupils to consistently look for "ear bones" which they asserted must be long and wide. The entire project was hopelessly stalled because the children could not understand why they could not find the ear bones. Although the teacher could have told them that a rabbit's ears do not contain bones, he elected to suggest an alternate way of thinking about the skeleton. The teacher asked the children why they thought the skeleton they were working with was that of a rabbit. The students replied that the bones of the back legs

[2] Educational Policies Commission, *The Central Purpose of American Education*, Washington, D.C.: NEA, 1961.

were shaped like a rabbit's back legs, and the skeleton was about the size that a rabbit's skeleton would be. These are both good reasons for supposing that the skeleton was that of a rabbit, and the teacher used both in providing the children an alternate way of thinking about the skeleton. The pupils were asked what other animals were about the size of a rabbit, and they named several, among which was the cat. The teacher then asked them if any of the animals they had just named might have back legs similar to a rabbit's. Before too long the children decided that a cat might. The teacher then said, "If your skeleton is that of a cat or any of the other animals you named rather than a rabbit, what kind of ear bones would you expect to find?" The children agreed they would probably not find any and began assembling the skeleton. Notice that the teacher did not in any way suggest that the pupils were wrong in their thinking about the ear bones of a rabbit. The children were simply provided with an alternate way of thinking about the skeleton to assist them in keeping the investigation moving.

Providing a clue to students who are stuck is a more direct process than suggesting alternate ways of thinking about a problem. Often, however, the clue that is provided is very specific and germane to the investigation only at a particular point and at a particular time in the investigation. For example, a teacher placed a mealworm in the middle of a 3 inch $\times$ 5 inch card and held the card above a table. The mealworm crawled off the edge of the card and fell to the table. The teacher asked a girl if what she had just seen suggested anything about whether or not mealworms could see. The girl answered, "If the mealworm can see, he shouldn't have fallen off the card." The girl was then asked what kind of clue her observation gave her about the belief that mealworms can see. (The girl had previously stated a belief that they could see.) The girl agreed that the observation had given her some ideas, but that more experiments would be needed to determine the meaning of the clue she had just received. Notice that the clue the teacher provided was one the girl could observe, and not a verbal one. Clues that provide actual data for children are the best (the girl is in the concrete operational stage), but sometimes verbal clues are the only ones that can be used. Teachers should not refuse to provide clues just because the clue is a verbal one.

Teachers, then, do have a particular responsibility to keep an investigation going by providing alternate ways of thinking about a problem, and clues to the solution of the problem when the investigation bogs down or when it has followed an incorrect direction to a point from which it cannot progress. In summary: *Teachers must be ready to provide alternate ways of thinking about an investigation and clues to a problem's solution when keeping an investigation going by using social transmission.*

> Make a list of nonverbal clues a teacher could give children during an investigation.

There is a common type of social transmission which takes place in every classroom regardless of the teaching method used. Every teacher asks questions.

> Ask yourself why teachers ask questions, and record your answers.

The first reason some teachers will give for asking questions is that they want to find out what the children know. That reason can represent a legitimate use of questions. Answers to such questions allow teachers to: (1) begin the learning cycle with the basic experiences the children need in learning a concept; (2) review the "Gathering Data" portion of the learning cycle before presenting the children with the idea the data represent, and/or (3) redesign plans for the activities the students will use in the "Expanding the Idea" portion of the learning cycle. Such questions can also be used to check such mechanical details as the use of a data recording system, vocabulary, the measuring system, or materials to be used in an investigation before it begins. This checking with questions can often save a great deal of time.

Notice, however, that the uses of questions just proposed *do not include* using questions to let the students find out what they must know. That is using questions to find out what a student knows in order that the student might be led to think as the teacher does. Unless students are led to change their minds through questions *asked about data the students have,* questions are used improperly. Not infrequently teachers ask a question to get an answer they have already decided upon. Such teachers rarely ask questions to find out what the students think, believe, have observed, or have found out. In other words, teachers too often want children to leave school knowing what they, the teachers, know. Teachers who use questions in this manner do not believe that the students can contribute to their own education. Such persons must, then, also believe that students must be fully educated for their futures when they leave school, because if they cannot make a contribution to their own educations while in school, they cannot be expected to have learned how to learn. They cannot, therefore, continue to learn on their own after leaving school. This is an absurd position for teachers to find themselves in, and is the result of teachers using questions to make a point they wish to make rather than using questions to assist students gather data or expand ideas. Asking students questions to find out if they think as the teacher does soon becomes a game for the students. After a few years in school answering questions becomes a matter of the students' attempting to read the teacher's mind. When that happens the students have stopped inquiring—developing their rational powers—and have begun to "figure people out."

When a teacher asks, "What do you think, Susan?" the teacher must be very sure of really asking Susan what she thinks, and not, "What do you think *I* think, Susan?" This means that when Susan tells the teacher what she thinks, the teacher is obligated to accept Susan's answer cheerfully. If a teacher asks questions and then tells the student giving the answer, "No, that is wrong," or "That's not what I had in mind," the student will attempt to become a mindreader, or will completely withdraw and simply say, "I don't know."

When students volunteer their best efforts in answering a question,

Figure 5–4   Teachers must ask questions, and they must also accept the answers children give them.

and those efforts are rejected again and again, the egos of the students are damaged. Students in such a classroom environment quickly learn not to put their egos in jeopardy by attempting to answer a question, and elect simply to not participate in the mindreading game.

Does this latter statement imply that teachers are obligated to accept all answers that students offer to questions? Our findings tell us that teachers should accept all honest answers to questions, and Karplus defends this position:

> . . . student's replies should be judged on their merit and not on the basis of conforming to the teacher's expectations. . . . One way of framing suitable questions is to address them to individual pupils. "What have you observed, John?" or "What evidence do you have that the objects interacted, Mary?". . . . The only incorrect answers to such questions would be very deliberate lies on the part of the pupils. As long as they are honest, their replies are automatically correct even if each child reports a different observation and none agrees with the teacher.[3]

A teacher asks questions to assist students in continuing their quest for information or in expanding an idea they have been presented. Such questions as, "How could you get the same results another way? What do your results tell you? How many times has that happened? Why do you think your experiment doesn't work? What did you find that made you feel you should do the experiment that way?" are examples of the types of questions that encourage the use of the rational powers and keep a student involved in the learning process. They are the types of questions that keep an investigation going.

If students are to move from one intellectual development stage to another, they must think. Questions can be used to keep students thinking. Consider such questions as these:

1. Is the circuit you are using correctly hooked up?
2. Was the water used in your experiment hot enough?
3. Did you get good results?
4. Are the three measurements you made all accurate?

These four questions have a common property. They can all be answered with a "yes" or a "no." Now "yes" or "no" questions are not conducive to stimulating the thought processes of a learner. In fact, they tend to stop the thought processes. When a teacher gets a "yes" or a "no" answer, there is no suitable follow-up question except the nebulous "Why?", and that question can be interpreted in only one of two ways:

---

[3] Robert Karplus, "Science in the Elementary School," *New Developments in Elementary School Science—A Conference,* Oklahoma City, Oklahoma: Frontiers of Science Foundation of Oklahoma, 1964, p. 11.

the learners can think they are being asked: (1) why they believe what they said is true; or (2) what reason can they give for what they saw happen.

Think back now to learners in the concrete operational stage. They think only with the immediate present or in terms of what they have concretely experienced in the past. In other words, they think only in terms of reality. Now if such learners believe they are being asked (1) above, they will revert to the concrete events of the situation and repeat their observations. That does not lead them to analyze, synthesize, infer, and use the other rational powers. If concrete learners believe they are being asked (2) above, they are being asked to go beyond the data and form conclusions based upon abstract reasons. You know that students who reason concretely cannot do that.

"Yes" or "no" questions—and the usual follow-up "why" question—are not conducive to leading students to make further observations, conduct additional experiments, figure out data currently in hand, or do any additional type of activity that might lead to additional data or better understanding. In fact, "yes," "no," or "why" questions are most often viewed by students as a chance to get their defenses properly organized because the teacher is quizzing them.

"Yes" or "no" questions are not productive questions which lead to increased intellectual development because they are representative of a class of questions that tend to restrict thinking. That class of questions focuses the attention of the learner on a specific factor in the investigation or gives the learner direct information; it is called *convergent*. A convergent question tends to cause the learner to look inward, toward what has been done, and not outward, toward what might be done; in other words, it tends to terminate an investigation. Such questions encourage the learner to concentrate on retaining facts rather than using the learner's head for something better, such as evaluating a suggestion from the teacher, analyzing what needs to be done to implement a thought triggered by a question from the teacher, or synthesizing data from an experiment and drawing inferences and generalizations.

Convergent questions can be used to advantage in inquiry-centered teaching *if* the teacher uses them to focus attention on a particular portion of an investigation with which the learner is having difficulty. "Yes" or "no" questions can be used here. "Is the dry cell you are using dead?" is a "yes" or "no" question that may help unravel why an investigation is not being fruitful. If the learners are led to engage in such activities as analyzing their errors or correcting faulty materials through a series of convergent questions, they can make the adjustments needed and move on. Once the learners are thinking in a convergent manner, however, the teacher has the responsibility for asking questions that will stimulate them to think in a wider scope. This type of question is a *divergent* question.

Divergent questions invite the learner to think in a multiplicity of directions and to consider a number of possible explanations for the data collected. The question, "What do you believe the best procedure is to collect information?" illustrates the best type of divergent question. A typical convergent question often asked by teachers is, "Does the information you have support the idea we have been studying?" Convergent questions tell learners that what is really important is not what they think or what their information tells them, but that the proper thing to believe is what they have been told. Divergent questions tell learners that it is what they have to say that is important. If your purpose in the classroom is the transmission of information about a particular discipline, divergent questions are of little value because they tend to lead the learner away from what is and toward what might be. The principal purpose of asking divergent questions is to find out the direction of the learner's thinking and what is being thought.

Earlier you were introduced to four questions that required "yes" or "no" answers. These questions are also convergent questions. How could these questions be made into questions which stimulate the learner to think, and lead toward divergent thinking? Reread the first "yes" or "no" question asked. Now consider this restatement of that question: "How could you show that your circuit is properly hooked up?" That question invites the learners to rethink how they hooked up the circuit and the reasons they had for so doing. (These reasons may include that they thought it would work that way.) The teacher is now in the position to use an effective divergent question: "How could you hook up your circuit another way and get the same results?" Such a question invites learners to utilize their rational powers and to learn more about electrical circuits. The foregoing would probably not have taken place if a "yes" or "no" question had been used.

Rewrite the "yes" or "no" questions 2, 3, and 4 into questions that cannot be answered "yes" or "no." Then for each write a divergent question that could be used following the reply made to the question you just constructed.

Often teachers use questions as a disciplinary measure. If the teacher is using a question to redirect the attention of learners from something nonproductive to something productive, or to help them focus their attention on the problem at hand, we would agree that a limited use of this technique can have a beneficial effect. If, however,

Figure 5–5   Questions during an experiment help develop under-standing.

the teacher uses questions to show the learners that they don't know something, have made an unacceptable interpretation of data, have improperly designed an experiment, or "haven't studied," we condemn such uses of questions. The teacher who follows this procedure risks destroying the morale of the child focused upon. In addition the students may begin to doubt that the teacher really wants them to gather data, generate all the ideas they can about those data, and expand any idea given. Questions can be used productively in a disciplinary way only if they are intended to focus (or redirect) the attention of students on the problem being considered.

How is a question asked? Perhaps the best way is to phrase the question as simply and directly as possible, to stop for just an instant, and then to call upon an individual student. Calling upon the student first and then asking the question is an invitation to the rest of the students to stop thinking about the specific question being asked. This will not always happen, but there exists that inherent danger. Sometimes teachers ask questions and then do not ask a specific student; this procedure leads the class to provide, and the teacher must then accept, a "gang" answer or chorus. While this procedure does stimulate the entire class to think about the question, gang answers could result in serious class-control problems. If the question is asked directly, and the teacher pauses—the entire class is stimulated to think. If an individual is then called upon, the possible loss of class control by the teacher is avoided.

One of the most important principles to remember in questioning is that the questions the teacher asks should not be trivial; they should be genuinely concerned with the problem being identified or the data being interpreted. The first question asked should be so directed that it begins the discussion about the most apparent aspects of the pending or completed investigation. A question such as, "How much have your plants grown since the last watering?" is direct, to the point, and suggests a definite pupil action. The foregoing question is superior to, "What effect has the water which we have been giving the plants had on them?" This question suggests that there should be some obvious effect that water has had on the plants (and there may be none) and also demands that the students begin to think in the abstract—an ability that elementary-school-age children do not usually have. Questions, therefore, should be direct and to the point. Questions must also not be too broad in scope, but should let the learner focus on a specific idea. "Name one property which your object has, Mike," is a superior question to, "What properties does your object have, Mike?" Each question asked should let the learner uncover just a bit more of the concept being developed and, in most cases, small steps or "bites" are best for this. Questions, then, should be important, direct, specific, and when used sequentially should lead the learner to the development of a concept.

Just as no one can tell you exactly how to establish and maintain discipline in your classroom, no one can tell you precisely how to ask questions. At one point in our research, we asked a group of 50 experienced, inquiry-centered teachers to contribute their ideas on asking questions. We have summarized their responses on the following pages. Each teacher was asked these six questions:

1. Why do you ask questions?
   (Responses)
   a. To start the learner thinking.
   b. To see if the learner is thinking in the direction of the problem.
   c. To put the learner on a definite track if necessary.
   d. To invite learner participation.
   e. To see what the learners know about a particular problem before beginning an investigation.
   f. To create interest.
   g. To allow learners to develop confidence.

2. What do you expect from a question?
   (Responses)
   a. An honest reply.
   b. A response that leaves both the teacher and the student free to ask another question (thus questions that invite a "yes" or "no" answer are of limited value).
   c. An opportunity for the student to ask him- or herself a question.
3. What do you want a question to do to the learning situation?
   (Responses)
   The question should:
   a. Free a student to ask questions.
   b. Personally involve the learner.
   c. Lead the learner or suggest to him.
   d. Stimulate interaction among the learners.
   e. Lead to further investigations.
4. What kind of question should be asked?
   (Responses)
   a. An important one.
   b. One to which the learner believes the answer is important.
   c. One that stimulates inquiry.
   d. A question devoted to one idea that is small enough to comprehend.
   e. A question that can be built on.
   f. A question that is not misleading.
   g. One that requires more than "yes" or "no."
   h. Use "why" questions sparingly, since they can be indefinite; instead of asking why something happened or is true, ask the student what evidence he can give that something happened or is true.
5. When do you ask a question?
   (Responses)
   a. When you want the learner to move on.
   b. When a learner's mind is wandering.
   c. To get learners back on the track or away from a dead end.
   d. To solicit problems and develop areas for investigation.
   e. To check the group's understanding.
   f. To stimulate group discussion.
   g. To improve a learner's self-image.
   h. To focus attention on the inquiry at its beginning.
   i. To see if a learner is ready to undertake an individual inquiry.
   j. To provide the teacher with the opportunity for conceptual invention.

      k. To initiate exploration.
      l. To begin discovery experiences.
      m. To lead the learner toward another concept.
      n. To find what the learner is doing and thinking.
  6. How do you ask questions?
     (Responses)
      a. Ask for the attention of the class.
      b. Ask with enthusiasm and genuine interest but easily and informally.
      c. Ask the question and then select a respondent.
      d. Encourage students first to listen carefully to the question and then to volunteer answers.
      e. Don't rush the student to respond.
      f. Generally use volunteers to answer.

You know, of course, that all answers must be accepted. These six general, teacher-made categories are presented to you not as rules but as data on which to build your own solutions.

Use the information on the last few pages as data and develop, in writing, a plan you believe will be effective for *you* to use in asking questions.

    Providing materials, clues, and opportunities for social transmission are all teacher responsibilities during the "Gathering Data" phase of the learning cycle. You have seen that the proper use of questions can provide the opportunities for much social transmission. That social transmission cannot take place, however, if the teacher does not listen to what the learners say.

    When a question has been asked the teacher must listen to the replies very carefully. Only then will that teacher know what questions to ask next. This is one important reason for listening, but there is a more important reason. When someone is asked a question, the one being questioned that usually assumes the response they give is important. If the teacher is not attentive, the students quickly learn that their answers are important only if they agree with the teacher's ready-made answer, and you are back to the mind-reading syndrome discussed earlier. The rapport between the teacher and the class has been decreased. Listening carefully to the children can greatly aid rapport, but leading them to understand that their replies are important is essential for another reason. It tells the children that they, as well as the teacher, have a responsibility in carrying out the activities of the class. Developing the ability to listen to what children have to say is not easy for an adult—adults usually feel that the learning can proceed much more rapidly if they interpret what has been said and, in short, tell the children what they should know. We, as teachers, must constantly remind ourselves that the principal goal we are reaching for is to assist children in learning why they know what they know (learning how to learn), and that goal can best be achieved if we use the contributions of the children in advancing their understanding of the topic under consideration. We cannot, however, utilize the children's contributions if we do not listen and find out what they are.

Earlier in this chapter the environment necessary to encourage pupils to become involved in gathering data was discussed. There is perhaps no better way to establish an environment conducive to inquiry than for the teacher to become a willing, involved investigator with the children. If the students do the investigating, collect and interpret the

Figure 5–6 If the teacher establishes an environment in which children can learn to investigate, the teacher too must be a willing investigator.

data about the problem under consideration, and the teacher then rejects the results of what the children have done, the students are going to conclude very quickly that the investigation process is a fake. They will begin to think that the teacher knew the answers all the time and, unless data are produced which allow them to conclude what the teacher wants them to conclude, their investigation has failed. If the teacher is sincere about teaching children to investigate, *all the results that are produced must be accepted.* When the teaching process is based on an investigation, the teacher will function best by becoming an investigator with the students.

Teachers can best show their intentions to be investigators during the time when data are being interpreted. When data are available for inspection and evaluation, they must be arranged in an order that will allow all the children to view them at the same time. A technique that is quite useful in allowing data to be efficiently displayed and in enabling the teacher to become a part of the investigation is to use the chalkboard and become the class secretary. The students should first be led to identify the several factors (variables) about which data have been gathered, and should then be asked to suggest procedures for arranging these data in a convenient order. If no suggestions for the arrangement come from the class, here is an excellent opportunity for the teacher to become an actual part of the investigation; a method can be suggested for arranging the data and the children urged to contribute to the discussion. If the teacher freely changes the data-arranging procedure to conform to the wishes of the class, the learners have seen a concrete demonstration that the teacher is an investigator too.

An additional behavior that will contribute to students' acceptance of the teacher as an investigator develops when the data placed on the chalkboard (or chart) are interpreted. This is a crucial time in maintaining a classroom environment that encourages or discourages active investigation by the students, and teachers demonstrate to the students which kind of classroom environment is maintained by their attitudes toward the data collected. If teachers show that they do not have faith in the information the children have gathered (by actually stating that the information is not believable or by acting skeptically toward it), the investigative spirit within the classroom has probably been lost. But if a teacher accepts the data as any member of the group does and continually asks about what those data tell, that teacher has shown that not only the information found but also the group's investigative procedures are accepted.

Because of the teacher's accepting attitude, the class believes their investigative procedures and data have been accepted. Now there are two avenues open to the teacher. The students can be led to summarize

Figure 5–7   An inquiry-centered class will involve the teacher in many class activities, including that of class recorder.

their data and, if the problem or situation under study warrants it, form a generalization, or the teacher can ask another question which must then be investigated. If, however, the teacher realizes that the students are reaching an unacceptable generalization or conclusion, a second approach is available which the teacher can use and still be accepted by the children as an investigator. This is the suggestion of an additional investigation to confirm the students' findings. The teacher would, of course, also suggest an additional experiment when such an investigation led the children to a generalization acceptable to the discipline of science and, of course, to the teacher. (The children must not be aware that the teacher views their results as unacceptable.)

The gathering-data phase of the learning cycle demands a great deal from the teacher *after* an appropriate curriculum has been selected. Specifically, the teacher is responsible for:

1. Material with which the students are to work.
2. Establishing an environment which invites the students to participate actively in investigations and engage in social transmission.
3. Keeping the investigation going by providing clues to the students, asking questions, listening to the students, and being a participant in the classroom activities.

Keep in mind that if teachers do not discharge the foregoing responsibilities they have damaged the process of assimilation, and without assimilation there is no disequilibrium, no consequent accommodation, and no mental-structure change. If a school does not lead students to mental-structure change, it does not lead them to achieve the central role of the school—the development of the ability to think. The primary role of the "Gathering Data" phase of the learning cycle, therefore, is assimilation, and that is a mandatory part of the learning process.

TEACHER RESPONSIBILITIES IN THE "GETTING THE IDEA" PHASE OF THE LEARNING CYCLE

To understand the teacher responsibilities in this second phase of the learning cycle the purpose of "Getting the Idea" must be clear. That meaning begins with the consequence of assimilation, which is disequilibrium. In Chapter 3 we referred to a mismatch between what is assimilated and existing structures. Now the process by which structures are revised—the mismatch is removed—is equilibration.

The experiences which learners have during the "Gathering Data" portion of the learning cycle have provided each of them with the concept of what is being dealt with. But there is no organizing principle, no framework, no language which the learners can use to express this concept. In order for the learners to leave the disequilibrium state, someone must *invent* a principle, the necessary framework, and the language, necessary for them to use to get the idea altogether. That "someone" may be the learner or the teacher, but the learner must encounter an organizing scheme that permits the formation of the idea. In the process the learner acquires a name, label or some other manner of identifying the concept in the future. The disequilibrium has now been removed. This entire process is quite plainly accommodation. The learner now has undergone the complete process of adaptation—assimilation and accommodation—or has put thought in accord with things. Stated another way, the learners have changed their structures to accommodate reality as they encountered it.

During this period the teacher has some important responsibilities. First, each of the class members must know the source of all the data that are used in the process of presenting them with the new idea. The experiments done, the measurements taken, the data collected—anything done in the experiment must be understood by the learners. However, do not expect the learners to understand what those data mean. If they do, they have invented the organizing scheme for themselves and already have the idea they are to obtain from the learning activity.

The second major responsibility of the teacher in the "Getting the Idea" phase of the learning cycle is to provide whatever the learners need to give them the organizing scheme to which they must accommodate. *Generally that includes the language of the concept.* In the example which follows, fourth grade children have experienced all manner of differences among familiar systems. These systems have included their classroom, the playground, and athletic teams. In short, they have experienced that there are many differences in what appears to be a common system. They next encounter the following "Getting the Idea."

GETTING THE IDEA[4]

As you have observed, the parts of a system can differ. For example, you can hold a baseball bat in different ways. You and the baseball bat make up a system. The bat is a part of the system. It can be held in different ways.

A part of a system that can be arranged in different ways is called a *variable.*

The position of your hands on a baseball bat is a variable. The way a basketball player holds the ball for shooting is a variable. The distance between you and your partner in a game of catch is a variable. In fact, any part of a system that can be changed is a variable.

Perhaps you have played a game of ping-pong with a friend. In order to win, you probably tried to vary the direction in which you hit the ball. You tried to vary the distance, too. The direction and distance that the ball traveled were variables in the ping-pong system. They were variables that you tried to use in order to play the game and win it.

The concept of variable can now be used by the children to do mental operations. In particular, the concept of variable can now be used in doing experiments. That, of course, is the "Expanding the Idea" phase of the learning cycle.

When meeting the "Getting the Idea" phase of the learning cycle for the first time, many persons fail to see the difference between: (1) letting the children have many experiences through gathering data and then presenting them with the concept; and (2) telling the children what concept they are going to study and then letting them have the experiences. Number (1) is, of course, using the learning cycle and the advantages of that have been thoroughly discussed.

Consider number (2) above. Whenever persons are told at the start of an experience what is to be gained from it, there exists the tendency for those persons to explore only those aspects of the situa-

[4] John W. Renner, Don G. Stafford and Vivian Jensen Coulter, *Variation,* Encino, California: Benziger Bruce & Glencoe, and New York: Macmillan, 1977, p. 45.

tion which provide data about what has been told to them. If, for example, children are told they are to find out which liquids allow the most light to pass through, they will concentrate only on the property of light transmission. They might miss such properties as thickness and stickiness. The directions given to the children narrow the observations they make. Suppose that a class knows magnets attract some kinds of metal and is told that they are going to work with the magnetic field which is found in the space around a magnet. The teacher provides them with metal objects and magnets and the children then do exercises that show that there is a space around a magnet that seems special. That space is special because when a metal object—like a thumbtack— is placed in it, that object moves toward the magnet. The children have experienced the magnetic field.

But now consider what has happened to the children. By naming the specific concept before it was experienced, the teacher told the children that assimilating data about anything but the magnetic field is unimportant. In other words, the children's assimilation has been restricted; the experience is convergent. As has been shown in this book, the experience of assimilation leads to disequilibrium, which in turn leads to accommodation and to new mental structures—new ways of transforming data from the environment. When children are given the concept *before* the experiences which lead to it, there is no need for them to experience disequilibrium. All that is necessary is for them to see that what they have been told is true. And without disequilibrium there is no accommodation, and without accommodation there is no mental structure change or development. We believe that the developing of new and rearranged mental structures represents learning. What happens when students are told what concept they are going to study and then are shown it in some way? These students accumulate information about the concept but *they do not develop an understanding of the concept.* The concept can be talked about but it cannot be used to incorporate other concepts or to study relationships which exist among concepts because the learners have not acquired the necessary mental structures to do so.

When the language of the concept—its name—is presented before the concept itself is experienced, the assumption is made that logic is based upon language. That assumption, according to Piaget, is not true (see Chapter 3). Rather, language must be based upon logic. That is, language is a stimulus that prompts the learner to use certain mental structures to make a response. But the mental structures must be there before the stimulus can be received. Therefore, when language is presented which should serve to help each learner identify a structure and the structure is not there, the language has no meaning. But if the learners have had experiences which have been assimilated, they are ready to receive an organizing idea and the language of that idea—they are ready to accommodate. Then, when the language is used in the future, it represents a stimulus which the learners can receive and use to activate the mental structures necessary to make a response.

The foregoing paragraphs demonstrate the importance of teaching methodology in science. Every teacher wants to lead students to develop thinking ability and facility with the concepts of the discipline. Many persons in education believe that providing materials and experiences with them will lead children to achieve these desirable goals. That belief is not necessarily true. If teachers supply the students with the language of a concept before the assimilation experiences needed to understand that concept, neither the use of the rational powers nor accommodation is necessary. Materials which accurately portray the discipline of science—that is, the quest for knowledge—are essential in the classroom. But the entire purpose of having the materials can be defeated if the teacher does not use teaching procedures that lead to assimilation, disequilibrium, and accommodation. Using such teaching procedures is, in our opinion, the most important responsibility of the teacher. Furthermore, if the learning cycle is not being used, an inquiry-centered classroom atmosphere does not exist.

TEACHER RESPONSIBILITIES IN THE "EXPANDING THE IDEA" PHASE OF THE LEARNING CYCLE

Study Figure 5–8; the diagram in the figure shows that from the beginning of the learning cycle all activities are focused at leading the student toward the idea, or concept, that will be invented. That process is convergent. In discussing question types earlier in this chapter the point was made that whenever a convergent question was used, a divergent question should soon follow. That same principle applies here. The students' thoughts have been converged through the "Getting the Idea" phase of the learning cycle. The learning cycle now has the responsibility to lead the learners to begin to think divergently with respect to the newly-invented concept.

How does a teacher lead students to begin to think divergently? Refer to Chapter 4 and the three questions listed there to be asked of every new idea that is introduced to students. Those three questions can be used as general guidelines in determining the specific responsibilities of the teacher during the third phase of the learning cycle.

Specific examples of teacher responsibility in this phase of the learning cycle often help develop understanding of it. The following activities represent a portion of the "Expanding the Idea" section which follows the "Getting the Idea" section included earlier. The concept invented there was "variable."

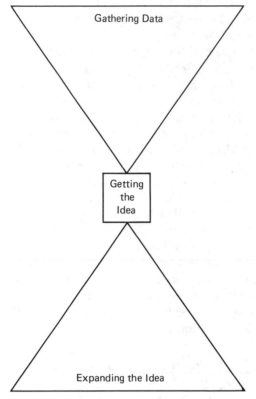

Figure 5–8   The operation of the learning cycle.

EXPANDING THE IDEA[5]

Experimenting   Do some experiments with a bow-and-arrow system.
Use rubber-tipped arrows so no one will be injured.

First, hold the bow in the same position each time. Shoot the arrow.
See how far it travels. Then vary the distance you draw the cord back.
See how this variable changes the distance the arrow goes.

Do the experiment another way. Vary another part of the system.
Draw the arrow back the same distance each time. But vary the position
of the bow. Shoot the arrow each time you change the position of
the bow. How does this variable change the distance the arrow travels?

How would you hold the bow-and-arrow system to make the arrow
go the farthest? Give a reason for your answer. Base your reason
on the results of your experiment. Consider the two variables you used.

Experimenting   Make a pendulum system. To make your pendulum, you
will need a stand, a string, and a washer. Use a string which is 100-cm

[5] Ibid., pp. 46–48.

long. Tie the washer to one end of the string. Then tie the string to the stand. Suspend the washer. You now have a pendulum system.

Pull the washer back and release it. Let the pendulum system swing. Notice how it moves back and forth. Let the pendulum swing for one minute. Count the number of times it moves back and forth in one minute. One complete swing, one back and forth movement, is known as a *cycle*. The time needed to make one cycle is called the *period*.

Experimenting   Now, do another experiment with your pendulum. Do this experiment with one variable. Change the length of the string to 20 cm. Then change the length of the string to 40 cm, 60 cm, and 80 cm.

Count the cycles each time you swing the pendulum. How many cycles does the pendulum go through in one minute? How many cycles does it go through in one minute with a length of 20 cm, 40 cm, 60 cm, and 80 cm? Keep a record. In this experiment the variable was the length of the string. Describe how changing this variable changes the number of cycles in one minute.

Analyze the foregoing "Expanding the Idea" activities and decide what responsibilities a teacher would have while they were being carried out. Make a plan to carry out those activities.

Your analysis of the foregoing "Expanding the Idea" section from *Variation* probably led you to a state of disequilibrium. That disequilibrium probably occurred because you found that the types of responsibilities a teacher would have in leading children to carry out the activities in the "Expanding the Idea" section were those that the teacher would have in a "Gathering Data" section.

Your finding is correct; the responsibilities of teachers in these two learning-cycle phases are identical, with one exception. In both phases the teacher needs to supply materials, provide clues to keep the investigation going, ask questions, and help record data. There is, however, one important difference in these two learning-cycle phases, and that difference concerns the exception just referred to. In "Expanding the Idea," the learners know the concept that they are investigating. They have been provided with the idea and have the language for that concept. The teacher has the responsibility of helping the learners consciously use the language of the concept and use it correctly.

In the activities involving the pendulum, for example, the children *are not* asked how changing the length of the string affected the number of cycles the pendulum made in one minute. Instead they meet this statement: "In this experiment the variable was the length of the string." They are then given this direction: "Describe how changing this variable changes the number of cycles in one minute." In the bow-and-arrow activities the children are asked to vary the distance the bow's cord was drawn back and asked to "See how this variable changes the distance the arrow goes."

In the "Expanding the Idea" section, therefore, the teacher has the responsibility not only to involve the children with activities and materials which use the concept, but the learners must also be involved with the language (or other labels) attached to the concept during the "Getting the Idea" phase of the learning cycle. The language (or other labels) associated with a concept must not be minimized; it represents the stimuli learners use throughout their lifetimes to call mental structures into operation. What does need to be minimized in most of today's schools is the use of language with children before they have had the opportunity to experience the concept and collect data about it. After this, and only after this, is a label useful.

Consider how the term "transistor" is used throughout our society. The majority of persons using that term could not explain what the concept of the transistor is. They have a language label but no mental structure on which to put that label. As was described in Chapter 2, this represents cheap recall and has nothing to do with leading learners to achieve the central purpose of education. The only structure that most persons who use the term transistor have is one that involves the fact that in some ways appliances having transistors are better than those not having them. In other words, the label becomes a classification device that has nothing to do with the concept of the transistor and what its function actually is.

The way to avoid such meaningless recall is to encourage students to gather data about a concept of which they can develop an understanding, to use those data in attaching language to such a concept, and then to provide extensive experiences using both the concept and the language. That procedure follows the structure of the discipline of science, it is inquiry, and it will lead the learners to develop their rational powers.

Look again at Figure 5–8. Notice that the two triangles shown in the figure are empty. The contents of these triangles represent what the children *actually must do* in order to "Gather the Data" and "Expand the Idea." What actual experiences must the children have? The discussion of these experiences is the subject of Chapter 6. When studying Chapter 6 keep in mind that each of the experiences discussed in terms of filling of the triangles of Figure 5–8 must demand that the children use some or all of the rational powers.

Chapter 6
Essential Science Experiences:
The Processes of Science

Three primary purposes of the science curriculum in the elementary school were listed in Chapter 2. These purposes are:

1. To develop in the learner a command of the rational powers.
2. To develop in the student the ability and confidence to inquire.
3. To lead the learner to develop an understanding of the changing nature of the environment in terms of matter, life, and energy, and their interactions.

Any content used in the elementary school classroom must allow and encourage the achievement of one or more of these purposes. The converse is also true—if what is being done in the science classroom is not leading learners to the foregoing purposes, it is of questionable educational value. Sometimes things are done in the classroom just for fun. Sometimes a learner can read about something that is nice to know. We applaud both of these reasons. But do not delude yourself that you are doing anything but having fun. Many science textbooks written for elementary school science introduce very abstract concepts, such as the atom. Such concepts are chosen because of adult appeal, but they are of no value to children in the preoperational and concrete operational stages of thought. Furthermore, if you again consider the purposes for which elementary school science is taught, such content does not fit with the pupils who are there.

The above-mentioned purposes of elementary school science serve as more than goals to lead learners to achieve. They also serve as criteria that can be used to evaluate the content being taught and how it is being used. The learning cycle—"Gathering Data," "Getting the Idea," and "Expanding the Idea"—represents inquiry, and only when a child experiences this will the child develop the ability and confidence to inquire. So when content and teaching procedures are selected for use in the elementary science classroom, the previously stated purposes serve as evaluative criteria. One ought not to be afraid to apply them rigorously to the materials and techniques selected for pupils to interact with.

There is, however, one question that as yet has not been explored. What specifically does a child do when that child is involved in the three phases of the learning cycle—"Gathering Data," "Getting the Idea," and "Expanding the Idea"? From the frame of reference of the teacher, what kinds of experiences do you provide for children to encourage them to undertake inquiries? We believe there are six specific experiences which are essential when using the learning cycle and which would make the classroom activities recognizable by a scientist as science. Those essential experiences are observing, measuring, interpreting, experimenting, model building, and predicting.

Figure 6–1 shows the relationship of these six essential experiences to the learning cycle and science. As Figure 6–1 suggests, "Gathering Data," "Getting the Idea," and "Expanding the Idea" used together properly represent doing or learning science. These three major aspects of doing science can be further reduced to simpler processes—the six blocks at the base of the pyramid labeled "Essential Experiences."

In order to do and to learn science, children must be involved in the learning cycle. But in completing the learning cycle children will be involved in observing, measuring, interpreting, experimenting, predicting, and model building—in other words they will use the "Essential Experiences." It should be emphasized, however, that the "Essential Experiences are not independent educational processes. That is, the "Essential Experiences" are not adequate in and of themselves for the learning of science. A program of activities could be developed which focused on each of these processes, but unless such activities were coordinated with the learning cycle, the objectives of teaching science could not be accomplished. The "Essential Experiences" are the processes by which "Gathering Data," "Getting the Idea," and "Expanding the Idea" are accomplished. This cycle is, in turn, the vehicle by which science is done or learned.

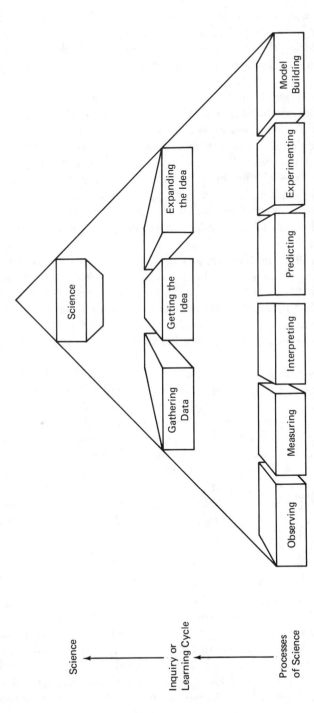

Figure 6–1 The basis of the pyramid of science is composed of the Processes of Science. These processes are essential in doing science.

153

In Chapter 5 the learning cycle was depicted using two triangles and a rectangle as shown in Figure 6–2. All six "Essential Experiences" may be used in arriving at the idea which is to come from the data collected during the "Gathering Data" phase. That idea is a concept of science, a model of some object or process, or a pattern or regularity in the data.

The processes, though not used in equal amounts of time, are used in an order or combination which will *culminate* in "Getting the Idea." For example, when a new aspect of nature is explored, a person would logically begin by observing and measuring to secure information. Then that person would proceed to interpreting, predicting, experimenting, and model building. It is not reasonable, for example, to begin to use model building and predicting until some information is available and some interpreting has been done. After the *idea* has been grasped, all six of the "Essential Experiences" can again be utilized in "Expanding the Idea."

By this time you have already done many explorations and experiments. In this chapter and following chapters, to make or emphasize a point, we will simply describe a type of experiment or refer to one you have already done. We do this because we wish to focus on expansion of the teaching-learning model idea. You will do activities, but they will be mental investigations because you can use formal reasoning.

Each of the six experiences is a process which is used in the practice of science or by someone learning science. As processes they are tools for use. These process tools have certain basic components that identify them whether they are being used to gather data or expand an idea. We will first explore the six processes by focusing on each in turn although, in many cases, more than one process will be involved in the activity used for reference. More activities will be used in the initial processes to help you to begin to relate the processes, the learning cycle, and classroom activities. We will also show how the processes can lead directly to "Getting the Idea" and how they are used in "Expanding the Idea."

OBSERVING

If you are interested in acquiring information about an object you are not familiar with, the most obvious thing to do is to look at it. Your observations can give you a great deal of specific information and can lead you to discover other types of investigations which will give you much more information. Observations, however, can be made in many ways. Feeling, squeezing, poking, rubbing, and listening are but a few of the methods (other than visual) which can be used to make obser-

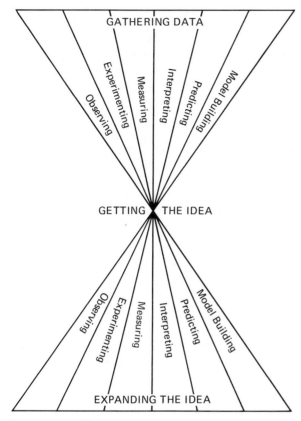

Figure 6–2   The Processes of Science are used in all phases of the learning cycle.

vations. Observing is the first action taken by the learner in acquiring new information. The curriculum must provide opportunities for the learner to have extensive experience making observations. How are such learning experiences provided?

It is axiomatic that if a learner is going to learn how to observe, the learner must have experience observing. This means being given the opportunity to watch, feel, squeeze, poke, and do other things needed to do what will enable the learner to describe the object being observed. Furthermore, the object the learner is observing must be one the learner feels comfortable with. The object must not be so foreign to the observer that the observer is afraid of it or uncertain of what can or should be done with it. When young children come to school they are probably more familiar with the objects found in the environment than with anything else. The beginning observations that children can be led to make, then, can be on the common things in their immediate environment. Objects such as plants, rocks, and small animals are naturally interesting to most children. These kinds of objects should provide an abundance of observing opportunities. We will also discuss some objects which are of human fabrication that are of particular interest and which often provide excellent opportunities for simple or beginning observing. The following activity uses such a fabricated object—baby pictures.

ACTIVITY: BABY PICTURES
Each child in a class brings his or her own baby picture. The picture should show the person at about 8–18 months. The pictures are then placed on a table so the children can look at them. The children are asked to try to identify the person in each picture. This is an ongoing activity for several days. During this time the children are sharpening their visual observational skills by looking for identifying characteristics. It is also a very enjoyable activity.

In the baby picture activity, the children are required to compare certain characteristics in a nonverbal manner, and to match those characteristics with a person. Such nonverbal observations are often used with children in kindergarten and first grade. The teacher, or a child, will hold up an object of a given shape and color to identify and then say, "Hold up an object like this." The teacher might then say, "This shape is a triangle. See how many other triangles you can find." The children then look for other triangular-shaped objects and point to them or hold them up.

Observations in which verbal descriptions are required are somewhat more difficult. These observations usually follow and are built on nonverbal observations which have developed an essential descriptive vocabulary.

The following is a very general outline of a learning cycle based on simple observation and description. As you will see, it is possible to use only one process skill in the entire cycle. For upper grades, however, this is rarely the case.

GATHERING DATA
Activity 1 The children at their desks observe wooden blocks cut into triangles, circles, squares, rectangles, and diamonds. The children learn to describe the shapes of the various wooden objects. The teacher provides the shape label as needed.

Activity 2 The teacher calls out a shape. Each child holds up an object of that shape from the child's own tray.

GETTING THE IDEA
The teacher collects many objects that are familiar to children, such as a plate, a cup, a picture, a book, a watch, a coin, a bell, et cetera. The

teacher holds up one object at a time, then asks some child to describe the shape of the object. After the teacher has gone over the collection of objects, she then verbally states the idea:

Objects have a shape.

EXPANDING THE IDEA

Activity 1   Have the children first find square objects in the classroom. Round, triangular, rectangular, and other shapes are found next.

Activity 2   Have the children observe and describe objects of a particular shape on the playgrounds, along the street, and at home. Be sure that both living and nonliving objects are included.

Another visual observing activity which allows children to extend from nonverbal visual observing to observing which includes verbal descriptions and grouping of objects can be done with buttons.

ACTIVITY: BUTTONS

Each child is given approximately 20 assorted buttons on a cardboard tray. The teacher then leads them to do the following activities.[1]

Sorting by Color   Distribute a tray and a handful of buttons to each child. Discuss with the class the properties of the buttons as well as their similarities and differences. Then suggest that the individual button collections be sorted by color. Children should choose their own methods and numbers of groups. For example, some may group all red buttons into one stack and all other colors into another. Some may sort each color into a different pile; others may even separate colors into shades. Accept all these choices as correct, and encourage individual pupils to describe their sorting procedures.

Sorting by Other Properties   After the previous discussion has been completed, ask the children to sort their buttons according to another property. The number of groups and the properties they use should again be left completely to the pupils. Offer suggestions only if a child seem very confused. Afterwards ask a few children to describe the methods they used and let others participate in the discussion. As your pupils exchange ideas they will probably ask for more opportunities to sort buttons.

Individualizing the Use of Buttons   Children may also group the buttons according to specified numbers of properties. Color might be one property, color and shape designate two properties, and so on. Ask children to tell you what properties they used for their groupings. If a child has trouble sorting his button collection, try giving him only

---

[1] Reprinted with permission from *Material Objects Teachers Guide,* p. 28, by the Science Curriculum Improvement Study, Chicago: Rand, McNally and Company. © 1970 by the Regents of the University of California.

eight or ten selected buttons during another session. Allow the children access to the buttons during free class periods. This additional work will help them analyze and further diversify their sorting methods.

The button activity expanded the observational process to include grouping objects by property. Use this activity as a "Gathering Data" activity for grouping objects. Then plan a "Getting the Idea" activity using *classroom objects* or pictures of common objects. The idea is, "objects with the same property can be put together." You will probably wish to modify the idea to present it to children.

Next, plan "Expanding the Idea" activities using objects in the same environment.

Children who participate in learning experiences such as these are having their abilities to describe phenomena developed. This, of course, also demands that development of a vocabulary that will allow the observer to express himself adequately. In such a learning situation the vocabulary that is acquired really belongs to the learner because it answers a felt need. If, for example, a child is describing a button and uses the word "bumpy" when the word "rough" is more appropriate, the invention of the word "rough" by the teacher will be accepted by the child and that word placed meaningfully in his vocabulary.

In addition to providing experience in observation, the foregoing "button" lesson demonstrated the contribution that experiences such as these can make to the development of the rational powers of the learner. The categorization of the buttons demands that properties be analyzed, buttons be compared, each comparison be evaluated, and that a generalization be reached about exact classifications.

Simple qualitative comparisons can be used in grouping or describing objects. Some objects can be placed together because they all have bumps on them or because they are all soft, or blue, or have holes in them. Comparisons often require the observer to move toward quantitative ideas or measurement. Although the following activity has observing as its principal thrust or focus, notice how observing merges naturally into other processes such as measuring and experimenting.

In order to reinforce the learning cycle and its use with the process of observing, synthesize a series of activities from the following materials and suggestions. The *idea* is *serial order.* Design "Gathering Data" activities, a "Getting the Idea" activity, and "Expanding the Idea" activities.

Objective

To develop and expand the idea of serial order.

Materials

A variety of balls and ball-like objects such as: a clay ball, a cotton ball, a rubber ball, baseball, golf ball, tennis ball, soccer ball, pool ball, and others.

SOME ACTIVITIES YOU COULD USE IN GATHERING DATA

1. Let the children describe each ball, pointing out similarities and differences using sight.
2. Let the children feel each ball and describe it. The children can rub, squeeze, or poke the balls.
3. Let the children drop the balls on a table top and listen to the sound.
4. Have the children close their eyes. Then drop one ball at a time. Let the children decide which ball sounds the loudest when it is dropped. Then let them choose the second loudest, and so forth.
5. Let the children arrange the balls from largest to smallest.
6. Let the children arrange the balls from lightest to heaviest.
7. Let the children arrange the balls from smoothest to roughest.
8. Another way the children could arrange the balls is from most bouncy to least bouncy.

   This serial ordering activity requires a carefully controlled observation—an experiment. The objective is to study the "bounciness" of balls. In order to do the experiment you would need to carefully plan the observation you are going to make. For example, you must decide how high you will hold the ball above the surface which it will strike. Also what data you will record to use in comparing the bounciness of the balls. Generally speaking, an experiment involves observing, but experiments also involve measurements. Such measurements as how high did the object go, how long did it take, how much did the objects weigh.

9. Refer to the activities with the balls and use them to develop the idea of serial order. Have the children begin to use the words "serial order."
10. Expand the idea of serial order using objects in the classroom.

MEASURING

After taking measurements of any object, investigators (adults or children) are able to make statements that are much more definitive than those they were able to make based only on qualitative observations. We cannot, for example, look at a plant today and specifically say it has grown in a definite quantity since yesterday. Our senses might tell us the plant has grown, but they certainly would not tell us how much. In order to be able to state how much a plant has grown in 3 days or in a week, we must be able to refine the measurements that our senses allow us to take. Not only are our senses inadequate to make a measurement as small as daily plant growth, but they are also woefully inadequate in accurately estimating large measurements, such as the distance to the sun, the velocity of sound, or the weight of an elephant. Measurements are necessary to extend our senses down to the infinitesimal and up to something approaching the infinite, because our senses are not reliable as measuring devices except in a very approximate way.

Measurements can be considered observations, but they are quantitative observations that can be repeatedly taken in the same manner at different times, and the results received will be approximately the same. There will be variations that occur in measurements due to growth (occurring in a living organism, if that is what is being measured) or due to inaccuracies or inconsistencies that occur in the application of the measuring standard. The concept of variation both by itself and in measurement is an extremely important one, and we shall return to a discussion of it later. To enable pupils to learn how to use observations from measurements in the same manner as the qualitative observations previously discussed are used, the elementary school science curriculum must provide appropriate learning experiences for pupils at all levels.

A learning experience which involves the process of measuring of a living organism can be done with seeds. The activity which is described next uses simple comparison measuring with concrete objects.

ACTIVITY: SEEDS

Very interesting and valuable learning experiences can occur if each child is given an envelope containing about a dozen seeds and seedlike objects. The children are then asked to sort objects into categories and identify which of the objects they feel are seeds and which are not. After sorting has been completed (in this portion of the activity the children are using their rational powers of comparing and classifying), each child is then invited to state which of his objects that child feels are seeds. Responses such as, "This is a seed because it has funny little marks on it," are representative of the responses children will give during this activity. At this point the teacher should ask (if one of the children hasn't), "How could we find out which of your objects are seeds?" and eventually the class will suggest planting all the objects and seeing which ones grow.

What follows is an interesting activity for first graders; they thoroughly enjoy setting up their investigation and observing which seeds mature and which do not. They will, early in the experiment, want to dig up some of the objects planted to see which of them have started to grow. Much good inquiry-centered teaching can be done while this is going on, and it keeps the children's interest in the activity very high. In a few days, the children will have decided which of the objects were seeds. At this point the teacher gives each child (or two children) additional objects like those found in the envelope, which were seeds. This will allow the pupils to see whether or not there are any general characteristics about seeds which they could establish. This seed-identification activity leads to the introduction of the measurement aspect of the unit.

Children do not at first see the need for measuring or do not think measuring is very important. These difficulties can be overcome, however, if the teacher directs their attention to their own plants with such questions as, "Whose plant is biggest today?" "Has your plant grown since last week?", and "How do you know?" Eventually one of the children might measure the plants, or the teacher may have to introduce the procedure.

After the children have accepted the fact that by measuring the plants they can answer questions about how their plants are growing, the problem of how the measuring is to be done has to be solved. With first-grade children it is probably unwise for the teacher to introduce a formal measuring unit, such as centimeters. All that is needed is a system by which the growth at different intervals can be measured.

Each child is given an envelope containing many strips of colored construction paper and asked how these can be used to measure the growth of the child's plant. The child will eventually come to the conclusion that one end of a paper strip can be placed at the base of the plant and a mark drawn on the paper which represents the height of the tallest leaf. While this idea will usually come collectively from the children, the teacher will probably have to suggest that each strip be dated, so as to enable them to know when the various measurements were taken.

In studying the growth of a plant, the learner must compare the various measurements that have been taken, synthesize these measurements into a complete picture of the plant's growth, and evaluate whether or not the plant is growing as well as the other plants in the room. Rational power development is an inherent attribute of this science activity.

In addition to the foregoing, this learning activity has another dimension, one that can be used to introduce the mathematical concept of graphing to children. After several measurements have been taken, the teacher should ask the children what they can do to compare their measurements. The pupils will usually line up the measured strips of paper on their desks in some arrangement. At times these arrangements will not be too meaningful. The teacher can then ask how the strips can be arranged to make a picture of how their plants grew from measurement to measurement (no doubt you will recognize this particular aspect of the activity as interpreting). Not too much time is needed before the entire class has the strips arranged in chronological order. At this point the teacher can suggest (if the children have not already done so) that these strips be pasted upon sheets of paper so that a permanent picture of the growth of each plant might be made, and this picture can then be easily added to as more measurements are taken. In this activity, measurements—how they are recorded and how these recordings can be interpreted—have been integrated in an understandable, meaningful way for the children. Measurement is a valuable curriculum area—one in which children can become interested and with which they are comfortable.

In an elementary school classroom, the children should be led to progress from qualitative observations to quantitative description or measurements. We do not intend to suggest that qualitative observations are not useful data. Some properties or aspects of an object or event are difficult, if not impossible, for an elementary school child to describe quantitatively. For example, odor, color shade, pitch and even roughness or smoothness are very difficult to measure.

There are many aspects of an object or event that can and should be expressed quantitatively. Review what you did in the rolling ball experiment (page 6). After a brief period of observing the path of the ball as it moved from the table top to the floor, and changes in the motion of the ball, you began to make very specific measurements of height and distance. Without these measurements, the experiment would not have progressed.

In the candle burning experiment (page 108) you placed a candle in a tray of water and lit the candle. Then you inverted a cylinder over the candle and observed what happened—bubbles escaped from the edge of the cylinder, the candle went out, then water rose in the cylinder. To construct a model to explain the event it was important that qualitative observations be made, but it was equally as important to know the order in which the events occurred. Describing the sequence of occurrences during an event allows the event to be reconstructed and discussed or pondered. Establishing an ordinal sequence, such as the sequence of qualitative observations, is an important type of measurement.

The activities in an elementary school science program should, over a period of time, allow the children to make many different kinds of measurements. For example, there should be activities in which distance, weight, temperature, and volume are measured. Measurements involving time should include, "How many times did the event occur in one minute (or one day, or one year, etc.)" Also, "How long did the event take?", and "When did it happen?"

It must be stressed that in each activity requiring a measurement, the level of intellectual development of the child must be taken into account. Children should be expected to take *only* those measurements that are appropriate for their intellectual level.

When children are involved in measuring and recording their measurements, the observation that not everyone gets the same value will soon be made. This does not mean that some are wrong and some are correct. It is simply an accepted limitation in making quantitative descriptions. Measurements will vary because of instruments, temperature, and other factors, including differences in the way individuals see things. Variations are to be expected. The idea of variation can be introduced and understood in measurements. But variation is not limited to measurements. People vary in such factors as height, skin color, and hair texture. Trees of the same kind vary in many ways, as do poodles, porpoises, and plankton. Histograms are often used to express variation and in college you no doubt will have the opportunity to use such ideas as mean, mode, and standard deviation to express or describe variation.

ACTIVITY: CHALKBOARD
Each member of a fourth grade class measured the length of a chalkboard. The measurements in meters were written on the end of the chalkboard.

5.25 meters	5.24	5.25
5.20	5.23	5.23
5.23	5.27	5.24
5.23	5.23	5.22
5.20	5.22	5.26
5.24	5.24	5.23
5.26	5.23	5.21
5.23	5.25	5.23

The teacher then drew a number line on the chalkboard, marked off equal divisions, and labeled it.

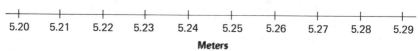

Meters

Figure 6–3

The teacher then let each child place an "X" in the place on the number line that represented the child's own measurement.

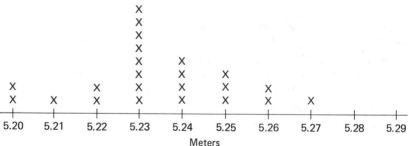

Meters

Figure 6–4 Each X represents a measurement. When more than one person has the same measurement, the X's are placed in a vertical column.

The next question that might be asked is, "What value will we report for the length of the chalkboard?" You will, no doubt, realize that this question does not involve a measurement. The question is answered by interpreting the data or measurements. When you make the interpretation, perhaps by choosing the value of 5.23 or the average value, then you have gathered additional data through interpretation. Suppose other classrooms in the building have chalkboards like the one in this room. What would you predict (or infer) their length to be? This prediction (or inference) becomes data that could be used.

Gathering data through observation and measurement leads directly to other processes which in time produce or make available new data.

The learning cycle—"Gathering Data," "Getting the Idea," "Expanding the Idea"—often involves several of the essential processes.

The entire cycle can be used, however, with the principal focus on the process of *measuring*. The following activity is an example of this taken from a fourth grade children's book.[2] Follow the cycle.

GATHERING DATA
Try this experiment. Mark a straight line for a starting line. Put your feet together, with the toes of both feet on the starting line. Hop as far as you can with your feet together. Measure the distance you hopped in centimeters. Again, hop as far as you can and measure the distance. Make a record of the two distances.

Compare the two distances you hopped. If the distances are not the same, take a part of the longer distance and add this part of the shorter distance. Make both distances the same. Compare this new distance with each of the distances you measured. How is the new distance different from each of the earlier distances?

Repeat what you did. Hop as far as you can. Then measure the distance. Hop again and measure the distance. Do this four times. After each time, make a record of the distance.

Now, take a part from each of the longer distances. Add these parts to the shorter distances until all four are the same. Make a record of this distance.

GETTING THE IDEA
You made all four distances the same. To do this, you took parts from the longer distances. You then added these parts to the shorter distances. The new distance you obtained is called the

average.

The new distance is the average distance you can hop. In many experiments, you will report the average result. You determine an average by repeating the experiment. An average often provides accurate data and is usually better than the result of only one experiment.

When you listen to people talk, you will hear the word "average" used to describe almost everything. People talk about average driving speeds, average salaries, average food prices, and even average people. There is even an average number of letters on each full line of print on this page. Perhaps you can find out this average.

Averages are important in your school studies. You will be working with averages in many ways in your mathematics, science, and social studies classes.

EXPANDING THE IDEA

Measuring Try this. Add together the four distances you hopped. Divide the sum by four. The number you get is also called the average.

[2] Renner, John W., Don G. Stafford, and Vivian Coulter, *Variation,* Encino, California: Benziger Bruce & Glencoe, 1977, pp. 54–58.

Compare this average with the average you got by taking away and adding on.

Sometimes it is very hard to get an average by taking away and adding on. For example, suppose you wanted to know the average height of the pupils in your class. It would take a long time to find the average by taking away and adding on.

Think about how you could find the average height of the pupils. What numbers would you need to add together? What number would you divide by?

UNDERSTANDING AVERAGE
1. Find the average height of the pupils in your class. Find the average in centimeters. Find the average in inches.
2. Find out the number of pupils in five different classrooms in your school. What is the average number of pupils in each class?
3. Determine the average age in months of the pupils in your class.
4. Find the average age of the members of your family. Which has more variation, the ages of your family or the ages of the pupils in your class?
5. One boy reported that the average time he spent coming to school each morning for one week was fifteen minutes. On one of the mornings it took twenty-two minutes. Explain how he could have an average time of fifteen minutes.

INTERPRETING

As data accumulate, a person who wishes to use the information tries to make it understandable. In an elementary school classroom data interpretation can have a variety of forms. Data interpretation usually follows observing and measuring and very often precedes experimentation, prediction, and model building in the "Gathering Data" phase of the learning cycle. Interpreting can be as simple as grouping objects into heavy and light or deciding if an object is rough or smooth, or as complex as building a model to explain patterns in data. Interpreting is "making sense out of data." Interpretation of data might lead directly to a generalization or pattern which can be stated as an *idea*.

For example, as you experimented with the pendulum (page 9), you found that the period of the pendulum increased as the length of the pendulum increased. This simple pattern could be stated as the idea:

> The period of a pendulum increases as the length of the pendulum increases.

Qualitative predictions could be made and tested using this simple idea.

> What qualitative prediction could you make about the period of a pendulum?

Interpreting can be the seed of an idea to explain an event. When you did the candle-burning activity (page 108), the bubbles which came from the tube might have caused you to think, "The air is expanding." The seed of interpretation then led, with others, to building a model to explain why water rose in the cylinder. The model which you developed could be the *idea* in the activity.

In almost every case, interpretation leads to experimenting and predicting. If, during the interpretation of data, a pattern or trend is discerned or suspected, this pattern or trend can be stated as a possible generalization (or perhaps an hypothesis). A carefully planned series of observations and measurements, an experiment, is then conducted to learn more about the relationship involved.

Interpreting involves the discernment of the various factors which appear to affect an object or event. When plant growth is observed and considered, the factors of light and water are almost intuitively associated with it. But other factors such as temperature, soil type, and mineral content might also be involved. Isolating these important factors, or variables, is an essential aspect of interpretation. Discovering that a particular variable is *not* important represents a significant finding. For example, in the pendulum activity, you found that the length of the string of the pendulum affected the period, but the mass of the object on the string did not.

The process of interpreting, no doubt, involves all ten of the rational powers of the mind. Interpreting then, is one of the most educationally fruitful aspects of the learning cycle. It is also one of the most abused parts of the learning process in classrooms. Teachers are usually willing to allow children to observe and measure. But when it comes to the interpretation, teachers have a tendency to take over. Interpreting data is fun and exciting—but unless the pupils do it, the educational value is lost. The teacher can act as a guide, but let the pupils interpret!

There are two procedures for teaching data interpretation—the individual and the group. In the individual method each pupil keeps personal records and with the assistance of the teacher or classmates, interprets, generalizes and concludes from them. What the pupil receives from this procedure is directly dependent on the child. In the group procedure, each pupil contributes personal findings to the entire group, and what the pupil gains is as much dependent on the data of others as it is on that personal data. This latter method, in addition to being useful in demonstrating the values of working together, leads a pupil to discover the scientifically sound concept of the value of more than one set of measurements or viewpoint. While there are values to be gained from each pupil's interpreting his own data, these values, as well as several others, will be achieved by group interpretation of data.

In this approach the teacher uses the chalkboard and serves as the class secretary. Each group of pupils states what was found and the teacher records it. At the end of such a session there are many data available for inspection and study. The entire class has the same data, and the attention of the entire group (including the teacher) can be focused on any part of the information. The class is then able to decide whether or not any of the variables being considered required the collection of additional information. This type of social interaction is important in learning.

Data interpretation frequently involves data organization. A collection of unorganized descriptions and measurements usually "makes no sense." Imagine a sports page randomly covered with pieces of information about the scores of baseball games for the entire season. Before you could begin to discern a pattern, you would almost surely have to decide on and implement some organizational scheme. You might begin by deciding to count and record the total number of wins and losses by each team. After that you might decide to serial-order the teams on the basis of most wins to least wins. The data would then begin to yield new information that could not be obtained directly from the random pieces of data. The new information might be that Team A has won 76 percent of its games, while Team D has won only 40 percent of its games.

The information showing the number of wins or losses by a team could be placed in a histogram, as shown in Figure 6–5.

The type of organizational scheme that will yield the most or best

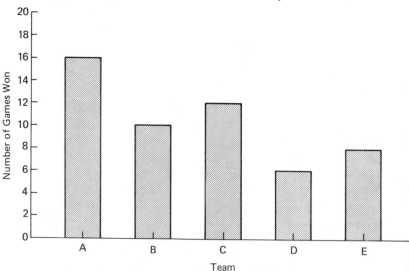

Figure 6–5 This is a type of histogram called a bar graph. The number of games won by each team can be readily compared.

data is also an interpretation. The teacher will need to provide considerable guidance in this area initially. This can be easily done by placing the lines and labels of a histogram (Figure 6–6) on the chalkboard. Then invite the children to place the data they have collected into it.

Another form of initial organization that is very useful, and one that often allows data to be brought into focus, is tabular form. The teacher can place the empty blocks of the table (Figure 6–7) and labels on the chalkboard. Each child or group can then put data in it.

The teacher should place the complete table, without the data, on the chalkboard. The teacher should then gradually involve the pupils in deciding on the labels. Finally, the pupils should be able, with some suggestions, to set up their own tables when they collect data. Data interpretation through use of organizing schemes can be taught, but it takes patience on the part of the teacher.

One organization of data sometimes suggests another. For example, data placed in tabular form might also be represented in a line graph or histogram.

Children in a fifth grade class determined their heartbeat rate by counting the number of times their heart beat in one-half minute, and then doubling this. The teacher had each child record his heartbeat rate in Table 6–1. The teacher then inquired and found the lowest heartbeat rate and had that child record that value first. Then each child, in order of heartbeat rate, recorded the child's own value. As you see, there were several cases in which the heartbeat rate was the same.

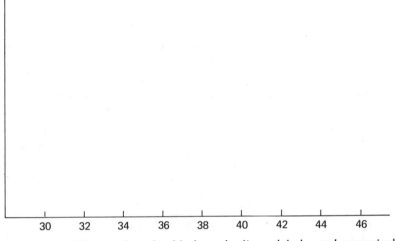

Figure 6–6   The teacher should place the lines, labels, and numerical dimensions on the histograms the first few times they are used in class. Then, gradually the children will become capable of constructing the histograms all by themselves.

Length of Pendulum in Centimeters	10	20	30	40	50	60	80	100
Group 1 — Period in Seconds								
Group 2 — Period in Seconds								
Group 3 — Period in Seconds								

Figure 6–7 The use of a data table will help children learn to organize data.

A class discussion of Table 6–1 leads to further interpretation and additional data. For example, the range of heartbeat rates for the class was from 74 to 90. More of the children in the class had a heartbeat rate of 80 than any others. The average heartbeat rate was 81.

Interpretation of the original data allowed the children to learn something about both themselves and the class. It also allowed them to gather some new data that could be used to describe the class. Intuitively, the children dealt with the idea of variation. They were also made aware that the average has meaning only for a collection of data—that no person in the class had the average pulse rate.

After the grouped data had been interpreted, the teacher asked if the data could be organized another way. It was agreed that a histogram could be used. The teacher, acting as the class secretary, placed the labels for the histogram on the chalkboard (see Figure 6–8).

Additional data and comparisons can be made from the grouped data. For example, the average heartbeat rate for boys and girls can be determined and compared.

Table 6–1 HEARTBEAT RATES OF CHILDREN
IN A FIFTH GRADE CLASS

NAME	NUMBER OF HEARTBEATS PER MINUTE	NAME	NUMBER OF HEARTBEATS PER MINUTE
Jill	74	Bob	80
Tom	76	Sally	82
Bruce	76	Judy	82
Jane	78	Polly	82
Jerry	78	Mary	82
Tim	78	Brook	82
Chico	78	Lori	82
Billy A.	80	Nancy	84
Billy C.	80	Chris	84
Jeffry	80	Joel	84
Ann	80	Mike	84
Andy	80	Jimmy	86
Sean	80	Marie	90
John	80		

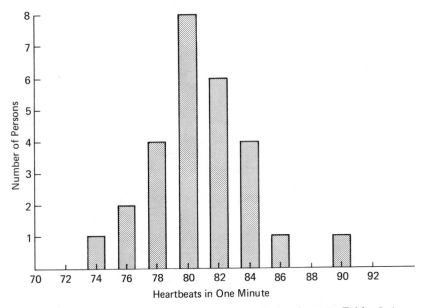

Figure 6–8 The heartbeat rates shown in tabular form in Table 6–1 are organized here into a histogram.

The following activity[3] follows the learning cycle. Notice that the idea is presented on the basis of data gathered through interpretation of charts. The children have, of course, already gathered data and produced the chart.

GATHERING DATA

You have been organizing information on a chart in order to represent the relationships among the organisms in a certain area. Now it is possible to look at the chart and to think about each section. You can see how one section is related to other sections.

You should have a section for producers, sections for two kinds of consumers, one section for decomposers, one section for raw materials, and a place to indicate light. Check your work to see if you have included all the sections on the chart. Be sure that you have labeled all the sections.

Interpreting Choose one section of the chart and imagine that it no longer exists. Imagine that the things represented there have all been destroyed. Write a paragraph about what might happen if that were true.

You have considered what would happen if organisms from an entire section in your chart were gone. Choose just one population. Imagine that all members of that population are gone. How would that affect any other population? Find a population which could be eliminated without an effect on any other population.

GETTING THE IDEA

Plants and animals within a certain area are shown on your chart. The chart summarizes the interactions among the living things. The food cycle is an example of interaction and of a relationship among the plants and animals.

Organisms in an area interacting in this kind of relationship can be called a

community.

Write the word "community" at the top of your chart.

The word "community" is probably familiar to you. You very likely refer to the area in which you live as a community. In some ways, the meaning is exactly the same. The word "community" is a reference to the things which are close to you and with which you have some kind of relationship.

The term "biotic community" is applied to organisms that are dependent upon each other for survival. The word "biotic" means of or

---

[3] Renner, John W., Don G. Stafford, and Vivian Coulter, *Action,* Encino, California: Benziger Bruce & Glencoe, 1977, pp. 326–331.

having to do with life." A biotic community is a community of living things. In this part of the book, the term "community" is a reference to the biotic community.

Each part of a biotic community is dependent upon other parts. There are interactions between one living thing and other living things. There are also interactions between living things and nonliving parts of the environment. One population is dependent upon another population. This dependency holds the community together.

EXPANDING THE IDEA
Depending on where you live, you may have several different kinds of communities near you. But, regardless of the kind of community or of the populations which compose it, every community must have the sections which you have represented and labeled on your chart.

Predicting Write a paragraph predicting what would happen if you removed "light" from your chart. What would happen to the community? Give data to support what you think.

Interpreting Think of some other kinds of communities. Choose a kind which is of interest to you and make a community chart which shows different organisms interacting in a food cycle.

Perhaps you will need to investigate organisms and food habits. Be sure that you have all the necessary parts of the community. Draw the arrows which show food transfer. When you are through, trade community charts with a classmate. Check to see that every organism listed in the community has a food source.

When you listed organisms on your chart, did you list people as part of the community? Discuss how people interact in a community. Compare the effect of people on a community with the effect of other organisms.

Make a list of the ways people affect a community. Indicate whether each way is helpful or harmful. Discuss your list with others. Then change your list if you think you should.

There is a problem from the traditional frame of reference associated with allowing pupils to interpret data. The pupils might interpret the data incorrectly and arrive at a wrong conclusion. Is this a dangerous or undesirable procedure?

No one, of course, likes to arrive at an incorrect answer—especially teachers. There is a good reason why teachers feel as they do—they (as children and students) were probably never allowed to accept an incorrect answer as having any value. Anything they needed to know was presented to them as a correct fact, and when a person has grown up in a tradition such as this, learning to appreciate the value of an incorrect answer (i.e., incorrect from the adult's point of view) is difficult. Such an attitude is unfortunate because: (1) it puts a premium on information; and (2) it represents a misunderstanding of what an answer is. Point (1) will not be discussed here because the questionable value of teaching factual information has been treated already. In addition to what has already been said, however, consider another aspect of overemphasizing information. When a premium is placed on factual information the importance of recall to the learner is greatly overemphasized. Recall is one of the rational powers, but it is only one of ten (10 percent). In many classrooms across the country, developing the 10 percent of the ability to think occupies more than 90 percent of the school day. The inequity of such a procedure is immediately evident.

The second reason listed above, however, is an extremely important one to consider at this point in our discussion, because the final result of data interpretation is an answer. But in order to fully appreciate and understand what data can do for us, we must have a relatively solid notion of what an answer actually is. To have an answer you must first have a problem or question, and an answer to that question or solution to the problem is what the data (information) which have been gathered tell you it is, nothing more. If an experiment has been used to acquire those data being considered, then perhaps variables can be manipulated in some way to enable more or different data, or both, to be accumulated. But when all the data that can be obtained from all the various experimental processes that can be designed are gathered, the answer to the question depends strictly upon what those data tell you. This belief does not exclude the use of common sense, intuition, or both in interpreting the data. If, for example, an investigator receives an intuitive insight while performing an experiment, that experience may completely change the investigator's experimental procedures. But the final answer arrived at will still be directly dependent on the manner in which the data received from the experiment (which has been redesigned to accommodate the "moment of intuition") are interpreted.

Science is a fruitful area to explore in order to demonstrate the use of intuition in investigation; the work of such men as Newton, Faraday, and Einstein provides excellent examples of how intuition is used to solve a problem or advance an idea. In every case, however, the final result—the answer accepted—depended on how the data received, whether following a procedure designed by intuition or logic, were interpreted. We, as teachers, must teach science as it is practiced; that is, the answers that our students give us should be based upon the data their observations, measurements, and experiments have given them. If we reject the answer formulated from the data and substitute (without test) what we feel is the answer, we are using the discipline of science incorrectly. In addition—and from an educational point of view more importantly—we are prohibiting our pupils from gaining confidence in their ability to solve their own problems through the interpretation of data. Such pedagogical procedures are harmful to the development of the pupils' rational powers—their ability to think— which is the principal purpose of all education. So if a wrong answer develops from the data that are collected, and the pupils give that answer with extreme sincerity, we, as teachers, must accept it. When a wrong concept or fact has been developed, what should be done?

The pupil must not be allowed to harbor an incorrect concept, but experience has shown that telling the learner he or she is wrong will not allow the learner to correct that concept. Probably, the learner will overtly accept your decision as adult authority, but will certainly not really begin to disbelieve what his or her own collected information has indicated and accept what you say. If a pupil is going to learn to classify, compare, evaluate, and use all the rational powers, that pupil must be given experience classifying, comparing, and evaluating without the feeling that what the pupil does is really not important because the teacher will say whether or not the pupil's own data are correct, and interpret them for the pupil. This notion about teaching tells us that if applying the rational powers to data delivered by an experiment has the adverse affect of leading learners to an erroneous concept, there is only one way for the learners to correct that concept for themselves. They must be provided the opportunity (or observation) to apply their rational powers to data from a second experiment that will result in developing a contradiction to the first experiment. The pupils must then decide which evidence is correct, and they have absolutely no basis for making such a decision. The only way they can approach the solution to that problem is to repeat both experiments or observations or measurements.

If the data and experiment delivered are leading the learner to an incorrect concept, then something that was done in the experiment was done improperly. Leading learners to see the necessity of repeating the experiments will also give the class an opportunity to review their procedures. If the class-determined procedures are carefully reviewed, the probability of recurrence of procedural errors (which will again result in the learners' arriving at an unacceptable concept) has been reduced. Therefore, if teachers are to lead learners away from a self-developed concept that is unacceptable to science, a second experiment must be available which, although using a different route, will provide data to enable the learners to arrive at the acceptable concept.

One of the pervasive concerns expressed in this book is that elementary school science experiences contribute to the development of a child's rational powers. We have referred several times to how the data interpretation can make such a contribution. Therefore, it is more fruitful, educationally speaking, to spend the time needed to make additional observations and measurements and allow the children, through their own interpretation, to arrive at a correct result than to short circuit the process by rejecting their interpretation and supplying your own.

EXPERIMENTING

Data interpretation can lead to new data through organization. Very often, however, data interpretation, when applied to observation and measurements, leads to other essential processes—experimentation, model building, and prediction. The results of using these processes require further interpretation.

When observations and measurements are initially interpreted, one or more possible trends, patterns, or relationships may be noticed or suspected. These possible relationships act as a guide to further explorations and are sometimes called "working hypotheses." These explorations, which will be designed to establish whether or not a relationship exists, must be carefully planned and controlled. When observations and measurements are made under planned and controlled conditions, an experiment has been done. Since experimenting requires controlled conditions, some data collection and data interpretation need to precede it. The data used come from many sources, such as observations, measurements, and the interactions of objects under consideration, so as "to see what happens." This last activity is an observation, but it is not in the strictest sense an experiment. If the investigator did not have some data related to the experiment, the investigator would have no idea what to control or what to observe.

Experiments do, of course, provide data, and are an essential part of the "Gathering Data" phase of the learning cycle. Some pupils in a fourth grade class had some familiarity with plant growth through simple observation. They had decided that certain factors were essential to plant growth and were ready to test them. The following is a series of experiments on plants. Notice how certain factors are controlled. Notice also how the directions or guidance given the children decrease as the experiments continue.

EXPERIMENTING[4]
Get three pots and fill them with soil. Plant three bean seeds in each pot. Give each pot the same amount of water.

---

[4] Renner, John W., Don G. Stafford, and Vivian Coulter, *Variation*, Encino, California: Benziger Bruce & Glencoe, 1977, pp. 240–245.

Set one pot in full light. Turn a box over the second pot. This pot then will be in the dark. Turn a box over the third pot, but make a hole in the box. This pot then will be in a small amount of light.

Each plant will get a different amount of light. But be sure that everything else is the same. Everything else in the environment must be the same. You are testing only one variable here. This one variable is the amount of light.

You have found out about light on bean plants. But what about light on other kinds of plants? What will happen if you use grass seeds? Predict what you think will happen.

EXPERIMENTING

Repeat the experiment with light. But use grass seeds instead of bean seeds. Put twenty grass seeds in each of the three pots. Keep your records as carefully as you did before. Control all the variables as well as you can.

What is the effect of light on bean plants? What is the effect of light on grass? What do you conclude?

You did controlled experiments with plants and light. Except for light, all the conditions were the same. Does the amount of water a plant receives make a difference? Can a plant have too much water?

EXPERIMENTING

Again, plant beans in three pots. Keep all variables the same except the amount of water. Keep the soil in one pot fairly dry. Give this plant only a little water. Keep the soil damp at all times in the second pot. Keep water standing on top of the soil in the third pot.

Observe the growth of the plants. Keep a record of what happens in each pot. Combine your data with the data of others in your class. What do you conclude about water and bean plants?

EXPERIMENTING

Get two small pots which are the same size. Decide on the kind of plant which you would like to grow. You might like to plant sunflower seeds instead of bean seeds. Or you might like to try this experiment with a flower such as the zinnia.

Plant only two seeds in the first pot. Plant a great many seeds in the second pot. Care for the plants in both pots in exactly the same way. Your only variable is the number of seeds which you planted in each pot.

Observe the growth of the plants. Keep a record of the growth. What information did you gather from the results of this experiment?

EXPERIMENTING

Next, do an experiment to test the effect of temperature on plants. List the materials which you will need. Plan how you will keep track of the results. Write a statement on what you conclude.

At the conclusion of this series of experiments, the idea (concept) "environmental factors" was used to focus on aspects of the environment that affect living things. The first two phases of the learning cycle have been completed.

Now plan some "Expanding the Idea" activities which would follow the experiment just done to gather data and the introduction of the idea of environmental factors. Plan at least two or three.

Some experiments, like the plant growth experiment, require days or weeks to complete. Other experiments require only a few minutes or hours. For example, if an experimenter wished to compare the bounciness of different balls, a plan to control certain variables, such as dropping height, must be made. Then the experiment is carried out. Measurements are then made, recorded, and interpreted. All of this could probably be accomplished in less than an hour. The experiment has three distinct phases. These phases are: (1) planning the experiment; (2) performing the actions and collecting the data; and (3) interpreting the data. Learners must be intimately involved in all three phases.

MODEL BUILDING

Model building is a very creative process in science. The models of nature created by children or adults enhance understanding or explain some aspect of nature. The atom and the globe are perhaps the two best known models of nature. But models, to be useful, do not have to be as comprehensive as these models. In fact, to develop the process of model building, you should begin with very simple models.

The following activity was developed for grade three. The children interact with concrete objects and that interaction leads to a model understandable by children at the grade three level.

AN ELECTRICAL PUZZLE[5]

You will need a circuit tester (Figure 6–9) to solve a puzzle. First, you will need to make a puzzle box. To make your puzzle, you will need six paper fasteners, copper wires, and a small cardboard box. A shoe box will do.

Punch six holes in the box top. Number each hole. Put the numerals beside the holes on the top side of the box top. Put one paper fastener in each hole. Then connect wires to paper fasteners 1, 3, 4, and 5. Make the connections on the underside of the box top (see Figure 6–10).

Find out which pairs of paper fasteners make a complete circuit. Use your circuit tester. Make your test by touching the light bulb and

[5] Renner, John W., Don G. Stafford, and Vivian Coulter, *Systems,* Encino, California: Benziger Bruce & Glencoe, 1977, pp. 116–117.

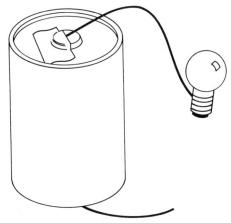

Figure 6–9   This system is called a "circuit tester," it is made of a flashlight cell, a bulb, two pieces of wire, and some tape. The bottom of the bulb is placed on one part of an object attached to the tester, while the wire from the bottom of the flashlight cell is touched to another part. If the light goes on, then the object completed the circuit.

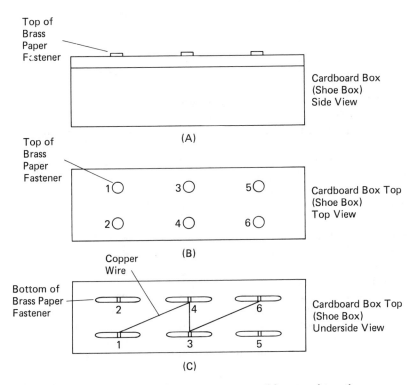

Figure 6–10   Different puzzles are constructed by attaching the copper wire to different numbered brass paper fasteners.

the wire of the circuit tester to paper fasteners. Start by testing paper fasteners 1 and 3. Which pairs light the light bulb?

Now, connect your wires to other paper fasteners. Change the connections. Then put the box top on the box. With the lid on the box, you cannot see the wiring. Exchange puzzle boxes with another girl or boy. Test the paper fasteners on the box that you get. Which pairs make a complete circuit? Test all the pairs that the six paper fasteners make. How many pairs can you make with the numerals 1, 2, 3, 4, 5, and 6?

A more advanced model, a simple molecular model, can be developed by sixth grade students. Notice that the model is developed from children manipulating the actual concrete objects. In the following series of model-building activities, the pupils have already observed the expansion and contraction of air and the diffusion of one material through another.[6]

GATHERING DATA

How could a gas move through a gas? How could a liquid move through a liquid? How could a solid move through a liquid? The following experiment provides a model which will help you to understand how diffusion works.

Experimenting   Fill a beaker with marbles. Fill the beaker with marbles level with the top of the beaker. The marbles are a model of a jar full of water.

Now answer these questions: How full of marbles is the jar? What do we mean by being full? How is the beaker of marbles in Figure 6–11 like a jar of water? How is it not like the jar of water?

Next, pour dry sand into the beaker (see Figure 6–12). Shake the beaker. Let the sand diffuse into the container of marbles. Fill the sand level to the top of the beaker.

Next, pour some water into the "full" container. Observe the water as it diffuses through the sand (see Figure 6–13).

Interpreting   Use the marble, sand, and water model to explain how one kind of matter could move through another kind of matter. Next, look at the picture. The picture provides data which can be used to answer the questions which follow.

Let the marbles represent water. Let the red sand represent red food coloring in the water. Now consider this question: Will the red sand diffuse upward through the marbles without someone stirring or shaking the container? What if you left the container on a shelf for several days or weeks. Would it make a difference? Try it and see.

[6] Renner, John W., Don G. Stafford, and Vivian Coulter, *Models,* Encino, California: Benziger Bruce & Glencoe, 1977, pp. 172–179.

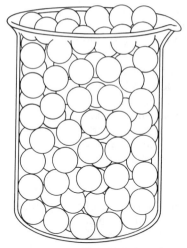

Figure 6–11 The container is "full" of marbles.

Figure 6–12 Even though the container is full of marbles, sand can be poured into it.

Figure 6–13 Even after the container is full of marbles and sand, water can be poured into it.

If the marbles and sand are moving, the particles of sand will diffuse upward through the marbles. Put the lid on the jar and shake it. Observe the sand and marbles system. Stop shaking the jar and again observe the system.

How is this model like the water and food coloring system? How is the model unlike the water and food coloring system?

For an odor to reach your nose, a gas which gives off the odor must move. For example, a gas is moving when the odor of a perfume, a flower, or a moth ball reaches your nose. The odor, let's say, moves through the air. It moves like the sand particles in the sand and marble system moved when you shook the beaker.

GETTING THE IDEA
The idea that gases, liquids, and solids are composed of tiny particles can be used to explain many things about matter. Consider water, for example. Water is composed of extremely small particles.

The smallest particle of a pure substance such as water is called a

molecule.

Water is a liquid. Liquids are composed of molecules. Gases such as oxygen are composed of molecules. Solids such as sugar are composed of molecules.

A molecule is the smallest particle of a substance. Molecules themselves are tiny objects. In your class, the individual pupils are the smallest units that make up the class. The class is made up of the smallest-sized packages, called pupils. You cannot divide a pupil into smaller packages while retaining the identity of the pupil.

A pupil in a class, then, is like a molecule of water in a drop of water. You can line up the pupils in a class in neat rows. Pupils are mixed together as they walk down a hallway. Or they can play on the playground, running, jumping, or just looking at an ant hill. But, whatever they do, they are still members of the class. They are the parts of which the class is made.

Interpreting According to our model, all matter is composed of very small particles. Matter is composed of molecules. The picture shows how the particles are arranged in a solid, and in a gas (see Figure 6–14). Why is what is shown in the picture a model? What does the model represent?

Observing Look at a sugar cube with a hand lens (see Figure 6–15). Break the sugar cube into pieces. Then look at the pieces with a hand lens. Crush the pieces to a powder. Examine the powder.

Suppose you could continue to break the pieces of sugar. Let's say you could break them into bits which are smaller and smaller. What determines how small a piece of sugar could be?

Interpreting Place some sugar in an empty tea bag. Then place the tea bag over the side of a beaker. Add water until the watch touches the

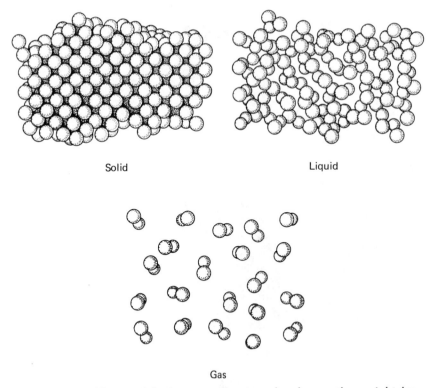

Solid

Liquid

Gas

Figure 6–14   This model of matter shows molecules as they might be in a solid, a liquid, and a gas. This model is probably too abstract for most sixth grade children.

tea bag. Observe the interaction of the water and the sugar. A mixture such as sugar and water is called a solution. How does the sugar get through the tea bag into the water? Use the molecule model to explain the diffusion of sugar and water. Use the model to describe a solution.

PREDICTING

The interpretation of data, as you have seen, can lead to model building. There is another use that can also be made of interpretations made from data. That use is exactly the same as the use that can be made of any past learning in increasing our ability to function more effectively in the future; that is, we use past learnings to *predict* what our future behavior should be. The interpretations that we make of our past experiences form the basis for our everyday behavior. A common example illustrates this very well. When you are standing at a corner waiting to cross the street and the light regulating the traffic turns red, you feel free (after a visual inspection) to cross. In the past you have

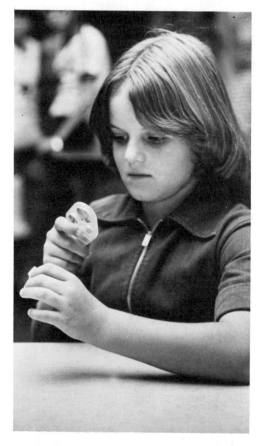

Figure 6–15   How small
can a piece of sugar be?
(Martin J. Lollar)

had direct experience that tells you that moving automobiles stop when confronted with a red light. From that data-interpretation experience, you predict that the moving automobiles you are watching will also stop when the traffic light becomes red. You are so convinced your prediction is valid that you are willing to risk your own personal safety by stepping into the street in front of automobiles approaching the red light. This behavior on your part did not come without a great deal of experience which occurred over a long period of time.

So it is with predictions that can be made from data received from experiments. If children are going to learn to predict future events and base those predictions on scientifically collected and interpreted data, they must be given the freedom to make predictions; we, as teachers, must provide experiences that will give them that experience.

You have seen in this chapter how observing, measuring, interpreting, experimenting, and model building can each provide the focus for "Getting the Idea" and "Expanding the Idea." But where and how does predicting fit into the learning cycle? Before we attempt to answer that question let us explore in greater depth just what a prediction is. A prediction is an estimate of the events to take place or the results to be achieved, or both.

You will immediately recognize that the description of a prediction does not differ greatly from that of an hypothesis, and your observation is quite correct. There is, however, a fundamental difference between them. An hypothesis is generally based on very limited experience with a particular problem or situation (as had been previously stated), and sometimes it is based on intuition. In other words, an hypothesis is a belief of an investigator of what the answer to a question actually is; although a great amount of evidence is not needed to support the investigator's personal belief, enough is needed to suggest further investigations and guidance for those investigations. Sometimes the information that an experiment delivers in its early stages is not definitive enough to allow one hypothesis to be stated; rather, the data suggest several hypotheses that can be tested. An hypothesis, then, could be described as a tentative assumption stated to enable the investigator to test its validity. Stating hypotheses that are believed to be false is often useful in an investigation because proof of such falsity narrows the number of possible explanations for a problem. Hypotheses are sometimes called "working hypotheses."[7] Such a literal interpretation of the term is quite useful in understanding it; that is, an hypothesis is a statement that guides further work.

Predictions, however, do not have the tentative, "work-guiding" nature of hypotheses; they are not stated for the primary purpose of being tested—hypotheses are. A prediction is made on the basis of ideas that have been tested over and over again. When, for example, the weather is predicted, these predictions are based on data from such variables as temperature, humidity, time of year, wind velocity, and direction. The effect of each of these factors on weather has been thoroughly investigated, and while that investigation was progressing many hypotheses about these factors' effects were tested. Now, however, meteorologists understand the effect of the various factors upon the weather and need not further hypothesize about them. Rather, the effect of such thoroughly tested factors can now be used to predict the weather. An hypothesis, then, is an assumption to allow the validity of a generalization or model to be tested, and a prediction is the utilization of tested generalizations or models in order to forecast the future behavior of an individual, the results of an experiment, or the outcome of an event.

[7] Chamberlain, T. C., "The Method of Working Multiple Hypotheses", *Science*, 148: 756, 1975.

What is the value to pupils of learning how to predict? Why is experience in this area an essential part of their experience in science? Perhaps the most basic reason for including experience in predicting in science education is that prediction is a definite, integral part of the structure of the scientific discipline. In many ways, prediction is at the apex of the scientific process; all that is done in a scientific investigation leads the experimenter toward the goal of stating results of a similar situation in the future. Since we feel that the elementary school science curriculum must be recognizable as science by a scientist (the integrity of the discipline must be maintained), prediction must be a part of that curriculum.

What is necessary in order to make a prediction? Data must be gathered, classified, compared, analyzed, and evaluated. Those data selected must then be synthesized into a generalized statement about the situation being considered. This generalization then allows the investigator to reason from the general to the particular about what will happen in a future situation. This is, of course, deduction. In other words, making a prediction demands that many of the learner's rational powers be used. The experience of predicting, therefore, assists learners in the development of their rational powers and leads them to construct a more complete picture of the structure of the discipline of science than they would if prediction were not included. Prediction is, in a sense, a practical application of one's understanding of nature.

Now to the question of, "Where does predicting fit into the learning cycle?" As you can see, predictions are based on *ideas* that have been formulated primarily through interpretation, experimentation, and model building. The natural place of predicting, therefore, is in "Expanding the Idea." Then why, you might ask, is predicting listed in the "Gathering Data" triangle (Figure 6–2) as well as in "Expanding the Idea"? The answer is simple. No idea stands alone. Each idea is linked to others in the structure of science. Even when one is expanding one idea, that person is gathering data with which to construct or invent a related idea. Thus prediction fits meaningfully into both triangles.

PLACING THE PROCESSES OF SCIENCE IN THE ELEMENTARY SCHOOL

Where in the elementary school education should pupils have the process experiences in science described in this chapter? A definitive answer to this question cannot be formulated because all pupils are different. A first-grade group of children in one section of the country may be completely unlike any other first-grade group of children anywhere else. Furthermore, large differences exist among the pupils in any given grade in an elementary school. Therefore, what will be said here about the specific grade placement of the various experiences in science must be tempered with the good judgment of the classroom teacher and the teacher's consultant. Do not be misled into believing that the suggestions made here refer to the mythical "average child." Rather, the following suggestions are based on what research has told us about children and how they learn. Our concern is to outline a general view of the sequence of science education experiences for children which will make a maximum contribution to the development of their rational powers. We are particularly concerned with outlining an educational program that can be used to accelerate all pupils in the area of science. For, as Celia Stendler has said, "sixteen-year-old thinkers can never be made of six-year-olds, no matter how carefully the educational program is planned."[8] But there are definite intellectual gains that children can make by being engaged in an explicit, carefully planned educational program. Regarding such a program, Professor Stendler has said that "if at the present time, as a result of chance experience, some adolescents build into their nervous system a structure of logic capable of handling abstractions, more youngsters could do so, if these experiences were not left to chance."

Although no one can outline in detail the specific, day-to-day experiences the pupils in any given classroom should have, certain general guidelines can be laid down which will prevent chance from being the primary factor that determines whether or not they will have science experiences that will help to develop their rational powers.

What is said here is largely based upon the work of Jean Piaget. The next few paragraphs will also serve as a review of what was said in Chapter 3. The first level of development with which we must concern ourselves is the preoperational stage. Understanding this phase of child development is important for primary-level teachers and particularly for first-grade teachers. In the preoperational stage a child is basically concerned with "establishing relationships between experience and action; his concern is manipulating the world through action."[9] This stage of development begins about the time the child starts to develop his language ability and continues until he can begin to manipulate symbols. In other words, when a child enters the first grade

---

[8] Celia B. Stendler, "Elementary Teaching and the Piagetian Theory," *The Science Teacher*, Washington, D.C.: National Science Teacher's Association, September 1962, p. 37.

[9] Jerome S. Bruner, *The Process of Education*, Cambridge, Massachusetts: Harvard University Press, 1962, p. 34.

he is an object-manipulator. Science is greatly concerned with the study of objects because the world around us (the investigative field for science) is made up of objects, from subatomic particles to the earth itself. Children's first experiences in science, then, should be concerned with objects and, since upon entering the first grade they are manipulators of objects, it is only natural that children be given the opportunity to study and manipulate objects.

How do first graders study an object? When given an object the first act they will perform is to look at, or observe, it. So the first of the essential experiences in science which the child should have is observation. Of course, all the necessary observational abilities cannot be provided for during a child's first few years of school. While this experience is the first one for a child to have, opportunities to have it must be provided throughout the learner's educational experience. Remember, as we previously discussed, that observation involves all the senses, and not just seeing.

Children in the preoperational stage have mastered the basic principles of a language (an extremely difficult act) by the time they enter school. They can talk about what they have observed. Letting them talk about their observations using words that have been newly developed for them or that they have invented is beneficial to their language development. You will remember from Chapter 3 that one of the factors involved in learning is social transmission. Talking is certainly a part of social transmission. Here, then, is a second expectation a teacher can have of preoperational children—they can report.

Since the child is a manipulator of objects, the ideas of measurement can be started in the first grade. These measurements will be quite crude and approximate and must definitely involve objects. The comparison of the height of a plant with a stick, a piece of paper, or a soda straw involves comparing the plant with another object and the manipulation of one or more objects. Do not expect children in the preoperational stage to make repeated application of some standard unit of length in measuring an object. That involves the conservation of length, which preoperational thinkers do not do. The techniques for and systems of measurement, which the child will need in later academic life and as a citizen, will be more thoroughly understood when met if the basis for measurement is developed in the early primary grades. This experience, like observation and reporting, should continue to be provided for preoperational learners.

In the concrete operational stage, the child is capable of performing some type of operation, as opposed to his preschool behavior, which was merely active. Childrens' attention can then be focused on a problem or situation which will cause them to do something definite "to see what will happen." Such operations furnish children with data about the real world which they can internalize and use in the solution of problems.

In most cases children have entered the concrete operational stage by late in their first year of school. Since that means they have begun to see the various states in transformation (which is what an experiment is), they can begin to do very simple experiments during the latter months of the first grade. One of Piaget's basic premises about children in the concrete operational stage is that they can use operations as a means of finding data to assist them in solving problems. An example of that premise is, as was discussed earlier, that if first-grade children are presented a group of seedlike objects (some of which are seeds) and asked how they can determine which are seeds, they will suggest planting them. Here is a concrete operation that six-year-olds are very willing to undertake. Children of this age do not normally hypothesize because they see the problem as an entity. They do not see the several variables, divisions, or both, of the problem—they see it as a whole. They can only say the seedlike objects will or will' not grow; they cannot hypothesize about any given portion of the experiment. The children have no reason for making such a statement—they have no information which would lead them to make it—and any statement they would make is a wild guess and not an hypothesis. Children should not be encouraged to make such wild guesses at an early age because bad intellectual habits could be formed that will have to be broken when they begin to form simple hypotheses.

The experiment described produces data and, according to Piaget, children in the concrete operational stage have the ability to use these data to assist them in answering their questions. When they do this, they are interpreting data. Experimentation and data interpretation, therefore, can be introduced into the elementary school science program at the late first grade level—when the children have entered the concrete operational stage. There is some evidence to support the notion that these two experiences will be most efficient if they follow a period of experience in observation and perhaps some acquaintance with measurement. Perhaps the idea of relative size is all the work with measurement that a child needs before beginning experimentation. This basic idea can be thoroughly taught by a comparative exercise during which the teacher will ask such questions as, "Who is the tallest?" "Which book is heavier?", and "Which stitch is longer?" After such introductory experiences the results provided by the childrens' experiments can be used as a vehicle to lead them to begin to understand measurement as a tool to be used to interpret those results.

The sequence, then, of the essential experiences in science is observation, the basic idea of size in terms of measurements, data interpretation, and simple experimentation. The experiences provided in each of these areas can be started in the first grade and need to continue and become increasingly sophisticated as the child progresses upward through the educational system.

As children move upward through the elementary school and continue to have inquiry experiences, they move deeper and deeper into the concrete operational stage. In the latter years of their elementary schooling they can begin to make data interpretations, construct models or make predictions, or both. They also begin to synthesize simple hypotheses and will be capable of more controlled experimentation. But the models they build, the predictions they make, or the hypotheses they state will be concerned with the objects and operations they are presently concerned with. They are deep into the stage of concrete operations, but they have not yet entered into the early phases of formal operations. In a study we conducted of 588 secondary school students we found that approximately only 25 percent of them had entered the formal operational stage. Do not expect, therefore, fifth and sixth graders to construct mental models, make predictions, or synthesize hypotheses about anything except reality. They will not usually take that step into the unknown and begin to relate what is possible but not real to them. Do not put your level of expectation beyond those of prediction or the construction of models which can be made by children using the information and objects they have directly in front of them.

You are going to be working with children in the concrete operational stage of learning; do not expect too much model building and prediction. Of extreme importance, however, is that children in the late concrete operational stage have model-building and prediction experiences; and that these experiences are essential in moving them toward achieving formal operational ability.

Chapter 7
Essential Concepts in Science

In order to accomplish the goals and objectives of elementary school science, pupils must be involved in doing science. In Chapter 7 six essential processes needed for doing science were presented. *We firmly believe that a program which does not involve pupils directly in these processes is not teaching science.* It is possible, however, to imagine a program strongly committed to allowing pupils to participate in the essential processes and yet still not be an effective science program. Involvement of pupils in the processes of observing, measuring, interpreting, experimenting, predicting, and model building would, no doubt, promote rational power development. This involvement might also, if the processes were used in a meaningful sequence, develop the pupils' ability and confidence to inquire. But in order to accomplish all three of the goals of science education in the elementary school, *direct involvement with the processes are essential, but they are, by themselves, not enough!*

The process skills are designed to allow a person to collect, organize, and interpret information about natural phenomena. Of course, these same process skills can be applied effectively to other areas as well. For example, the process skills are essential in the logical study of economics, politics, sociology, and psychology. If, however, a person wishes to develop and understand natural phenomena, that is, *to develop an understanding of the changing nature of the environment in terms of matter, life, energy, and their interaction,* there are certain basic or fundamental concepts that must be understood. There are, we believe, ten concepts that are essential to the understanding of natural phenomena. They are *matter, space, time, energy, balance, variation, change, property, system,* and *model.* These concepts strongly enhance a person's ability to think about nature. A complete science program in elementary schools must develop the six process skills and it must also develop an understanding of the ten essential concepts.

Now it must be strongly emphasized that understandings of these concepts are also gained through their active use by pupils or by active investigations involving them. The essential concepts are not passive ideas like a person's name or the name of an object which can be transferred to another person in a simple spoken word. A two-year-old child can learn that a dog's name is Sam, but that does not mean that the child understands dogs. It should also be emphasized that understanding of these concepts does not come quickly. Understanding of the essential concepts develops gradually as they are used during investigations to think about nature. Some of the essential concepts, such as property, system, and variation, can be introduced by name in elementary school using the learning cycle after limited experiences in the "Gathering Data" phase. Other concepts, such as energy, should be formally introduced by the learning cycle only after very extensive experience to develop intuitive understanding. Still other concepts, such as space and time, might never be formally introduced in elementary school. Each of the ten essential concepts will be discussed individually later in the chapter.

Perhaps you are wondering about other science concepts that are often found in elementary school programs—concepts that deal with specific areas or aspects of nature. Are they not also essential? The answer is "yes" if you must help pupils learn about that specific area. Each content area has its own specific concepts. In order to learn about a particular content area, one must learn the specific concepts involved in that area. For example, if the content area of magnetism is chosen, the specific concepts of attraction and repulsion, magnetic poles, and magnetic field should be learned. These specific content concepts allow one to think about and discuss magnetic phenomena. It is nice to know about magnetic phenomena, but a person could do science very effectively in many areas of nature and have no knowledge of magnetism. In fact, we believe that *there is no specific list of concepts about the various aspects of nature that must be learned in elementary school science.*

It is not possible to learn about all content areas of science in elementary school—trying would be foolhardy. There are, however, certain areas of nature that are traditionally dealt with in science. We will take no position for or against the selection of particular traditional aspects of nature and the specific concepts of nature for study. Certain topics or areas might be chosen because of the interest of the children or the importance of the understanding as viewed by the teacher. Our primary concern is that the topics or concepts selected, and the way in which pupils are expected to develop an understanding of them, are compatible with the level of intellectual development of the child. Keep in mind also, that although many of the concepts about specific areas of science are nice to know, *they are not essential!*

THREE DIVISIONS OF THE TEN ESSENTIAL CONCEPTS

The ten essential concepts can be separated into three categories that reflect the nature of the concept.

Basic or Fundamental Concepts: Time–Space–Matter–Energy

By basic or fundamental, we mean that there is hardly anything that can be done or thought that does not involve these concepts. Children at a very early age begin to interact with objects (pieces of matter) around them and explore spatial relationships. Intuitive development of space-matter relationships begins to take place in the crib as a child reaches for objects. At an early age, children develop the understanding that an object is permanent—even when the object cannot be seen, it still exists. Spatial relationships are further explored as the child crawls and walks.

A sense of time appears to be built into many animals and plants. Man has some innate time sense, but for the most part must depend on external events for time measurement and awareness.

The concept of energy is listed as fundamental, but it does not appear to develop in children from some innate seed. This concept is perhaps the most abstract of all concepts dealt with in elementary school. It is, in fact, so abstract that we would not choose to introduce it in elementary school if it were not essential to understand natural phenomena.

People are, in a sense, locked into a matter–space–time–energy context. It is impossible to explore any area or even think without involvement of these concepts, whether consciously or subconsciously, either formally or intuitively. For these reasons, the development of these fundamental concepts is essential. An elementary science program must include a rich variety of activities which enhance and develop these essential concepts.

Universal Condition Concepts: Change–Variation–Balance (Equilibrium)

A widely accepted notion in science is that everything is in a condition of continuous change. Paint is used to cover buildings to slow the inevitable change in wood or metal. Additives are put into food to slow the spoilage. People use creams and other substances to slow the aging of the skin, but, although it is slowed, change continues. Try to think about some aspect of nature that does not change; then you will become convinced of the universality of the concept of change.

You have, no doubt, heard that no two people are identical, not even identical twins. As a matter of fact, it is probable that no two objects in nature are exactly alike in every minute detail. Variation in objects, events, and measurements is universal.

Objects and events all differ to some extent, and they are continuously undergoing change, yet science continues to search for patterns of change. The search not only for change but for the ranges of variation of such change is essential to science.

Balance (or equilibrium) is found in all systems from the solar system to the single atom, or from the total animal to the single cell. You can confine air with a balloon, but let the tiniest hole appear and the tendency toward balance between the air inside and outside the balloon immediately becomes apparent.

The concepts of change, variation, and balance (or equilibrium) are essential to the description of every collection of objects or events in nature. To understand any aspect of nature is: (1) to understand patterns of change in objects or systems; (2) to understand how objects or events vary and the range of that variation; and (3) to understand how opposing factors tend to bring a system into a stable condition or a state of balance.

Describing and Organizing Concepts: Property–System–Model

The attributes of an object or event that are used to identify or distinguish it from other objects or events, or simply to tell about objects and events, are called *properties*. At all levels of scientific activity and in all areas of nature people begin with information about the objects and events they are studying. Such information as shape, color, odor, texture, boiling point, melting point, cleavage, alive or dead, reactivity, density, and size is considered important.

When two or more objects or two or more phases of matter are investigated together, the objects or phases of matter are called a *system*. You are aware, no doubt, that the system concept is used extensively in many other areas of knowledge as well as science. We talk about transportation systems, communication systems, solar systems, political systems, school systems, and body systems. The system concept allows an investigator to mentally isolate for study two or more objects from all others in the universe. The systems concept also allows a person to communicate ideas and relationships about the system. For example, when a person refers to the school system of a city, a distinct set of buildings and groups of people are mentally isolated from all the others.

In order to explain some aspect of nature or to communicate ideas about a system to someone, models are used. Models can be very simple. A simple sketch of a house with objects in it is a model that a primary level child can make. This model can be used to explain or communicate ideas about the house. Models can also be very complex and abstract. The atomic models used to explain chemical reactions are examples of very complex models.

It is unthinkable that elementary school children would be expected to use very complex models. It is unfortunately true, however, that most elementary school science programs introduce many very abstract models to children. This probably happens because the authors of such programs do not fully understand the use of models in reasoning. In learning to use models, children must begin with very simple models and *slowly* progress to more complex ones.

The concepts of properties, systems, and models are indeed essential concepts in science. But they are not used in science alone. These concepts are used in many other areas of knowledge.

ESSENTIAL PROCESSES AND CONCEPTS OF SCIENCE AND EDUCATIONAL TRANSFER

The education of a child should not be administered as a series or collection of unrelated packages. One part of the educational program should be supportive with others. We believe that a science program should be organized around the essential processes and the essential concepts. If a science program is organized in this way, the objectives of elementary school science can be achieved. But that is not all. The processes and concepts that we have labeled as essential can be applied in all discipline areas to collect, organize, interpret, use, and communicate information and ideas. A program organized in this way would, therefore, have maximum potential for transfer from one curriculum area to another.

ORDER OF INTRODUCTION OF THE ESSENTIAL CONCEPTS

Each of the ten essential concepts can be introduced *in some form* at almost any level in the elementary school. In some cases, however, the concept must be introduced in a series of steps that extends over a period of years. Only after a learner has had many experiences with lower level concepts can the essential concepts be formally introduced.

The concepts of property and change, for example, are readily grasped by children in the first and second grades. On the other hand, children will need to make many comparisons of objects and events that develop an intuitive understanding of variation before that concept is formally introduced. The concepts of matter and energy require even longer periods and will probably not be formally introduced before grade five. A common error of teachers and curriculum writers is to introduce the names of concepts such as matter and energy by means of a definition. These teachers apparently assume that if a child is able to use the word for the concept, the child has an understanding of it. That belief is, of course, only wishful thinking. Not only is just teaching a child to use a word a naive approach to teaching, it might be harmful because it tends to give children the feeling they know something without real learning and understanding. Since the foundational intuitive structures and ideas have not been developed, gaps in the conceptual structure will be left. If, on the other hand, adequate experiences with the concept precede the introduction of the word or label, the word or label becomes a focusing idea that can enhance understanding and allow expansion into other related ideas.

How should the essential concepts be introduced into the curriculum? The answer is, "With a great deal of thought and planning!" If a teacher uses a commercially developed program, most of the thought and planning should have already been done for the teacher by a curriculum developer. The learning cycles should be obvious. If the curriculum developer understands the intellectual development of children and the conceptual and process structure of science, the developer will be able to carefully and logically plan the teaching and learning cycle for each concept.

The following is a very general plan for the teaching and learning of the concept of matter. Notice that there are several learning cycles associated with preliminary and expanding concepts. Notice also that there is a comprehensive learning cycle which extends over the six year elementary school period.

MATTER

Matter is the most tangible real thing because it can often be held in the hand and examined. This allows children to interact with matter directly and they should begin at the start of the program to do so. The word matter should not be introduced, however, until later in the program—perhaps at grade level four or five. There are many preliminary aspects of matter that need to be investigated first.

As shown in Figure 7–1 the first level of activities with matter should involve identifying pieces of it as things or objects. Children need to become aware that there are many different kinds of objects in their environment.

The next level at which matter can be investigated is that objects that have different shapes and appearances can be made of the same "stuff" or material. The material of which an object is made can exist as a solid, a liquid, or a gas. The change of a material from one condition or state of being to another is a physical change. A change of one material into another is a chemical change.

After many investigations have been done—that is, many learning cycles have been completed—the word matter can be introduced. Then

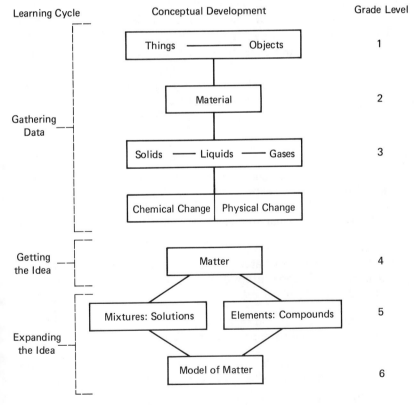

Figure 7–1   Learning cycles are used to develop individual concepts and processes. There is also a more comprehensive learning cycle that can be superimposed over the entire elementary school science program.

the concept matter can be expanded. The first area of expansion of matter might be to identify mixtures or solutions or both. Other areas of expansion should be to identify substances—materials that are homogeneous. These substances can then be expanded to include the ideas of elements and compounds.

In grade six a simple model of matter can be developed through concrete investigations. The tendency of many teachers is to carry the model too far. They can hardly resist the temptation to talk about atoms, electrons, protons, neutrons, and such. Resist this temptation. The children are, at best, just beginning to enter the stage of formal thought. Many children in grade six are not yet in this stage. In either case, the concept of atoms and atomic structures is too abstract.

Figure 7–1, which you have just explored, shows how the development of an essential concept over a period of several grade levels can and should also follow the "Gathering Data," "Getting the Idea," and "Expanding the Idea" cycle. The "Gathering Data" and "Expanding the Idea" portions of the cycle are themselves composed of several learning cycles. Each of the cycles develops a concept closely associated with the essential concept "matter." The development of the other essential experience concepts can be placed into a structure like Figure 7–1. The following is an example of the development of one of the associated concepts shown in Figure 7–1. The concept is "chemical change." The learning cycle through the "Getting the Idea" phase, where the concept of "physical change" was invented, has already been completed by the children.

EXPANDING THE IDEA[1]
To observe some physical changes, you can do some experiments. A change will occur in each experiment. Some of the changes will be physical changes. Others will not be physical changes. You will test each change. Use what you have just learned about finding physical changes.

System A   Put sugar into water. Stir it up. Describe what happens. Is the change you observe a physical change? What evidence can you find to support your answer?

System B   Mix dirt and sand together. Do you produce a physical change? Find evidence to support your answer.

System C   Light a candle. Watch it burn. Describe what happens. Is the burning a physical change? What evidence do you have to support your answer?

[1] John W. Renner, Don G. Stafford, and Vivian Jensen Coulter, *Systems* (Grade 3), Encino, California: Benziger Bruce & Glencoe, 1977, pp. 70–76.

Figure 7–2 Conclusions in science should be supported by evidence.

What do you believe happens when a physical change occurs? State a rule which helps to explain what happens. Be sure your rule explains what happened in System A and System B.

GATHERING DATA
There is another kind of change. To study this other kind, you need to explore with System D. The objects in System D are a candle, a wooden clothespin, a piece of aluminum foil, and a teaspoonful of white sugar.

System D   Fold the aluminum foil three times. You need a folded piece ten centimeters long and five centimeters wide. Fasten the clothespin on one edge of the aluminum foil tray. Put a teaspoonful of sugar in the tray. Light the candle. Hold the tray and sugar over the candle. Use the clothespin.

Carefully observe System D for any changes that occur. Make a record of all the changes you observe.

GETTING THE IDEA
Remember your rule for a physical change. Describe the sugar when the experiment is finished. The sugar looks different. But the change you observe is more than a change in how it looks. You cannot get the sugar back. You cannot call the change a physical change. The change you observe in the sugar is a

chemical change.

There are many common examples of chemical changes. The rusting of iron is a chemical change. The tarnishing of silver is another chemical change. An acid interacting with a metal brings about a chemical change. The burning of a candle is a chemical change. Burning produces a chemical change.

EXPANDING THE IDEA
Make a rule about a chemical change. First, ask yourself, "Can a chemical change be undone?" Base your rule on your answer to this question. The rule helps you to know whether a change is a chemical change or a physical change.

Sometimes chemical changes and physical changes are hard to tell apart. Evidence from experiments will give you some clues. You are going to do some experiments. The evidence will help you to see chemical changes.

System E   Measure 20 milliliters of vinegar and put it into a beaker. Add one teaspoonful of baking soda. Is the change you see a physical or a chemical change? What evidence do you have for your answer?

System F   Put a teaspoonful of copper chloride in a tea bag. Fill a beaker with water. Place the tea bag and copper chloride in the water. Stick the tea bag to the side of the beaker. Is the change you see a physical change or a chemical change? What evidence do you have for your answer?

System G   Boil an egg. Boil it until the material inside is solid. What kind of change has happened? What evidence do you have for your answer?

ENERGY

As you can see, matter is a very important concept. An understanding of this concept is essential to understanding the environment. But an understanding of the concept of matter is developed through a logically planned sequence of learning activities—learning cycles. We have already referred to matter as a very tangible part of reality. You can hold it in your hand to feel it and describe it. Now if this very tangible aspect of nature required a very carefully planned program of hands-on activities prior to the introduction of the label, what about a very abstract concept such as energy? The answer is simple. The activities in elementary school can only begin the development of this concept. Some teachers and curriculum developers attempt to define energy by referring to the concept of work which is, as used in science, abstract and complex. To define one abstract concept using other concepts, whose meaning is not understood by the learner, is not teaching. A more meaningful approach to the development of understanding of energy is to use learning cycles that extend through several grade levels and which lead the learner to investigate such concepts as motion, heat, light, sound, electricity, magnetism, gravity, pushes and pulls, or actions and reactions. These concepts can be explored through concrete activities. For example, concrete activities can help the learner to see that motion can be changed to heat or light, heat can produce motion, or electricity can produce heat or motion. Since heat, light, electricity, and motion can each be changed into the other, they must be forms of the same thing. This "thing" can be labeled energy. But even after all of the carefully planned development, do not expect the learner to understand the concept of energy at an abstract level when the label is provided.

HIERARCHY OF ESSENTIAL CONCEPTS

A concept cannot be developed in isolation. Activities in which a child are involved might have as their principal focus the development of the concept of system. But it would be impossible to design activities to develop the concept of system without some direct involvement of the concepts of objects (matter), property, and change, and indirect involvement of the concept of variation. Thus, there is a logical hierarchy of the development of the essential concepts. Fortunately, the sequence of concepts in the hierarchy can be established so that it is both logical and remains in accord with the intellectual development of the child. Figure 7–3 shows one arrangement of the conceptual hierarchy.

Actually, all of the ten concepts are in use throughout all levels of science. The hierarchy scheme Figure 7–3 only suggests at what level the concept is formally introduced and can be *focused* upon. The concept is then added to the learner's reservoir of "thinking and talking" ideas used in studying and understanding nature.

The concept of matter is informally introduced as "things" or objects in the primary grades and then progresses through a series of other ideas to its formal introduction in upper elementary grades. On

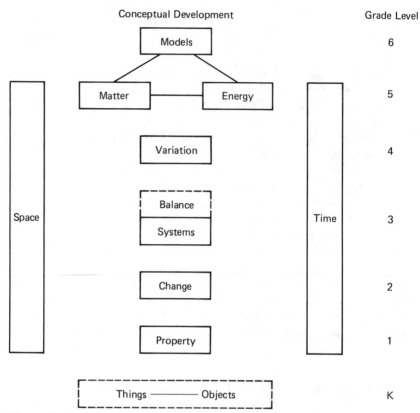

Figure 7–3 A conceptual hierarchy must be developed which allows ideas to be presented in a logical order with respect to both content and the child.

the other hand, property is formally introduced at the primary level. Its meaning and use should be expanded throughout the elementary school program.

As Figure 7–3 suggests, both space and time are used at all levels of the elementary school program. No particular level in Figure 7–3 is designated as the "proper" level to present and focus on the concepts of "time" and "space." Introducing something about these concepts is possible at almost any level on an intuitive basis. Discussions on "When did it happen?" "How long did it take?" "Show me how big the balloon was." "Which glass has more juice in it?" all take advantage of early learning that is common to all children and lead learners toward an understanding of space and time through the essential concept and process experience in science; however, a conscious and continuous attempt should be made by the teacher to refine and bring the two concepts of space and time into focus.

EXAMPLES OF ACTIVITIES TO DEVELOP THE ESSENTIAL CONCEPTS

If the school at which you teach has already selected a science program, examine it thoroughly. Determine whether or not every essential concept has been dealt with adequately. If not, it is your responsibility to supplement the text with activities that will lead the learners to develop those concepts. Hopefully, by now you will be able to design your own activities and implement them. You can also get ideas from other books, from periodicals, or from other teachers. In any case, you owe it to your pupils to provide them with opportunities to develop their understanding of the essential concept experiences in science.

The remainder of this chapter is designed to give you an opportunity to consider how activities can be developed to introduce or supplement the learning of the essential concepts. To do this we have introduced learning cycles concerning the essential concepts which have one or two phases of the cycle incomplete or missing. (Since we have already done several activities with the concept of matter, we will not deal with it again here.) Complete each learning cycle in writing. Then proceed to write and discuss your plan for comparison with others.

PROPERTY

The children in a first grade classroom have spent 2 weeks describing objects. They have learned to use shape words such as square, circle, triangle, and diamond. They have used color words, texture words, and size words. The teacher now feels that the children are ready to use the word "property."

The teacher, having placed several objects on a table at the front of the room, has the children watch and listen. The teacher then holds an object (a scarf) up so that all of the children can see it and says, "I am going to ask some of you to tell me one thing about this object. Do not tell me its name or what it is used for." The children describe the object by giving its color (red), its size (large), its texture (soft and smooth), and its shape (square). The teacher then says, "The words that you used to tell about the object are called properties." The teacher then has the children repeat the word several times. The teacher then holds up another object from the table and asks, "Who wants to give me a property of this object?" After the children have named three or four properties for each object, the teacher then selects another object.

> Now it is your turn. Think about how you could further expand the idea of property. Plan three or four activities. Be sure at least one of the activities deals with living things.

CHANGE

The children in your second grade room examined bean seeds. They then planted the seeds and observed them as they sprouted and grew. The children have described differences in their homes and school at different times of the day. They have observed an ice cube melt.

> You are now ready to introduce the idea of change to the class. Tell exactly how you would do it. Next, plan one or more "Expanding the Idea" activities involving the concept of change and each of the following.
>
> Changes in people.
> Changes that take place in the weather.
> Changes in food.

SYSTEM

The book that you are using refers to systems of the body such as the skeletal system. But the book does not develop the concept of system through concrete activities. It simply suggests that the children should refer to the dictionary to learn the meaning of the word "system."

> Create some activities that help the children develop an intuitive knowledge of the concept of system using the following systems and others that you think of.
>
> 1. A flashlight battery, bulb, and wire.
> 2. The children and chairs in your classroom.
> 3. Chalkboard and chalk or pencil and paper.
>
> Next, plan how you will introduce the idea of a system to the class. Remember that a system can be made of any objects that are considered together for some special reason.
> Now, plan some "Expanding the Idea" activities using system. You might have children identify systems and tell why they are a system. What systems would you use?

VARIATION

When children begin to describe and compare objects, they become aware of differences. Buttons are different colors and shapes. Children in a classroom are of different heights. The food in the cafeteria or their lunch boxes differs from day to day. Children develop an intuitive understanding of the idea that objects usually have both similarities and differences from a variety of activities designed to teach or develop other concepts. But there comes a time when the concept of differences is inadequate. This usually happens when children compare several objects of the same kind. For example, the children might examine a group of sea shells, or leaves, or guppies. In any group of naturally occurring objects of the same kind there are variations in one or more properties.

Plan some "Gathering Data" activities on variation using two or more of the following suggestions or others you think of.

1. How fast the children in a classroom can run.
2. The pencils used by the children.
3. A collection of leaves from the same tree.
4. Measurements of the length of a wall in the classroom.

Plan a class session with the children to introduce the idea of *variation*. Then expand the idea. Plan some activities in which the children report and discuss variation in their environment. One child might describe variations in trees, another in poodles, and another in automobiles. Plan one or two specific activities designed to focus on a variation that is related to something else. For example, how people dress depends on or varies with the weather or the kind of activity in which they are involved.

ENERGY

The children in a fifth grade class have done the following experiments.

1: Equal amounts of crushed ice were placed into two plastic bags and sealed. One bag of ice was placed on a table top. The other was passed from one child to another and the ice was held between their hands and squeezed. After the children had passed the bag from one child to another for 5 minutes, both bags were opened and the amount of water from each was measured.

2. A ruler with a groove down the middle was leaned on a book as shown in Figure 7–4. A marble was released at the top of the ruler and allowed to roll down the ruler, across the table top and onto the floor. The children measured how far from the table the marble hit the floor. The children repeated the experiment with a stack of two books, three books, and four books. Then they discussed how speed of the marble varied from one experiment to the next and how this speed is related to where the marble lands.

3. An unlighted candle was examined by the students. Then the candle was lighted. A beaker of water was held above the candle. The temperature of the water was measured every minute for 10 minutes.

4. The children have shot beans at a cardboard box target with large rubber bands. The rubber bands were placed on the thumb and index finger. A bean was then projected from the stretched rubber band.

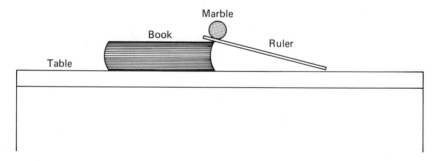

Figure 7–4

Now it is your turn. How would you use the data the students received from the four "Gathering Data" activities to introduce the concepts energy source, evidence of energy transfer, and energy receiver. Have the children draw from past experiences to give examples of an energy source, energy transfer, and energy receiver. You might have to give some examples to get the children started. For example, a sailboat and wind, a bowling ball and bowler or pins, a quarterback and a forward pass. What activities would you use to help the children expand the concepts you just introduced?

MODEL

Developing a model to explain patterns or properties of a particular part of nature is perhaps the most creative aspect of science. It is, therefore, an aspect of science that must be developed by using parts of nature that are capable of being explored. The human body is excellent for learning to develop models. For example, a model of seeing, or hearing, or breathing can be used. A model of muscle and bone action is easy to use.

Children can also experiment with magnets and develop a model of a magnetic field. Or they can develop a model to explain how electricity moves in a closed circuit, such as a model including a flashlight cell, a wire, and a bulb.

Suppose you have (through "Gathering Data" activities) introduced the children in your class to the concept of the model. They have expanded the concept by developing body models, a model of matter, and models of electricity and magnetism. Now you want to help the children see that other areas of knowledge use models too. Plan several activities that involve models in other areas. For example, you could develop a family model, or a friend model, or a government model, or a school system model.

BALANCE

The concept of balance with respect to objects in the environment is gradually developed intuitively over a period of years. Books laid on the edge of a table can fall to the floor. A mobile must have objects placed at just the right distances from the point of suspension. Chairs tilted too far back will topple. But the extension of the concept to the whole of nature is difficult and can only be partially done in elementary school.

Some ideas of balance are essential to the understanding of the environment. For example, suppose there were several animals and plants in the region. Some of the animals (coyotes, for example), used other animals for food. These animals that were used for food (rabbits, for example) used, in turn, plants for food. How is the idea of balance important to this community? What would happen if a disease killed off most of the rabbits?

Pretend you are a sixth grade teacher. Make a list of six or eight aspects of nature in which balance can be readily identified. Develop activities or problems to be solved by children that will expand the concept of balance.

SPACE AND TIME

On these two concepts, you are on your own. Select one of them and plan a series of "Gathering Data" activities, then help the children "Get the Idea" and "Expand the Idea." Decide how you will distribute the development of the activities by grade level. Be sure the activity is suited to the intellectual level of the child. Good luck!

If you are given the opportunity to serve on a committee in your school to evaluate and select a science program, make certain that all six essential processes and the ten essential concepts are dealt with. Of course, no particular science program might deal with the concepts and processes entirely as you would like it done. However, keep in mind this important idea. Remember, you are the teacher. Modify or supplement any planned program as you see the need to do so. As a professional teacher it is not only your prerogative, *it is your responsibility.*

Chapter 8
Curriculum Models

Suppose you were selecting a new piece of clothing. You probably would select a particular garment because of its styling, color, the way it fits you, what others in your age group are wearing, price, and other such factors. There are certain *criteria* that would lead you to select a specific garment over all others available to you. You use a similar procedure when you make many important decisions about your life, such as where you live and work, the types of furniture you will buy, and the kinds of food you eat. Your entire life is spent using criteria which lead you to make choices that greatly affect your life. In fact, the criteria you use to make decisions are constantly undergoing revision.

You are going to teach science to elementary school children. You must have something to teach them. That "something" is the *curriculum*. We do not believe that the curriculum consists only of the units or the textbook or the activities you select. The curriculum is what you select, but it also is how you, the teacher, use that selection with children. In other words, the curriculum is *what* you use and *how* it is used.

Oftentimes teachers say that they cannot have any influence on the curriculum because they are given a particular textbook which *is* the curriculum. Such teachers believe that only *what* is used constitutes the curriculum, and have ignored that *how* something is used is probably much more important than what is used. Recently a study[1] was made to test whether or not the *how* is as important as the *what*.

CONCRETE AND FORMAL TEACHING

Two classes of ninth grade physical science were taught *exactly the same material* by the same teacher during the same amount of time each day for one semester. The two participating classes were selected from the six classes available because of the time of day at which they were taught. The first group saw lots of demonstrations by the teacher of the concepts to be learned, was shown movies and filmstrips, given questions to answer and problems to work in class while the teacher was available and willing to help, given short lectures which were well illustrated on the overhead projector and the chalkboard, specifically directed what to read, and told what was to be on the test. This group was also not only allowed to see what happened in a demonstration but was told exactly why it happened. When an electric current lighted a bulb, for example, the group was told not only that the light was evidence of interaction among the elements in the circuit, the students were also told that an electric current is a flow of electrons. In other words, whether the concept was concrete or formal was unimportant. This kind of instruction was called *formal teaching*.

The second group was given the materials needed to gather the data required to allow the teacher to present to them the idea (the concept). The students in this group worked in pairs or trios and were given a minimum of directions, and the teacher worked with one group after another or with any group that needed help. After the students had gathered the needed data ("Gathering Data") the group was assembled and the teacher used their data to introduce them to the concept ("Getting the Idea"). Care was taken to insure that all concepts introduced were concrete concepts. The students were then given an experiment to do that used the language of the concept and the concept itself, and were told that the experiment they were doing involved the concept they had just met. This type of instruction used the learning cycle and was designated as *concrete teaching*.

[1] Schneider S. Livingston, *Relationships Between Concrete and Formal Instructional Procedures and Content-Achievement, Intellectual Development and Learner I.Q.*, Norman, Oklahoma, University of Oklahoma: unpublished Ph.D. dissertation, 1977.

The students who participated in this study were evaluated on their knowledge of the content studied and how this educational experience affected both their level of intellectual development[2] and their intelligence quotient[3] (I.Q.). The level of intellectual development and I.Q. were measured in September 1976, when the experiment started, in January 1977, when the experiment was concluded, and again in May 1977. The knowledge of content was measured at the end of each unit studied and exactly three months later.

The students who experienced concrete teaching outgained the group experiencing formal teaching at the end of each unit except one. The significant factor in this study is that the concrete teaching group far outscored the formal teaching group on knowledge of content *three months* after the conclusion of *every* unit they were taught. In other words, concrete teaching, using concrete concepts, enabled the students to remember specific facts and principles longer than formal teaching, which does not distinguish the level of a concept. (See Figure 8–1.) The concretely taught group also outgained the formally taught group in intellectual development. Both verbal and nonverbal I.Q. were measured. (See Figure 8–2.) The concrete group made large gains in nonverbal I.Q., and the formal group's nonverbal I.Q. scores declined. The two groups were equal in gain in the verbal portion of the I.Q. scale despite the emphasis given to language in the formal teaching group. (See Figure 8–3.)

USING SCIENCE TEXTBOOKS THAT TELL STUDENTS WHAT TO KNOW

The experiment just described demonstrates that how a teacher uses the curriculum is of more importance than what is in the curriculum if knowledge of content, intellectual development, and I.Q. are of importance to that teacher. So, if you are presented with a textbook which tells the children everything they are supposed to know, remember the experiment just described. Just giving the learners the information is not the procedure to use in leading them to the greatest gains in knowledge of content, intellectual development, and I.Q. What this means is that if the textbook you are given has reading which gives the children experiments to do and then tells them the answers, the children should not have the textbook in their hands. Instead, present the children with the materials to be used and instruct them

---

[2] The tasks designed by Piaget and Inhelder that measure progress toward formal thought given in Appendix D were used.

[3] As measured by E. T. Sullivan, W. W. Clark, E. W. Teigs, *Short Form Test of Academic Aptitude,* Level 5, Monterey, California: CTB/McGraw-Hill, 1970.

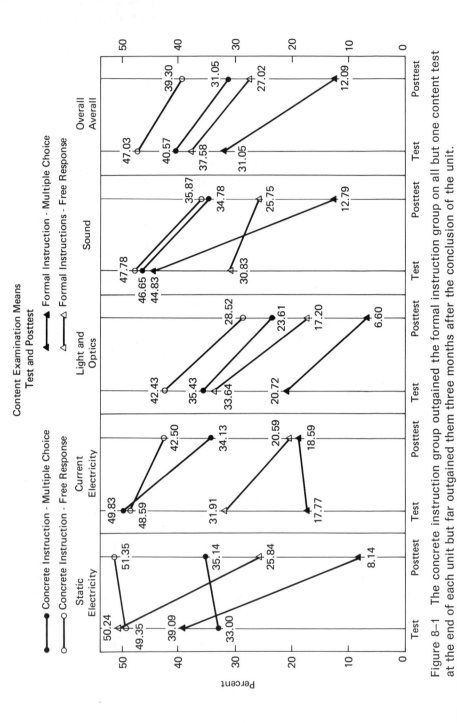

Content Examination Means
Test and Posttest

● Concrete Instruction - Multiple Choice   ▲ Formal Instruction - Multiple Choice
○ Concrete Instruction - Free Response   △ Formal Instructions - Free Response

Figure 8–1 The concrete instruction group outgained the formal instruction group on all but one content test at the end of each unit but far outgained them three months after the conclusion of the unit.

212

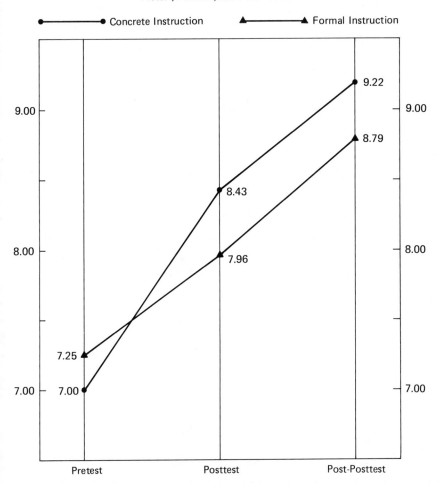

Intellectual Development Means
Pretest, Posttest, and Post-Posttest

●————● Concrete Instruction   ▲————▲ Formal Instruction

Figure 8–2 The group receiving concrete instruction outgained the ground receiving formal instruction during the experiment. The groups both received concrete instruction between the posttest and the post-posttest. Notice how similar the gains in intellectual development are.

in how to use those materials in order that they can gather the data needed to allow you to present the idea (or concept). Perhaps after the idea has been presented the book can be used for additional experiments involving the concept and/or some reading about the concept. Thus, you do have an option when presented a reading curriculum for science. You can turn it into a curriculum that uses the learning cycle by becoming the "keeper of the books" yourself.

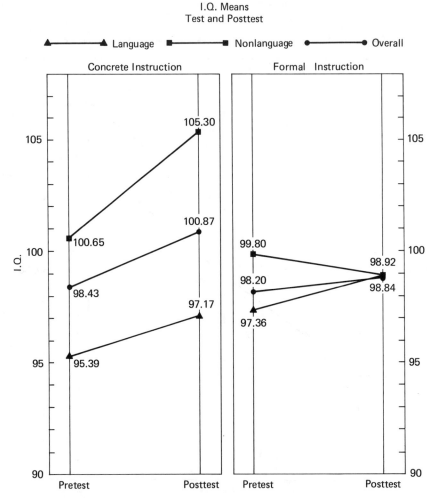

Figure 8–3 Concrete instruction greatly increases nonverbal I.Q., while producing the same gains in verbal I.Q. produced by formal instruction. Notice that formal instruction decreases nonverbal I.Q. slightly.

Reading about science is not science, but there is no doubt that reading, in general, represents a learning activity. You are engaged in it right now! Much valuable learning can come from reading about things. There are, however, two primary factors that limit the use that should be made of reading in elementary school science.

First, reading about any object, event, and/or situation before having any kind of actual experience—opportunities for assimilation —has to result in abstract thinking. The data presented in Chapter 3 clearly demonstrate that children populating elementary schools are definitely in the concrete operational stage of thought. This means that any mental operations used and assimilations expected of the children must be in terms of the experience they have had. Reading about something actually experienced (assimilated and accommodated to) can be helpful. That is why reading during the "Expanding the Idea" phase of the learning cycle is beneficial. Reading in science books about such topics as atomic structure, the DNA molecule, and nuclear energy may be excellent reading experiences, but are probably not making a significant contribution to the development of the child's conceptual framework of science because such reading experiences do not change mental structures through assimilation and accommodation. Reading does not permit children to develop their concept of science in terms of the relationship between process and content. They necessarily see the content side only, because they have not been involved in the process—gathering the data, discussing the new idea, and then expanding it. Elementary school science textbooks which concentrate upon telling children what to know, therefore, cannot lead children to develop mental structures about the nature of the discipline of science; such books primarily teach the skill of reading.

The second reason why reading is of limited value in teaching elementary school science has to do with evaluation (the topic of Chapter 9). Science, to make its maximum contribution to the intellectual development of children, must be taught as a system of investigation that yields data that can be used to introduce ideas and expand ideas. Evaluations, therefore, must be made just as the teaching is done. If the science program concentrates upon reading, there can be no investigations and, consequently, no evaluations can be made of children in terms of how proficient they are in science; they must be evaluated in terms of what they have read. Since science is not the area where the teacher grades on reading *skill*, the only other choice is to grade the children on how well they remember the content. That is, of course, grading on memorization (which *is not* science), and not upon the ability of children to explain something in their world in terms of the information they have gathered from experiences (which *is* science).

CRITERIA FOR JUDGING ELEMENTARY SCHOOL SCIENCE CURRICULA

From what you have just read you have probably decided that the first criterion to use in judging the value of an elementary school science program is that:

1. The curriculum must be constructed around the learning cycle or it must be capable of being accommodated to the learning cycle.

The observation is sometimes made that the three phases of the learning cycle are suited to many disciplines other than the science of the natural world—natural science. Such an observation is indeed true. The content of elementary school science, however, is to be selected from the natural sciences and should be judged accordingly. This includes experiences in ordering, grouping, and describing properties and all other activities associated with teaching children to collect analyze, and interpret data. The second criterion to use in judging the efficacy of an elementary school science curriculum is as follows:

2. The curriculum must draw its content from the natural sciences.

At several points throughout this book, the importance of using concrete concepts with learners in the concrete stage has been emphasized. The results of the teaching experiment described earlier in this chapter demonstrate that a concrete concept taught formally resulted in less educational gain than when care was taken to insure that concrete concepts were used with students capable of concrete reasoning.

Suppose a teacher gave elementary school science students several different chemicals that would ionize when they are in solution, as well as directions for many experiments to be done to gather data. After the data have been gathered the teacher next uses the data and presents the students with the concept of ionization. That is followed by a great deal of student experimentation with and reading about the concept and language of ionization. The instructor certainly has used the learning cycle and there is no doubt that the content is from the natural sciences. The students, however, would not learn the concept of ionization; they would only learn the name, which is not the concept. The reason for the lack of comprehension is that the concept is a formal concept and elementary school children reason concretely. The third evaluative criterion to use in judging an elementary school science curriculum, therefore, is:

3. The curriculum must be constructed with concrete concepts.

Refer to the objectives of elementary school science given in Chapter 2 and restated in Chapter 5. Describe how an elementary school science curriculum that satisfies the foregoing three criteria will lead children to achieve those objectives.

PART 1—INVENTING CURRICULUM MODELS

In the early 1960s science programs for the elementary school years were the subject of much attention. A series of conferences was held throughout the country to ascertain the opinions of persons engaged in all levels and phases of education as to what direction newly developed programs could take and receive acceptability. All of this activity— actually some small efforts were begun in the late 1950s—resulted in the establishment of several projects concerned with the production of science materials for elementary schools throughout the country. The Universities of California, Utah, Illinois, Minnesota, and New York were some of the locations where elementary school science curriculum development was taking place. Persons from the natural sciences, psychology, early childhood education, science education, elementary schools (teachers and principals), and educational evaluation made up the research and development teams that provided a new direction in elementary school science curricula.

In addition to involving many different kinds of persons from the field of education, the science curriculum projects of the 1960s had two additional operational criteria in common. These projects were funded by national organizations. For probably the first time in American education, curricula received funding at a national level in the late 1950s. These curriculum projects were aimed at the science curriculum in the secondary schools. In the 1960s that support was extended to elementary school science. The National Science Foundation, United States Office of Education, Carnegie Foundation, and Ford Foundation were some of the organizations which provided national-level funding for research and development in elementary school science. Some persons in education are always skeptical about accepting funding from national and governmental organizations. Their contention is that accepting an organization's financial support is accompanied by accepting their control of the project. We can say from first-hand experience with funded research and development in elementary school science that the prediction of the financial sponsor assuming project control was not true.

The third operational criterion the elementary school science curricula had in common was their concern for testing their materials with elementary school children. Each lesson, unit, and yearly program was taught to children from the inception of the idea to the final, published product. One of the organizations developing elementary school science curricula—the Science Curriculum Improvement Study (SCIS)—tested their materials in five different locations. These locations—called trial centers—were East Lansing, Michigan; Honolulu, Hawaii; Los Angeles, California; New York City; and Norman, Oklahoma. One or more schools in each location was designated as a "trial center school." The teachers in those schools were given special instructions in the use of the SCIS materials, and the trial center coordinator worked closely with the schools and various classes within the schools. When each portion of the program was completed, it was taught at the appropriate level. The teachers and trial center coordinator then isolated the strong points, weak points, and unacceptable points of each part of the newly developed curriculum and transmitted that information to the project headquarters (SCIS headquarters were at the University of California, Berkeley). The SCIS trial centers operated for approximately 7 years.

Of the several elementary school science curriculum projects which began in the early 1960s, three will be described here. Those projects are the SCIS, Science—A Process Approach (SAPA), and the Elementary Science Study (ESS). The project headquarters for the ESS were located at the Educational Development Center, Newton, Massachusetts; the SAPA headquarters were located with the American Association for the Advancement of Science, Washington, D.C. Each of these curriculum projects developed teachers guides and kits of materials, and many parts of each program also had worksheets, record books, or both for the children. None of the projects, however, developed reading materials for the children which give them information they "should know."

Completed versions of the materials of all three of these projects were available by the late 1960s. Materials from each of the projects have undergone one or more revisions since their completed versions appeared. These revisions will be discussed later in this chapter. What follows are descriptions of the *original* versions of the materials of each of the projects. We believe that to gain an understanding of the accomplishments of the innovation of the early 1960s of group-developed curricula, the original versions of the products of the SCIS, ESS, and SAPA should be studied. Prior to these projects children generally studied the facts and principles—most of which were formal concepts—from textbooks; the books contained what the child should know. The curriculum project era changed that; studying the *original* versions of the SCIS, ESS, and SAPA can lead you to see how.

The Science Curriculum Improvement Study (SCIS)[4]

Central to the curriculum developed by the SCIS—and to modern science—is the concept that changes take place because objects *interact*

[4] The material found in this section has been taken and adapted with permission from the Science Curriculum Improvement Study, *SCIS Sampler Guide,* Chicago: Rand McNally, 1970.

in reproducible ways under similar conditions. Interaction occurs among objects or organisms that do something to one another, thereby bringing about a change. For instance, when a magnet picks up a steel pin, the magnet and the pin are interacting. The *observed change itself;* the pin jumping toward the magnet, is *evidence of interaction.* Children can easily observe and use such *evidence.* As they advance from a dependence on concrete experiences to the ability to think abstractly, children identify the conditions under which interaction occurs and predict its outcome.

The SCIS program utilizes four major scientific concepts to elaborate the interaction concept—matter, energy, organism, and ecosystem. Children's experiences and investigations in the physical science sequence are based on the first two; the last two provide the framework of the life science sequence.

Matter, perceived as the solid objects, liquids, and gases in the environment, is tangible. It interacts with human sense organs, and pieces of matter interact with each other. Material objects may be described and recognized by their color, shape, weight, texture, and other properties. As children investigate changes in objects during their work in the SCIS physical science program, they become aware of the diversity of interacting objects and of their properties.

The second major concept is energy—the inherent ability of an animal, a flashlight battery, or other system to bring about changes in the state of its surroundings or in itself. Some familiar sources of energy are the burning gas used to heat a kettle of water, the unwinding spring that operates a watch, and the discharging battery in a pocket radio. Each of these objects provides evidence that energy is present. The counterpart of an energy source is an energy receiver, and a very important natural process is the interaction between source and receiver that results in energy transfer.

The third concept is that of a living organism. An organism is an entire living individual, plant or animal. It is composed of matter and can use the energy imparted by its food to build its body and be active. The organism concept therefore represents a fusion of the matter and energy concepts; but it is also broader than these, so it is identified and described separately.

As children observe living plants and animals in the classroom or outdoors, they become aware of the amazing diversity of organisms and their life cycles. They observe how plants and animals interact with one another and with the soil, atmosphere, and sun in the vast network of relationships that constitute life. The focus of the SCIS life science program is the organism-environment relationship.

The study of life focused on organism-environment interaction leads to the ecosystem concept. Thinking about a forest may help you understand the ecosystem. A forest is more than an assemblage of trees. Living in the shade of the trees are shrubs, vines, herbs, ferns, mosses, and toadstools. In addition the forest swarms with insects, birds, mammals, reptiles, and amphibians. A forest is all of these plants and animals living together. The animals depend on the plants for food and living conditions. The plants use sunlight, carbon dioxide, water, and minerals to make food to sustain themselves and other organisms in the forest. The interrelated plants, animals, sun, air, water, and soil constitute an ecosystem.

What you have read so far has probably led you to conclude that the SCIS is a content-centered program. We interpret it as being exactly that. You will also notice, however, that investigations the children perform have also been referred to several times. The SCIS program was constructed on the basic premise that the first task of the curriculum maker was to isolate that content which can be taught through investigation to children in the preoperational and concrete operational stages. But in addition to the scientific concepts just described the developers of the SCIS program believe that there are four process-oriented concepts—property, reference frame, system, and model—with which children should have experience if they are to develop scientific literacy. These concepts, together with others that relate to specific units, are at the heart of the processes of observing, describing, comparing, classifying, measuring, interpreting evidence, and experimenting.

The concept of property by which an object may be described or recognized has already been referred to. A property is any quality that enables you to compare objects. Properties also enable you to describe or compare concepts. For example, the term "climate" (hot, cold, temperate) summarizes the properties of weather in a specific region, and food production is a property of green plants.

Every description and comparison of natural or social phenomena reflects the observer's point of view or frame of reference. To the young child, who relates objects to himself rather than to others, the discovery of other frames of reference is a challenge.

In science, where the position (location) and motion of objects are important subjects of study, the reference-frame idea has been developed into the awesome relativity theory. Yet the basic concept, as included in the SCIS program, is simple—the position and motion of objects can be perceived, described, and recognized only with reference to other objects. When you say, "The car is at the south end of the parking lot," you describe the location of the car relative to the parking lot. In this example the parking lot and compass direction serve as a reference frame. However, when you say, "The car is to your left," the listener's body serves as a reference frame. A child who considers

Figure 8–4 Children learn the concept of property in the *Material Objects* units of the SCIS.

several reference frames thereby overcomes the usual self-centered viewpoint.

The third process-oriented concept is that of a system, which SCIS defines as a group of related objects that make up a whole. It may include the battery and circuits that make up an operating pocket radio, or it may consist of a seed and the moist soil in which it is planted. The system concept stems from the realization that objects or organisms do not function in isolation but exist in a context while interacting with other objects or organisms.

A subsystem is part of another system. Thus, moist soil is itself a system comprised of clay, sand, water, and decayed matter. It is at the same time a subsystem of the seed-moist soil system. The seed, with its coat, embryo, and stored food, is another subsystem.

Sometimes it is hard to decide what to include when defining a system. Does the soil-seed system include the air that permeates the soil? Ordinarily children would not include air because moisture is usually the most important factor in germination. However, if a child were to deprive the soil-seed system of air, the result would make him aware of its importance to plant growth.

A system becomes a new system whenever matter is added to or removed from it. When nothing is added or removed a system retains its identity, even though it may change in form or appearance. When selecting a system, children focus their attention, organize their observations, and relate the whole system to its parts (objects or subsystems). They become skillful in tracing a system through a sequence of changes.

The fourth process-oriented concept is the scientific model, which was discussed in Chapter 6. The SCIS program explains why children should experience the models concept:

> Scientific models permit children to relate their present observations to previous experiences with similar systems. Models satisfy the children's need for thinking in concrete terms. Models also lead to predictions and new discoveries about the system being investigated.[5]

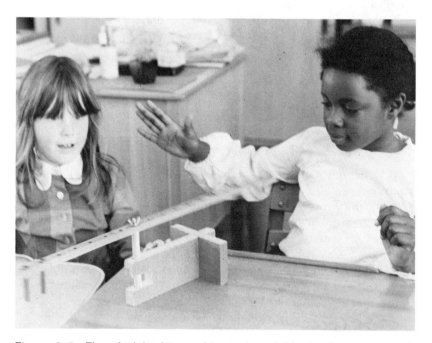

Figure 8–5 The whirlybird is used to study variables in the unit entitled *Subsystems and Variables* of the SCIS program.

[5] Ibid., p. 9.

The SCIS program begins at the kindergarten level and that portion of the program has the title *Beginnings*.[6] When the SCIS kindergarten program is studied, the fact that it is organized differently from the other units becomes apparent. Kindergarten children have a propensity for assimiliation so the "Gathering Data" phase of the learning cycle is extremely important to them. During this time the children can make the observations about which they will then communicate. The "Getting the Idea" phase of the learning cycle should probably not be emphasized because most concept formation other than that involving their immediate surroundings and physical needs is beyond children in the preoperational stage. As a result of that limitation the use of the "Expanding the Idea" phase of the learning cycle with preoperational children is also restricted. In other words the majority of the time the children spend in the learning cycle is spent in the assimilation phase. The following quotation[7] shows how the developers of the SCIS program viewed the importance of the dominance of assimilation for this educational level.

> In *Beginnings*, children observe and describe a wide variety of objects and organisms in the classroom and outdoors. Through suggested games, puzzles, and other activities, you help develop the children's ability to describe and compare objects by their color, shape, size, texture, odor, and sound. Ideas of number . . . and volume are introduced in simple activities such as weighing objects, counting beads, and measuring quantities of water. Changes that occur through time are considered in Part Nine, "Organisms," where the children work with seeds, seedlings, and plants. The children are introduced to spatial relationships when they describe the positions of objects in relation to other objects and when they reproduce printed patterns. The experiences in this unit contribute to a growing understanding of science and to language development.

The teacher instructions the SCIS prepared to teach one topic from the SCIS program follows.

ORGANISMS

OBJECTIVES
To observe and describe plants and animals.
To describe a series of events in sequence.

---

[6] Science Curriculum Improvement Study, *Beginnings, Teacher's Guide*, Chicago: Rand McNally, 1974. All the materials in this section have been taken from *Beginnings* with the permission of the publisher.
[7] Ibid., p. 14.

MAKING LEAF PRINTS

ADVANCE PREPARATION
Collect leaves and press them for several days between newspapers weighted with books or blocks. Read the activities in this chapter to decide which kinds of leaf prints you would like the children to make; assemble the necessary materials.

TEACHING SUGGESTIONS
Children enjoy making leaf prints. The described activities not only allow children to express their creativity but also help further their understanding of the similarities and differences among leaves.

Leaf book Mount some leaves on tagboard or construction paper and label them. Assemble the pages into a book for children to look at during their free time.

Crayon rubbings Invite the children to place a leaf, ridge side up, on a flat surface and cover it with a sheet of lightweight paper. Tell them to rub back and forth over the leaf with the side of a crayon until the leaf print appears.

Paint prints Ask the children to paint the ridge sides of leaves with tempera which has been mixed with liquid starch. Tell them to place the painted side down on a sheet of construction paper, put a piece of newspaper on top, and roll with a block print roller or rub with the back of a spoon. Carefully remove newspaper and leaf and let print dry.

Spray prints You can make negative prints while the children watch. Pin leaves to sheets of construction paper and spray paint around the edges of the leaves. Remove the leaves after the paint dries.

Clay prints Give each child some sturdy, well-veined leaves and a lump of clay that is lightly coated with salad oil or petroleum jelly. Tell the children to flatten the lump and press the veined side into the clay. If you use firing clay, the children can paint or glaze their "leaves."

Wax paper prints Invite children to place leaves and small pieces of colored tissue paper between pieces of wax paper. Then press the sheets together with a warm iron. The leaves and tissue paper pieces will be permanently embedded between the wax paper sheets. These can be used to make a mobile or hung in a window.

In order to continue the implementation of its content, which is begun at the kindergarten level, the developers of the SCIS program made the decision that children should have experiences with the physical and life sciences each year during grades one through six.

The SCIS program, therefore, consists of 12 units which present in learning cycles the content of the SCIS program which has been explained. When the concepts inherent in that content were matched with the intellectual levels of children in the several grades, the following units were the result.

	PHYSICAL SCIENCE UNITS	LIFE SCIENCE UNITS
FIRST LEVEL	Material Objects	Organisms
SECOND LEVEL	Interaction and Systems	Life Cycles
THIRD LEVEL	Subsystems and Variables	Populations
FOURTH LEVEL	Relative Position and Motion	Environments
FIFTH LEVEL	Energy Sources	Communities
SIXTH LEVEL	Models: Electric and Magnetic Interaction	Ecosystems

The phases of the learning cycle are not labeled for the students, and the program produces record books in which the children record data from the various experiments. (There are no student-readers for the SCIS program.) Nevertheless, the SCIS curriculum model employs a consistent teaching strategy throughout each unit. The children are provided materials which they are allowed to interact with in their own way; they are, in other words, allowed to *explore* the materials thoroughly and completely; the "Gathering Data" phase. The data from these explorations allow the teacher (or the children, or both) to *invent* ("Getting the Idea") concepts that can be used to explain what has been seen, or to develop models.

After the child has a newly invented concept, the child can begin self-questioning on many things about this concept. Finding items of information about the new conceptual invention is, of course, discovery ("Expanding the Idea"). Discovery is, therefore, only a part of the teaching method used by the SCIS program.

You might be tempted to think that the information the SCIS units provide children could be told to them in much less time than is required for using the units. You are, of course, correct; *but* the purpose of the SCIS units is *not* to transmit information (even though the children do gather much information). Rather, their purpose is to achieve the educational objectives that have already been discussed. The SCIS program does not believe that transmitting scientific information to children is educating them in that discipline; they believe, as the units demonstrate, that educating children in science is providing them with experiences that will permit them to *learn how to learn.*

Keep in mind that the group developing the SCIS model structured the work of the children by electing to lead them toward developing conceptual structures about matter, energy, organism, and ecosystems. They also elected to use exploration, invention, and discovery (inquiry) —the natural way of learning—to lead children to develop these structures. The materials were developed according to the intellectual development model of Piaget. In other words, the SCIS model permits and encourages children to learn within a structured system, but not all children are expected to do or learn the same things.

Use the curriculum-evaluation criteria given earlier. Evaluate the SCIS.

In reviewing the entire SCIS program, the following statements seem to describe the general character of that curriculum:

1. The SCIS developers first selected a conceptual hierarchy; the content which was to represent the discipline of science was of paramount concern. There is specific content to be taught at each grade level and the content taught in later grades assumes that the content in the early grades has been studied. Each later unit does provide for review.

2. Using the SCIS program requires that teaching be done in learning cycles—exploration, invention, and discovery. The phases of the learning cycle are not labeled in the children's record books but they are so labeled in the teacher's guide. The learning cycles in the SCIS units tend to focus on large, important concepts.

3. The intellectual levels of the learning materials of the program are matched to the intellectual levels of children in kindergarten through the sixth grade.

4. The underlying philosophy of the SCIS program stresses that the investigations in the program must be made by the children, but that no specific scientific processes or experiences are considered essential.

Elementary Science Study (ESS)[8]

Your frame of reference for discussing this curriculum model can best be established by quoting directly from the ESS group itself.

---

[8] The material in this section has been taken and adapted with permission from *A Working Guide to the Elementary Science Study*, Newton, Massachusetts, Education Development Center, 1971.

No group—ESS or any other—can design a single curriculum which will be suitable for the enormous variety of schools and school systems in this country and elsewhere. Planning a curriculum involves decisions which should be made only with knowledge about particular adults and children: their educational goals, their financial resources, and the circumstances in which they live and work. Those people whom the curriculum affects should be responsible for its shape and substance.[9]

The ESS group has simply said that there is no content that they feel should have precedence over any other. They explain their content frame of reference thus: "We have not proceeded primarily from theories about the structure of science or from a particular conceptual scheme of learning."[10] Not only, then, did the ESS group not operate from a content structure they wished to teach children (as the SCIS group did), but they were not at all concerned about using a model of how children learned. How, then, did the ESS group construct its curriculum? ". . . we relied upon taking what we thought were good scientific activities into classrooms to see how they worked with children. We have tried to find out what . . . six-year-olds, and nine- and ten- and thirteen-year-olds find interesting to explore."[11] The ESS took many kinds of materials into many different kinds of classrooms, watched what the children did, listened to them very carefully, and made decisions on the basis of what seemed to interest both the children and the teachers. On the bases of those data the ESS group developed ideas about units and put them into teacher's guides, films, film loops, equipment, and printed materials that would assist a teacher in leading children to become involved with the ideas being taught. All materials developed were subjected to vigorous classroom testing.

The ESS curriculum can best be characterized as a series of classroom resources which a school can use to develop its own curriculum. Each school must decide upon where an ESS unit is to be taught or serious overlapping could occur, and the antimotivational "we-had-that-last-year" syndrome will appear. To assist a school in preparing its science curriculum model, the ESS group has provided data about where they have found each unit to be successful. Those data on all 56 ESS units are shown in Figure 8-6. The line in the chart indicates the range of grades for which the unit is primarily intended.

The ESS program, then, requires that teachers thoroughly understand their educational purpose and the conceptual structure of science

[9] Ibid., p. 4.
[10] Ibid., p. 2.
[11] Ibid.

Elementary Science Study

The Elementary Science Study has been in existence since 1960 as one of the curriculum-development projects of the Education Development Center, Inc., a private, non-profit organization. Supported by the National Science Foundation, ESS has as its principal aim the production of materials of high scientific quality and proven appeal to children. The units are the unique products of joint efforts by scientists and teachers from many disciplines and levels of education. These specialists have produced a series of activity-centered units that make the classroom an exciting laboratory and take advantage of the child's natural curiosity about the world around him. He develops methods fro devising and carrying through his own investigations and records his conclusions systematically. Students work with a wide variety of materials — from specially designed microscopes to simple, everyday objects — all of which help them to see new dimensions in their environment. These flexible units free your pupils from the traditional, book-centered approach and let them learn through their own experiences. The chart below will give you a thumbnail sketch of each unit now available as well as appropriate grade level and area of science study. Note that units involving General Skills appear in criss-cross design; Biological Science in shaded design; Earth Science, blank; and Physical Science in diagonal-line design.

| Unit | | Grades | | | | | | | | |
|------|--|K|1|2|3|4|5|6|7|8|9|

Unit	Description	Grades
Light and Shadows	In their exploration of light and shadows, children find new meanings in a number of ordinary objects and phenomena. They use many shapes and their own movements to examine light sources and the shadows they cast. An opportunity is given for young children to experiment with spatial relationships in simple ways.	grades 1–3
Growing Seeds	Through continuing observation, children learn to distinguish seeds from objects which closely resemble them. They learn to define a seed in terms of what it does and to make strip graphs to represent the growth of their plants. It gives primary age children an opportunity to discover ways to find answers to their own questions about the world.	grades 2–3
Match and Measure	This resource book suggests interesting activities for primary children to learn about measurement in an informal way, using measuring sticks, tape measures, calipers, measuring wheels and a Geo-board.	grades 1–3
Mobiles	Children gain experience — in playful and dramatic terms — with some of the laws and problems of balance, balance systems, weight, and symmetry by constructing and hanging simple mobile.	grades 3–4

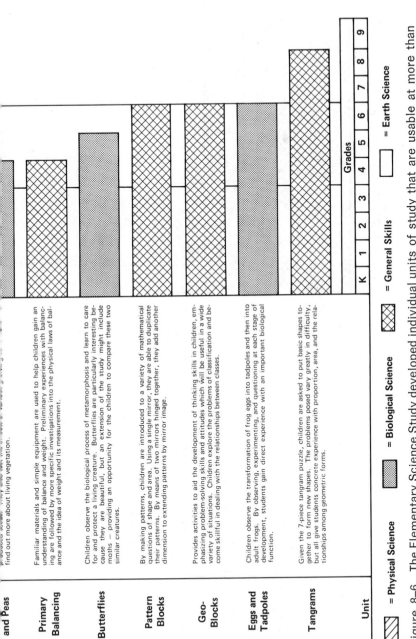

and Peas ... find out more about living vegetation.

Primary Balancing — Familiar materials and simple equipment are used to help children gain an understanding of balance and weight. Preliminary experiences with balancing are followed by more specific investigations into the physical laws of balance and the idea of weight and its measurement.

Butterflies — Children observe the biological process of metamorphosis and learn to care for and protect a living creature. Butterflies are particularly interesting because they are beautiful, but an extension of the study might include moths – providing an opportunity for the children to compare these two similar creatures.

Pattern Blocks — By making patterns, children are introduced to a variety of mathematical questions of shape and area. Using a single mirror, they are able to duplicate their patterns. By means of two mirrors hinged together, they add another dimension to extending patterns by mirror image.

Geo-Blocks — Provides activities to aid the development of thinking skills in children, emphasizing problem-solving skills and attitudes which will be useful in a wide variety of situations. Children explore the problems of classification and become skilful in dealing with the relationships between classes.

Eggs and Tadpoles — Children observe the transformation of frog eggs into tadpoles and then into adult frogs. By observing, experimenting, and questioning at each stage of development, students gain direct experience with an important biological function.

Tangrams — Given the 7-piece tangram puzzle, children are asked to put basic shapes together to form new shapes. The problems posed vary greatly in difficulty, but all give students concrete experience with proportion, area, and the relationships among geometric forms.

Unit

Grades

| K | 1 | 2 | 3 | 4 | 5 | 6 | 7 | 8 | 9 |

= Physical Science = Biological Science = General Skills = Earth Science

Figure 8–6   The Elementary Science Study developed individual units of study that are usable at more than one grade level.

229

Unit	Description	K	1	2	3	4	5	6	7	8	9
						Grades					
Musical Instrument Recipe Book	All about how to make over 20 stringed, wind, and percussion instruments from inexpensive, readily available materials. Activities provide uniquely satisfying experiments in learning about the physical properties of devices that produce sound.			▨	▨	▨	▨	▨	▨	▨	▨
Attribute Games and Problems	Provides activities for children using a set of hardwood blocks of many shapes and sizes which have been carefully designed to give experience with geometric shape and stimulate interest in linear, surface area, and volume relationships.			▨	▨	▨	▨	▨	▨	▨	▨
Animals in the Classroom	Here is a teacher's resource book, showing methods for keeping a variety of animals in the classroom — and, how to make them a focus point for language, mathematics, social studies, and science activities.			▨	▨	▨	▨	▨	▨	▨	▨
Spinning Tables	Children are familiar with motion in a straight line. A spinning table allows them to explore the paradoxical behavior of things which move in circles. They are both delighted and puzzled to find that their predictions about circular motion are wrong — and thus are motivated to explore further.		▨	▨							
Brine Shrimp	Seeing living things hatch from eggs is fascinating to children, and these small crustaceans are easily hatched and cared for, as well as providing experience in the workings of a life cycle. The children watch their own animals hatch, grow, and eventually have young of their own.				▨	▨	▨				
Changes	Provides children with an opportunity to see, distinguish, and understand something about the natural changes that are caused in familiar substances by the growth of living organisms — such as bacteria — as well as those not brought about by living organisms — such as rusting and melting.				▨	▨	▨				
Printing	With a printing press as part of the classroom, children begin to develop a feeling for creating and communicating. They discover that not only is printing a useful tool and that the printed text is a legible, easily reproduced ...							▨	▨	▨	▨

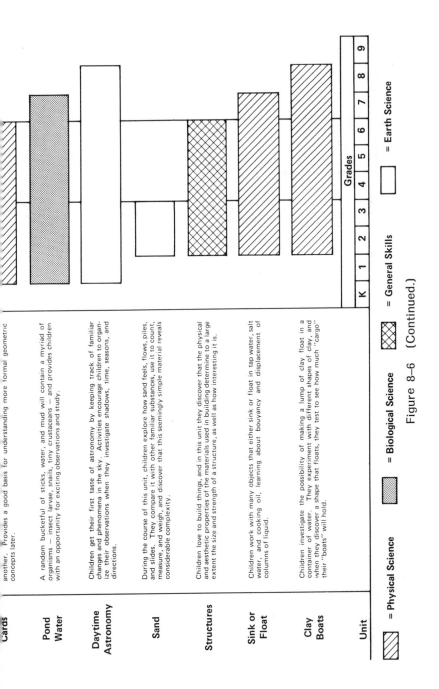

Cards — another. Provides a good basis for understanding more formal geometric concepts later.

Pond Water — A random bucketful of sticks, water, and mud will contain a myriad of organisms — insect larvae, snails, tiny crustaceans — and provides children with an opportunity for exciting observations and study.

Daytime Astronomy — Children get their first taste of astronomy by keeping track of familiar changes and phenomena in the sky. Activities encourage children to organize their observations when they investigate shadows, time, seasons, and directions.

Sand — During the course of this unit, children explore how sand feels, flows, piles, and slides. They compare it with other familiar substances, use it to count, measure, and weigh, and discover that this seemingly simple material reveals considerable complexity.

Structures — Children love to build things, and in this unit they discover that the physical and aesthetic properties of the materials used in building determine to a large extent the size and strength of a structure, as well as how interesting it is.

Sink or Float — Children work with many objects that either sink or float in tap water, salt water, and cooking oil, learning about bouyancy and displacement of columns of liquid.

Clay Boats — Children investigate the possibility of making a lump of clay float in a container of water. They experiment with different shapes of clay, and when they discover a shape that floats, they test to see how much "cargo" their "boats" will hold.

Unit / **Grades** — K 1 2 3 4 5 6 7 8 9

= Physical Science   = Biological Science   = General Skills   = Earth Science

Figure 8–6 (Continued)

231

Grades

Unit	K	1	2	3	4	5	6	7	8	9
Drops, Streams, and Containers			▨	▨	▨					
Mystery Powders			▨	▨	▨					
Ice Cubes			▨	▨	▨	▨				
Rocks and Charts				☐	☐	☐	☐			
Starting from Seeds			▦	▦	▦	▦	▦	▦		
Where Is the Moon?				☐	☐	☐	☐	☐		
Colored Solutions			▨	▨	▨	▨	▨	▨	▨	

Drops, Streams, and Containers

This unit invites young children to explore -- in a leisurely, informal manner -- the behavior of water and other common liquids. Suggestions are given to encourage each child to pursue those facets which interest him most, with a minimum of direct teacher intervention.

Mystery Powders

Students become familiar with some ordinary white powders and the use of indicators in identifying them and detecting their presence in mixtures. In learning to identify the powders and devising ways of distinguishing them from one another, students use some methods and techniques of investigatory science.

Ice Cubes

Activities and questions designed to provide a first look at the effects of heat, surface area, specific heat, and conductivity on melting rates. Children learn to use thermometers and learn something about freezing point, melting point, and density.

Rocks and Charts

Children become involved in the classification of some common minerals. As well as discovering the characteristics of the individual rocks, children learn something about setting standards for comparison by developing charts on which they can compare the attributes of more than one specimen.

Starting from Seeds

Children are given seeds and vermiculite as well as containers to grow their own plants in. They learn how seeds grow best by performing individual experiments and keeping their own records.

Where Is the Moon?

Students investigate the changing positions of the moon over a three-month period by direct observations. They are asked to predict its motions and appearance in the future, which requires that they find an order and regularity in its movements.

Colored Solutions

Children perform experiments associated with density and the layering of liquids. The results of their experiments form a foundation of facts from which they are able to make predictions and draw reasonable conclusions.

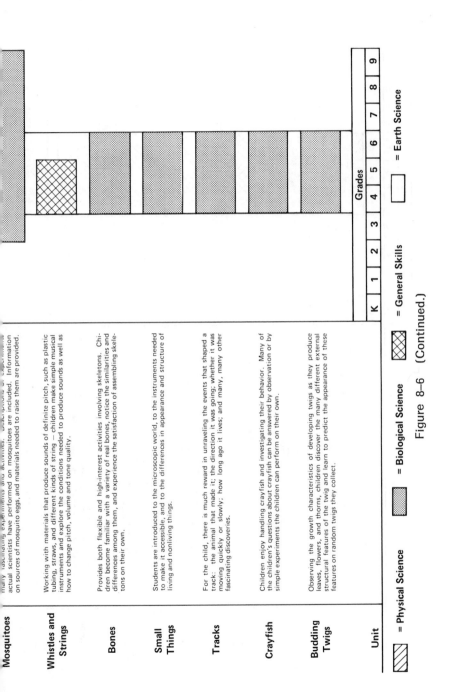

Mosquitoes

...many fascinating experiments and activities. Descriptions of experiments actual scientists have performed on mosquitoes are included. Information on sources of mosquito eggs, and materials needed to raise them are provided.

Whistles and Strings

Working with materials that produce sounds of definite pitch, such as plastic tubing, straws, and different kinds of string — children make simple musical instruments and explore the conditions needed to produce sounds as well as how to change pitch, volume and tone quality.

Bones

Provides both flexible and high-interest activities involving skeletons. Children become familiar with a variety of real bones, notice the similarities and differences among them, and experience the satisfaction of assembling skeletons on their own.

Small Things

Students are introduced to the microscopic world, to the instruments needed to make it accessible, and to the differences in appearance and structure of living and nonliving things.

Tracks

For the child, there is much reward in unraveling the events that shaped a track: the animal that made it; the direction it was going; whether it was moving quickly or slowly; how long ago it lives; and many, many other fascinating discoveries.

Crayfish

Children enjoy handling crayfish and investigating their behavior. Many of the children's questions about crayfish can be answered by observation or by simple experiments the children can perform on their own.

Budding Twigs

Observing the growth characteristics of developing twigs as they produce leaves, flowers, and thorns, children discover the many different external structural features of the twig and learn to predict the appearance of these features on random twigs they collect.

Unit

Grades: K 1 2 3 4 5 6 7 8 9

= Physical Science = Biological Science = General Skills = Earth Science

Figure 8–6 (Continued.)

Grades

Unit	Description	K	1	2	3	4	5	6	7	8	9
Animal Activity	Children use several techniques for examining the behavior of mice, gerbils, and other small animals, noting how diet, age, size of cage, noise, and time of day affect their liveliness.					▓	▓	▓			
Earthworms	By watching and experimenting with their own earthworms, children learn much about the habits and developmental stages of one of man's most helpful friends. They test their classroom experience by predicting where they will find the most worms outside, and develop confidence in their ability to find out things about an animal by themselves.					▓	▓	▓			
Peas and Particles	Through informal activities with common household items, children are given an understanding of large numbers and estimations. They begin to see the useful applications of rough estimation in many areas of mathematics, science, and the social studies.					▩	▩	▩			
Batteries and Bulbs	An introduction to the study of electricity and magnetism. Each child carries out experiments with simple and safe equipment — flashlight batteries, small bulbs, various kinds of wire, magnets, and a compass — and draws conclusions based on his observations.					▨	▨	▨			
Optics	Children discover and analyze, through direct experimentation, many of the fascinating properties of light. They also develop their critical powers through situations in which their curiosity and thoughtful inquiry are rewarded with new understanding and insight into how the world works.					▨	▨	▨			
Pendulums	Gives children an opportunity to observe, investigate, and contemplate the many physical phenomena associated with swinging objects. Bobs differing in size, weight, and shape lend the interest of variables to the investigations.					▨	▨	▨			
Micro-Gardening	Children are introduced to the molds — a group of microscopic living things very different from the growing things with which they are familiar. Students become familiar — through their own experimentation — with principles and procedures that have contributed to man's knowledge over the past 200 years.								▓		

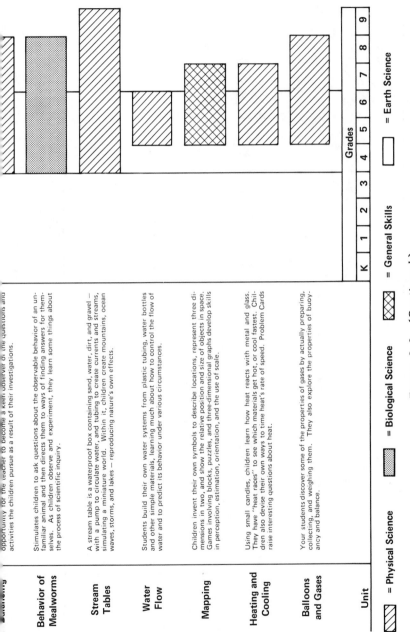

opportunity for the teacher to become a keen observer of the questions and activities the children pursue as a result of their investigations.

Behavior of Mealworms — Stimulates children to ask questions about the observable behavior of an unfamiliar animal and then directs them to ways of finding answers for themselves. As children observe and experiment, they learn some things about the process of scientific inquiry.

Stream Tables — A stream table is a waterproof box containing sand, water, dirt, and gravel — with a pump to circulate water, and tubing to create currents and streams, simulating a miniature world. Within it, children create mountains, ocean waves, storms, and lakes — reproducing nature's own effects.

Water Flow — Students build their own water systems from plastic tubing, water bottles and other simple materials, learning much about how to control the flow of water and to predict its behavior under various circumstances.

Mapping — Children invent their own symbols to describe locations, represent three dimensions in two, and show the relative position and size of objects in space. Games involving blocks, puzzles, and three-dimensional graphs develop skills in perception, estimation, orientation, and the use of scale.

Heating and Cooling — Using small candles, children learn how heat reacts with metal and glass. They have "heat races" to see which materials get hot, or cool fastest. Children also devise their own ways to time heat's rate of speed. Problem Cards raise interesting questions about heat.

Balloons and Gases — Your students discover some of the properties of gases by actually preparing, collecting, and weighing them. They also explore the properties of buoyancy and balance.

Unit

Grades: K 1 2 3 4 5 6 7 8 9

= Physical Science   = Biological Science   = General Skills   = Earth Science

Figure 8-6 (Continued.)

235

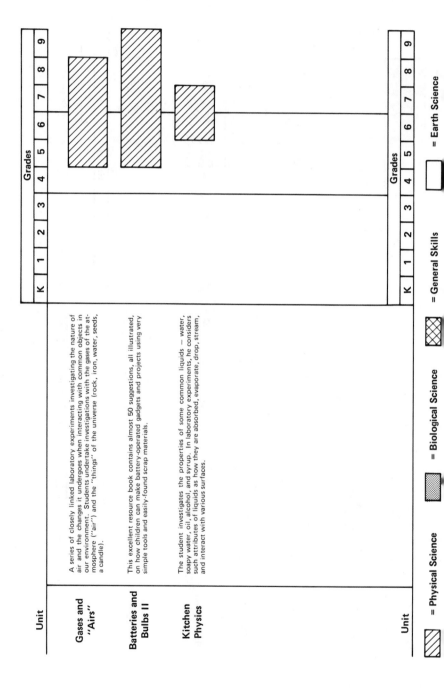

Unit | **Grades**

Grades: K 1 2 3 4 5 6 7 8 9

Gases and "Airs"

A series of closely linked laboratory experiments investigating the nature of air and the changes it undergoes when interacting with common objects in our environment. Students undertake investigations with the gases of the atmosphere ("air") and the "things" of the universe (rock, iron, water, seeds, a candle).

Batteries and Bulbs II

This excellent resource book contains almost 50 suggestions, all illustrated, on how children can make battery-operated gadgets and projects using very simple tools and easily-found scrap materials.

Kitchen Physics

The student investigates the properties of some common liquids — water, soapy water, oil, alcohol, and syrup. In laboratory experiments, he considers such attributes of liquids as how they are absorbed, evaporate, drop, stream, and interact with various surfaces.

Unit | **Grades**

Grades: K 1 2 3 4 5 6 7 8 9

= Physical Science   = Biological Science   = General Skills   = Earth Science they want to teach. The teacher selects from the 56 units available what their individual curriculum should be. If you carefully examine Figure 8–6, you will see that the teacher can easily have a balance among life, physical, and earth science. Furthermore, all types of content are available for all grade levels.

After selecting units, how does the teacher use them in the classroom? The ESS group describes the implementation of its units as follows:

> ESS units will be most effective in classrooms where inquiry is encouraged: where teachers are able and willing to listen more than to talk, to observe more than to show, and to help their students to progress in their work without engineering its precise direction. Students will need their teachers to help them observe carefully, ask questions, design experiments, and assess the results of their work. To do those things without telling or directing too much requires a restraint that is born of self-confidence, as well as confidence in, and respect for, children. We have seen our materials reinforce these qualities in teachers. *We have also learned that in the long run these qualities are more important to the teaching of ESS units than is a substantive knowledge of science.*[12]

Describing each of the 56 ESS units (see Figure 8–6) is not possible here. Nor is giving an overview of the content of the entire program (as was done with the SCIS curriculum) possible because the ESS program does not have any conceptual, content hierarchy. What follows are descriptions of several of the ESS units.

Before reading the descriptions of the ESS units you are reminded that there are no books for the children. Furthermore, the learning cycle is not a part of the ESS program. The ESS materials, however, lend themselves to being formed into learning cycles, but the teacher must do the formation.

1. *Animal Activity—Grades Four to Six*   This unit introduces children to several techniques for observing and measuring the activity of mice, gerbils, or other small animals. Using an exercise wheel coupled to a counter which records the number of times the wheel turns, children gather data on the activity of animals under varying conditions. They can test the effect on an animal's liveliness of such factors as diet, age, size of cage, time of day, and noise.

The student booklet, *Experiments on Animal Activity*, gives accounts of several ingenious experiments performed by biologists investigating the activity of mammals. The case studies make good starting points for discussions and can help children to see the possible

---

[12] Ibid., p. 3. (Italics added.)

value and interest of their own investigations to others. The unit is best taught on a flexible schedule. The study generally entends over a period of 2 months. Since most experiments take many days to complete, only a few minutes may be needed for the unit each day. Informal work with small groups has been most effective.

2. *Balloons and Gases—Grades Five to Eight* This unit gives children an opportunity to prepare and collect gases and to discover some of their properties. Preliminary work is done with acids and bases and a colored indicator, bromothymol blue. Students generate a number of common gases and conduct tests that enable them to distinguish between the gases. The Teacher's Guide contains recipes for making "mystery gases" that students can generate and attempt to identify on the basis of their previous experience. The chemical reactions by which the gases are produced offer interesting avenues for further study.

3. *Batteries and Bulbs—Grades Four to Six* The activities included represent an introduction to the study of electricity and magnetism. Each child makes experiments with his own simple equipment (flashlight batteries, small bulbs, various kinds of wire, compasses, magnets). Children investigate such things as way to light several bulbs with one battery, what happens when more than one battery is used, what is inside a battery, and how a bulb works. The materials are simple but sufficient for investigations at almost any level of complexity.

4. *Behavior of Mealworms—Primarily for Grade Six* This unit stimulates children to ask questions about the observable behavior of an unfamiliar animal and then directs them to ways of finding the answers for themselves. As children observe and experiment, they learn some things about the process of scientific inquiry while they gather information about the sensory perception of the mealworm. The primary objective of the unit is to help children learn how to carry on an investigation.

Mealworms are convenient subjects for animal behavior experiments. They exhibit reasonably consistent and definite behavior, they require practically no care, and they can be purchased very inexpensively from a number of sources.

5. *Daytime Astronomy—Grades Five to Eight* This unit is built around children's observations of the shadows the sun casts on the earth at different times of the day and throughout the year. Children become familiar with the apparent motion of the sun by recording changes in the length and direction of the sun's shadows. The resulting "shadow-clocks" are used for telling time, for finding directions, and for developing theories about the movement and relative position of the earth and sun. Working with globes indoors and outdoors, children can

investigate conditions that occur all over the real world. An earth-moon scale model allows them to simulate the role that sunlight plays in phases and eclipses.

6. *Musical Instrument Recipe Book—Grades Kindergarten to Adult* Making musical instruments combines craftsmanship with an exploration of the physical properties of devices that produce sound. There is great satisfaction to be derived from building an instrument that is pleasing and that works. This resource book contains illustrated instructions for making over 20 stringed, wind, and percussion instruments from inexpensive, readily available materials. It can be used as a construction manual and as a source of ideas for building original instruments.

Instrument making brings together many curriculum areas— science, crafts, social studies, and music. An instrument-making project can also yield a variety of instruments for classroom use at little cost.

7. *Peas and Particles—Grades Four to Six* This is a unit on large numbers and estimation. Children deal with numbers informally, devising ways to estimate and approximate large amounts, sizes, and distances.

At first youngsters estimate large numbers of peas, marbles, or other objects in jars. In the process they develop a variety of counting methods which can be compared and refined. The numbers generated by their estimations can also be the basis for discussions of the usefulness of approximate numbers, "rounding off" numbers, and so forth. Later the children apply similar strategies to problems of their own choosing.

The activities give children experience with numbers and counts as we often meet them in newspapers, budgets, surveys, and other areas of everyday life, rather than as exact figures in textbook problems.

8. *Pond Water—Grades One to Seven* The fantastic variety of life in a pond can serve as the basis of an almost endless study. *Pond Water* has three main components: a field trip to a pond, classroom observation of the water and mud brought back, and experimentation. The *Teacher's Guide* suggests ways of dealing with the problems of "which animals are the same" and offers a number of questions that have interested children.

A set of cards contains information on aquarium building, keeping animals alive, and making slides, as well as identification of a few of the most common animals, culture information, and suggested experiments.

9. *Structures—Grades Two to Six* Children love to build. *Structures* give them a chance to develop some trial-and-error problem-

solving techniques as well as to explore the relationship between the materials used in construction and the structural and aesthetic design of the objects that can be built with them.

Some of the materials used for building are paper, index cards, straws, modeling clay, wood scraps, Tri-Wall, cardboard, and spaghetti.

Activities in the *Teacher's Guide* include making clay towers, building with straws and pins, designing scale model communities, large-scale construction with wood or Tri-Wall, and many others.

10. *Whistles and Strings—Grades Three to Six* Working with materials that produce sounds of definite pitch—such as stiff and flexible plastic tubing, straws, and different kinds of string—children explore the relationships between objects and the sounds they make. By altering and combining these and other materials, they investigate the physical conditions necessary to produce sounds and to change the pitch, volume, and tone quality of sounds. They construct sound-making contraptions for experiments and make simple musical instruments. Some children compose music for their instruments and play music together.

Whistles and Strings has been used as a science activity and as a combined music-science project.

Keep in mind that the ESS units must be looked upon as a reservoir of material from which to construct a program—the SCIS materials constitute a sequential program.

Use the three curriculum-evaluation criteria. State your evaluation of the ESS materials in writing.

When reviewing the ESS units of study the following seem to describe the general character of those learning materials.

1. Each unit is based upon a sound scientific principle but the ESS developers did not feel that a conceptual hierarchy to guide the program from kindergarten through the sixth grade was either necessary or desirable.
2. There is no inherent teaching method in the ESS materials.
3. The ESS program leaves to the teacher the task of matching the intellectual levels of the learners and what is to be learned.
4. The *underlying philosophy* of the ESS materials stresses that the investigations must be made by the children but no specific content or scientific processes and/or experiences are considered essential.

Science—A Process Approach (SAPA)[13]

The group that developed the SAPA program focused their attention on what they believed to be the *processes* of science. They described these processes as those things scientists do when they investigate. The processes of science can also be thought of as ways of processing information. The SAPA program provides children with experiences that result in a cumulative and continually increasing degree of understanding of and capability in the processes of science.

There are 13 processes emphasized in SAPA, and these processes are spread throughout the seven levels of the program, from kindergarten through grade six. During the primary grades, children conduct investigations that utilize the processes of observing, using space/time relationships, classifying, using numbers, measuring, communicating, predicting, and inferring. According to the SAPA group the foregoing are the basic processes and provide the foundation for the integrated processes that are emphasized in the intermediate grades. The integrated processes are controlling variables, interpreting data, formulating hypotheses, defining operationally, and experimenting. The processes on which the SAPA program is based are defined and used as follows:[14]

1. *Observing* Beginning with identifying objects and object-properties, this sequence proceeds to the identification of changes in various physical systems, the making of controlled observations, and the ordering of a series of observations.

2. *Classifying* Development begins with simple classifications of various physical and biological systems and progresses through multi-stage classifications, their coding and tabulation.

3. *Using Numbers* This sequence begins with identifying sets and their members, and progresses through ordering, counting, adding, multiplying, dividing, finding averages, using decimals, and powers of ten. Exercises in number using are introduced before they are needed to support exercises in the other processes.

4. *Measuring* Beginning with the identification and ordering of lengths, development in this process proceeds with the demonstration of rules for measurement of length, area, volume, weight, temperature, force, speed, and a number of derived measures applicable to specific physical and biological systems.

---

[13] The material in this section has been taken and adapted from *Commentary for Teachers of Science—A Process Approach*, Washington, D.C.: American Association for the Advancement of Science, 1970.
[14] Ibid., *Purposes, Accomplishment, Expectations*, pp. 5–7.

5. *Using Space-Time Relationships* This sequence begins with the identification of shapes, movement, and direction. It continues with the learning of rules applicable to straight and curved paths, directions at an angle, changes in position, and determinations of linear and angular speeds.

6. *Communicating* Development in this category begins with bar-graph descriptions of simple phenomena, and proceeds through describing a variety of physical objects and systems, and the changes in them, to the construction of graphs and diagrams for observed results of experiments.

7. *Predicting* For this process, the developmental sequence progresses from interpolation and extrapolation in graphically presented data to the formulation of methods for testing predictions.

8. *Inferring* Initially, the idea is developed that inferences differ from observations. As development proceeds, inferences are constructed for observations of physical and biological phenomena, and situations are constructed to test inferences drawn from hypotheses.

9. *Defining Operationally* Beginning with the distinction between definitions which are operational and those which are not, this developmental sequence proceeds to the point where children construct operational definitions in problems that are new to them.

10. *Formulating Hypotheses* At the start of this sequence, children distinguish hypotheses from inferences, observations, and predictions. Development is continued to the stage of constructing hypotheses and demonstrating tests of hypotheses.

11. *Interpreting Data* This sequence begins with descriptions of graphic data and inferences based upon them, and progresses to constructing equations to represent data, relating data to statements of hypotheses, and making generalizations supported by experimental findings.

12. *Controlling Variables* The developmental sequence for this "integrated" process begins with identification of manipulated and responding (independent and dependent) variables in a description or demonstration of an experiment. Development proceeds to the level at which the student, being given a problem, inference, or hypothesis, actually conducts an experiment, identifying the variables, and describing how variables are controlled.

13. *Experimenting* This is the capstone of the "integrated" processes. It is developed through a continuation of the sequence for controlling variables, and includes the interpretation of accounts of

scientific experiments, as well as the activities of stating problems, constructing hypotheses, and carrying out experimental procedures.

The content used in the SAPA model to teach the processes just described is selected from the physical, biological, and behavioral sciences and mathematics. The concepts[15] the program leads children to develop are:

1. Physical sciences
   a. Solids and liquids and their properties
   b. Gases and their properties
   c. Changes in properties
   d. Temperature and heat
   e. Force and motion
2. Biological sciences
   a. Observing and describing living things
   b. Modes of living and behavior of animals
   c. Human behavior and physiology
   d. Microbiology
   e. Seeds, seed germination, and plant growth
3. Mathematical topics
   a. Numbers and number notation
   b. Measurement
   c. Graphing
   d. Probability
   e. Geometric topics

Each of the 7 years of the SAPA program is guided by a carefully developed set of behavioral objectives. Those objectives clearly state what an individual child is expected to be able to do when that child has successfully completed an exercise or a unit. The attainment of these objectives can be demonstrated by the child because the child can do specific things that can be observed. Examples of behavioral objectives which the SAPA program leads children to achieve follow.

1. The child should be able to *identify* the following three-dimensional shapes: sphere, cube, cylinder, pyramid, and cone.
2. The child should be able to *distinguish* between statements that are observations and those that are explanations of observations, and *identify* the explanations as inferences.
3. The child should be able to *construct* an inference to explain the movement of liquid out of an inverted container when air moves into it.
4. The child should be able to *describe* and *demonstrate* that the

[15] Ibid., pp. 179–187.

farther an object is located from the center of a revolving disc, the greater its linear speed, although its rate of revolution is the same.

5. The child should be able to construct predictions from a graph about water loss from plants over a given period of time.[16]

Earlier the 13 processes that the SAPA model is constructed around and the content that was selected to lead children to develop facility with those processes were listed. The SAPA group then matched processes and content necessary to learn them with the *intellectual* maturity of children in grades kindergarten through six. Each of the content topics was treated at several grade levels. The concept of magnetism, for example, is first met in Part B[17] by the children observing the magnet's properties. Magnetism next appears as a principal topic in Part D, when the children make observations on magnetic poles. In Part F the concept of magnetism furnishes the content for a data interpretation experience; the children study magnetic fields particularly with reference to the earth. The content conceptual structure of science is included in the SAPA model, but the child does not develop an entire concept at one grade level.

In order to give a general notion of the manner in which the SAPA curriculum model is constructed, the processes taught and content used to teach them from Part D are listed below. The number in parentheses following each process indicates how many lessons, including the Part D lesson, have been taught up to this point of the program.

Inferring (3)—Observations and inferences
Inferring (4)—Tracks and traces
Predicting (3)—Describing the motion of a bouncing ball
Using numbers (10)—Dividing to find rates and means
Inferring (5)—The displacement of water by air
Measuring (13)—Describing the motion of a revolving phonograph record
Measuring (14)—Measuring drop by drop
Using numbers (11)—Metersticks, money, and decimals
Communicating (10)—Using maps
Communicating (11)—Describing location

---

[16] Ibid., p. 22.
[17] The SAPA program is keyed to educational levels. In implementing the program, the following coding system may be used: Part A—Kindergarten; Part B—First Grade; Part C—Second Grade; Part D—Third Grade; Part E—Fourth Grade; Part F—Fifth Grade; Part G—Sixth Grade. There is increasing experimentation with other distributions.

Measuring (15)—Measuring evaporation of water
Inferring (6)—Loss of water from plants
Predicting (4)—The suffocating candle
Observing (16)—Magnetic poles
Using space/time relationships (14)—Rate of change of position
Measuring (16)—Describing and representing forces
Observing (17)—Observing growth from seeds
Communicating (12)—Reporting an investigation in writing
Using space/time relationships (15)—Two-dimensional represen-
    tation of spatial figures
Classifying (10)—Using punch cards to record a classification
Using space/time relationships (16)—Relative position and motion
Observing (18)—Observing falling objects

Each of the seven parts of the SAPA model has its own unique distribution of content and processes as shown in Part D. You will also observe that some of the processes have been used many times before; observing, for example, has been used 15 times in Parts A, B, and C, while inferring has been used only twice. That process distribution clearly demonstrates an emphasis on continuity of process skill development. There is also continuity in the content, but it is not as tightly structured as is the process continuity.

When reviewing the seven levels of the SAPA curriculum the following seem to describe the general character of the SAPA learning materials.

1. The science content of each unit was drawn from the familiar areas of science—the biological, physical, and earth sciences—but that content is the vehicle to teach the processes to be learned in that particular unit.
2. The SAPA materials are not organized into learning cycles, but the *underlying philosophy* of SAPA stresses that the investigations are to be made by the children.
3. The intellectual compatibility among levels of process, content, and child is built into the SAPA programs.
4. The developers of the SAPA materials believe that children having experiences with certain, specific scientific processes is essential.

A Comparison

The three curriculum models presented here all lead children toward the same purposes and these purposes are those subscribed to in this book. There are, however, differences among the three models.

The SCIS model is a content-centered model that utilizes the natural interests and intellectual abilities of children to teach them a conceptual structure of science as well as the processes they need from time to time to uncover that structure for themselves. The SAPA model devotes its attention to teaching the processes scientists use as they investigate, and utilize that content which interests children and which allows the processes to be taught. A conceptual structure of science emerges, but it is not as clear-cut and evident as that from the SCIS model. On the other hand, the process-structure that emerges from the SCIS model is not as evident as that from the SAPA model. The ESS model utilizes those science topics found to be of interest and that can be taught to children. The conceptual structure of science must be put into the program by the teacher through selection of units. The ESS units can be taught only by utilizing the complete involvement of the child in the processes of finding out. Neither the conceptual structure of science nor its process structure is as evident in the ESS model as in the other two models. The selection of a model can only be governed by the purposes children are being led to achieve.

In all three models, however, there are four threads of continuity that can be extracted and utilized to blueprint a generalizable curriculum model. In all three models the children focus their attention upon a *concrete object, event, and/or situation* that can be studied in a concrete way. The utilization of abstraction as the focus of investigation does not exist. This reflects the concern of each model for the intellectual level of the learner.

Each of the models leads the learners through an *investigation of* the objects given them. That investigation produces *data* the learner is led to *interpret*. In other words, the data allow concepts to be invented for or by the learners. The generalizable curriculum model which can be used with any type of learning materials, therefore, must reflect *objects, investigation, data gathering,* and *interpretation,* or, stated another way, exploration, conceptual invention, and the expansion of the newly invented concept (discovery). When an elementary school curriculum reflects these traits it is aimed toward the educational purposes outlined earlier. Quite evidently, the teacher controls the content being taught by the objects, events, and/or situations selected for the children to study. In our opinion, that is the proper role of the teacher. If exploration, invention, and discovery are used the process structure will evolve because of the interaction that takes place between the teacher, the children, and the materials.

PART 2—EXPANDING CURRICULUM MODELS

Revisions of SAPA, SCIS, and ESS

The original curriculum development projects SAPA, SCIS, and ESS are now public domain. They were developed with government funds and, in a sense, they now belong to the people of the United States. Not only were the projects written and trial tested with government financial support, but hundreds of government supported programs taught teachers how to use the new curriculum materials in the classroom. These teacher education programs developed a broad base of intellectual support for each project. Intellectual support for these projects also developed in college faculties both in science and science education. They were the people who promoted one or more of the curriculum projects in summer workshops, institutes, or in-service teacher programs. There is, therefore, a well established base of support for the curriculum projects.

It was inevitable, and certainly not at all contrary to the original purpose of the curriculum development projects, that when the original publisher no longer had exclusive rights to publication, new and improved versions of the original projects would be produced. Some of the revisions or second generation projects are now commercially available. As expected, each has a few changes from the original version, but, for the most part, the changes are superficial and cosmetic. The basic philosophies and content of the original projects are intact. Presently there are only a few revisions commercially available. It is entirely possible and probable, however, that other versions of each project will be produced in the near future. The revisions which are currently available are as follows.

• **SAPA II.** Science—A Process Approach II, is a revision of the original SAPA. This approach is available through Ginn and Company, A Xerox Education Company. Xerox was the commercial publisher of the original SAPA.

This new version of SAPA is designed to reflect the innovations of science education during the past decade. These innovations are, according to the planners of SAPA II: (1) a deep concern for and understanding of the environment and its problems; (2) a greater need for and commitment to individualized learning; and (3) new and important advances in educational technology.

As evidence of a new or stronger focus on understanding of the environment, SAPA II advertising materials give these examples of application of the science process to the environment:

Observing activity—with soils
Classifying activity—with a terrarium
Predicting activity—the impact of a clean-up campaign on the school yard environment
Inferring activity—effect of liquids on plant cells
Communicating activity—a tree diary maintained throughout the school year
Number activity—counting birds
Defining operationally—heat conservation
Interpreting data—limited earth
Formulating hypothesis—environmental protection

SAPA II is composed of a continuum of 105 ungraded modules. In graded schools modules 1 through 12 or 15 usually constitute kindergarten, 13 through 24 or 16 through 30 constitute grade 1, and so on in groups of 12 to 15 modules per year. The 105 modules of SAPA II are shown in Figure 8–7.

Figure 8–7   SAPA II

MODULE NUMBER	MODULE	PROCESS
1	Perception of Color	Observing/a
2	Recognizing and Using Shapes	Space/Time/a
3	Color, Shape, Texture, and Size	Observing/b
4	Leaves, Nuts, and Seashells	Classifying/a
5	Temperature	Observing/c
6	Direction and Movement	Space/Time/b
7	Perception of Taste	Observing/d
8	Length	Measuring/a
9	Sets and Their Members	Using Numbers/a
10	Spacing Arrangements	Space/Time/c
11	Listening to Whales	Observing/e
12	Three-Dimensional Shapes	Space/Time/d
13	Numerals, Order, and Counting	Using Numbers/b
14	Animal and Familiar Things	Classifying/b
15	Perception of Odors	Observing/f
16	Living and Nonliving Things	Classifying/c
17	Trees in Our Environment Change	Observing/g
18	Using the Senses	Observing/h
19	Soils	Observing/i
20	Counting Birds	Using Numbers/c
21	Weather	Observing/j
22	Same but Different	Communicating/a
23	Comparing Volumes	Measuring/b
24	Metric Lengths	Measuring/c
25	Introduction to Graphing	Communicating/b
26	Using a Balance	Measuring/d
27	Pushes and Pulls	Communicating/c
28	Molds and Green Plants	Observing/k

Figure 8–7   (Continued.)

MODULE NUMBER	MODULE	PROCESS
29	Shadows	Space/Time/e
30	Addition Through 99	Using Numbers/d
31	Life Cycles	Communicating/d
32	A Terrarium	Classifying/d
33	What's Inside	Inferring/a
34	About How Far?	Measuring/e
35	Symmetry	Space/Time/f
36	Animal Responses	Observing/l
37	Forces	Measuring/f
38	Using Graphs	Predicting/a
39	Solids, Liquids, and Gases	Measuring/g
40	How Certain Can You Be?	Inferring/b
41	Temperature and Thermometers	Measuring/h
42	Sorting Mixtures	Classifying/e
43	A Plant Part That Grows	Communicating/e
44	Surveying Opinion	Predicting/b
45	Lines, Curves, and Surfaces	Space/Time/g
46	Observations and Inferences	Inferring/c
47	Scale Drawings	Communicating/f
	A Tree Diary	Communicating/g
48	The Bouncing Ball	Predicting/c
49	Drop by Drop	Measuring/i
50	The Clean-Up Campaign	Predicting/d
51	Rate of Change	Space/Time/h
52	Plants Transpire	Inferring/d
53	The Suffocating Candle	Predicting/e
54	Static and Moving Objects	Measuring/j
55	Sprouting Seeds	Observing/m
	Magnetic Poles	Observing/n
56	Punch Cards	Classifying/f
57	Position and Shape	Communicating/h
58	Liquids and Tissue	Inferring/e
59	Metersticks, Money, and Decimals	Using Numbers/e
60	Relative Motion	Space/Time/i
61	Circuit Boards	Inferring/f
62	Climbing Liquids	Controlling Variables/a
63	Maze Behavior	Interpreting Data/a
64	Cells, Lamps, Switches	Defining Operationally/a
65	Minerals in Rocks	Interpreting Data/b
66	Learning and Forgetting	Controlling Variables/b
67	Identifying Materials	Interpreting Data/c
68	Field of Vision	Interpreting Data/d
69	Magnification	Defining Operationally/b
70	Conductors and Nonconductors	Formulating Hypotheses/a
71	Soap and Seeds	Controlling Variables/c
72	Heart Rate	Controlling Variables/d
73	Solutions	Formulating Hypotheses/b
74	Biotic Communities	Defining Operationally/c
75	Decimals, Graphs, and Pendulums	Interpreting Data/e
76	Limited Earth	Interpreting Data/f

Figure 8–7   (Continued.)

MODULE NUMBER	MODULE	PROCESS
77	Chemical Reactions	Controlling Variables/e
78	Levers	Formulating Hypotheses/c
79	Animal Behavior	Formulating Hypotheses/d
80	Inertia and Mass	Defining Operationally/d
81	Analysis of Mixtures	Defining Operationally/e
82	Force and Acceleration	Controlling Variables/f
83	Chances Are	Formulating Hypotheses/e
84	Angles	Interpreting Data/g
85	Contour Maps	Interpreting Data/h
86	Earth's Magnetism	Interpreting Data/i
87	Wheel Speeds	Interpreting Data/j
88	Environmental Protection	Defining Operationally/f
89	Plant Parts	Defining Operationally/g
90	Streams and Slopes	Interpreting Data/k
91	Flowers	Defining Operationally/h
92	Three Cases	Formulating Hypotheses/f
93	Temperature and Heat	Defining Operationally/i
94	Small Water Animals	Controlling Variables/g
95	Mars Photos	Interpreting Data/l
96	Pressure and Volume	Experimenting/a
97	Optical Illusions	Experimenting/b
98	Eye Power	Experimenting/c
99	Fermentation	Experimenting/d
100	Plant Nutrition	Experimenting/e
101	Mental Blocks	Experimenting/f
102	Plants in Light	Experimenting/g
103	Density	Experimenting/h
104	Viscosity	Experimenting/i
105	Membranes	Experimenting/j

• **SCIS II and SCIIS.** There are presently two commercially available SCIS revisions. SCIS II is the revision by American Science and Engineering. SCIIS is the revision published by Rand McNally & Company. Both of these companies were involved in the original SCIS program. Rand McNally published the printed materials—the teachers guides and student record books. American Science and Engineering produced and sold the SCIS materials kits.

• **SCIS II.** An author team of six persons headed by senior author Lester Paldy produced SCIS II. The revision of the SCIS program follows both the philosophy of science education and the conceptual and process content of the original SCIS. There are, of course, some changes in the activities and some new materials. For example, SCIS II contains activity cards designed to provide individual and small group activities. The activity cards also relate science to mathematics and language arts. There are new activities and content in the areas of earth science in the fourth and sixth grade physical science teacher's guides. The traditional student manuals of SCIS have been replaced in SCIS II with more flexible duplicating master booklets. The units and conceptual structure of SCIS II are shown in Figure 8–8. Notice that there is still a physical science unit and a life science unit for each level from level one through six. Levels four and six also have new names.

· SCIIS. SCIIS is the new Rand McNally version of SCIS. The author team for this program includes several of the directors of the original SCIS programs including Robert Karplus, Herbert Thier, Robert Knott, Chester Lawson, and Marshall Montgomery. SCIIS appears to have made even fewer changes in the original SCIS than SCIS II.

There does appear to be an attempt to focus some attention on the earth science aspects of the original SCIS by changing the titles of the two major divisions of units. The divisions which were entitled "Physical Science" and "Life Science" are now entitled "Physical/Earth Science" and "Life/Earth Science." A title change in level six of the physical science units from "Models: Electric and Magnetic Interaction" to "Scientific Theories" in SCIIS suggests a broadening of this unit to include other phenomena—primarily light, color, and simple optics.

The SCIIS program retains the student manuals, evaluation packets, and teachers guides. It also includes the kindergarten unit, *Beginnings*. In addition to these traditional parts of SCIS, the revision has included EYE cards (Extending Your Experience). The SCIIS levels, unit titles, and concepts are shown in Figure 8–9.

· ESS. No group has undertaken a general revision of the ESS program. There has been, however, a revision of many of the 56 individual units or modules, and 38 module materials kits are available from American Science and Engineering. The revised units available from Webster/McGraw-Hill Book Company are as follows:

Attribute Games and Problems
Batteries and Bulbs
Behavior of Mealworms
Bones
Brine Shrimp
Changes
Clay Boats
Colored Solutions
Crayfish
Eggs and Tadpoles

Figure 8–8   SCIS II

ORGANISMS		MATERIAL OBJECTS	
Organism	Food Web	Object	Change
Birth	Detritus	Property	Evidence
Death	Growth	Material	Serial Order
Habitat			

LIFE CYCLES		INTERACTION AND SYSTEMS	
		Interaction	System
Life Cycle	Biotic Potential	Evidence of	Electric Circuit
Growth	Plant	Interaction	
Development	Animal	Interaction-at-	Magnetic
Metamorphosis	Genetic Identity	a-Distance	Interaction
Generation	Germination		

POPULATIONS		SUBSYSTEMS AND VARIABLES	
		Subsystem	Evaporation
Population	Prey	Variable	Solution
Food Chain	Plant Eater	Histogram	Temperature
Food Web	Animal Eater		
Community	Plant-Animal	MEASUREMENT, MOTION,	
	Eater	AND CHANGE	
Predator	Dispersal	Reference	Reference Object
		Frame	
ENVIRONMENTS		Relative	Change
Environmental	Seasonal Change	Position	
Factor		Polar	Distance
Environment	Temperature	Coordinates	
Range	Response	Rectangular	Direction
Optimum		Coordinates	
Range		Relative Motion	Measurement

COMMUNITIES		ENERGY SOURCES	
Community	Food Transfer	Energy Transfer	Energy Receiver
Producer	Raw Materials	Energy Chain	Temperature
Consumer	Reproduction		Change
Decomposer	Food Cycle	Energy Source	
Food Source	Photosynthesis		

ECOSYSTEMS		MODELING SYSTEMS	
		Model	Electrical Energy
Ecosystem	Food-Mineral	Electricity	Air Temperature
	Cycle	Magnetism	Barometric
Water Cycle	Evaporation		Pressure
Oxygen-Carbon	Condensation	Circuit	Atmosphere
Dioxide Cycle	Gas		
Pollutant			

Figure 8–9   SCIIS

LEVEL

K   **BEGINNINGS**

CONCEPTS:

Color	Odor	Quantity
Shape	Sound	Position
Texture	Size	Organisms

1.

PHYSICAL/EARTH SCIENCE

MATERIAL OBJECTS

CONCEPTS:

Object	Serial Order
Property	Evidence
Material	

LIFE/EARTH SCIENCE

ORGANISMS

CONCEPTS:

Organisms	Habitat
Birth	Food Chain
Death	Decay

2.

INTERACTION AND SYSTEMS

CONCEPTS:

Interaction	System
Evidence of Interaction	
Interaction-at-a-Distance	

LIFE CYCLES

CONCEPTS:

Growth	Genetic Identity
Development	Plant and Animal
Life Cycle	Metamorphosis

3.

SUBSYSTEMS AND VARIABLES

CONCEPTS:

Subsystem	Histogram
Solution	Variable
Evaporation	

POPULATIONS

CONCEPTS:

Population	Animal-Eater
Plant-Eater	Food Web
Biotic Potential	Plant-Animal-
Predator-Prey	Eater

4.

RELATIVE POSITION AND MOTION

CONCEPTS:

Reference Object
Relative Position
Relative Motion
Polar Coordinates
Rectangular Coordinates

ENVIRONMENTS

CONCEPTS:

Environment	
Environmental	
Factors	
Biotic	Range
Abiotic	Optimum

5.

ENERGY SOURCES

CONCEPTS:

Energy Source
Energy Receiver
Energy Transfer
Energy Obtain

COMMUNITIES

CONCEPTS:

Pyramid of	Consumers
Numbers	
Raw Materials	Decomposers
Reproduction	Photosynthesis
Community	Food Transfer
Producers	Competitors

6.

SCIENTIFIC THEORIES

CONCEPTS:

Scientific Theory	Electricity
Magnetic Field	Light Ray

ECOSYSTEMS

CONCEPTS:

Ecosystem	Food-Mineral
Water Cycle	Cycle
Oxygen-Carbon Dioxide Cycle	

Gases and Airs
Geo-Blocks
Growing Seeds
Ice Cubes
Kitchen Physics: A Look at Some Properties of Liquids
Life of Beans and Peas
Light and Shadows
Match and Measure
Microgardening
Mobiles
Mystery Powders
Peas and Particles
Pendulums
Pond Water
Primary Balancing
Rocks and Charts
Small Things: An Introduction to the Microscopic World
Tangrams

Eight new ESS type units or modules, called McGraw/Hill Process Science Modules, have been included. These modules appear to be generally earth science or environmentally oriented. For the primary grades the titles are "Astronomy—D₂ y and Night," "Physical Sciences—Magnetic Properties," "Classification—Sets," "Weather—Winds, Clouds, and Rain." For intermediate grades, titles are "Ecology—Polluted Ecosystems," "Geologic Processes—Changing Earth," "Weather—Weather or Earth," "Astronomical Time—Keepers—Measuring Time."

Because ESS units de-emphasize "book learning," the units work well with nonverbal or bilingual students, and some have been adapted for special education classes. A *Special Education Teacher's Guide*[18] has been developed by Daniel W. Ball that allows teachers to adapt ESS materials for use with these students. The units for use in special education have been placed into three groups as follows.

The Perceptual Group
Attribute Games and Problems
Geo-Blocks
Mirror Cards
Pattern Blocks
Tangrams
Tracks

---

[18] Daniel W. Ball, *ESS/Special Education Teachers Guide*, New York: McGraw-Hill, 1978.

The Psychomotor Group
Batteries and Bulbs 1 and 2
Clay Boats
Drops, Streams, and Containers
Ice Cubes
Mapping
Mystery Powders
Primary Balancing
Sink or Float

Other Appropriate ESS Units
Behavior of Mealworms
Brine Shrimp
Butterflies
Changes
Colored Solutions
Earthworms
Growing Seeds
Life of Beans and Peas
Starting from Seeds
Match and Measure
Mobiles
Music Instrument Recipe Book
Peas and Particles
Pond Water
Small Things
Rocks and Charts
Structures

Synthesizing Curricula

You have just been informed about how the three curriculum models described in the first portion of this chapter have been revised. Such revisions are essential to any curriculum. SAPA, SCIS, and ESS materials were all carefully prepared and tested in many classrooms. When these materials were used in a broad range of classrooms, with teachers having many different teaching philosophies, the need for revision after several years was inevitable. Furthermore, the first editions of the SAPA, SCIS, and ESS materials were tested with children and teachers in the late 1960s. Children and teachers change too.

Even though the materials are now available bearing names related to the original projects, keep in mind that these revisions are just that, revisions. The original products were the starting points and those persons who revised them corrected what they felt were deficiencies in those original products. The overall philosophy, content and teaching procedures inherent in the original versions of the SAPA, SCIS, and ESS materials are, in general, also found in the revisions.

There are elementary school science curricula now available which represent a synthesis of many of the characteristics of the three original curriculum models discussed earlier. *The Learning Science Program* (LSP)[19] is a curriculum model which represents such a synthesis.

LSP begins by accepting the empirical fact that children in the elementary school have content and structures that reflect concrete operational reasoning and who function concretely. (If you have any doubts about meaning of the concepts, content, structure, and function, return to Chapter 3 and review.) The program, therefore, leads chil-

Figure 8–10   Children in the *Learning Science Program* have actual experience with the phenomena of science. (Photograph courtesy of Benziger Bruce & Glencoe, Encino, California.)

[19] John W. Renner, Don G. Stafford, and Vivian Jensen Coulter, *Action,* Encino, California: Benziger Bruce & Glencoe, and New York: Macmillan, 1977, p. 185.

dren to develop understandings of concrete concepts. The following example illustrates that point.

The fifth grade portion of the LSP is entitled *Action,* and one of the major concepts taught at that level is energy. Now energy is one of the most abstract concepts in all of science as it has been taught throughout the years. Generally the learners were given the definition "energy is the ability (or capacity) to do work" and were asked to accept it. At best they were given that definition as the reason why gasoline (it makes an automobile move) and electricity (it runs an electric motor) are sources of energy. The importance of the concept of energy in today's world makes teaching it necessary, *but it must be taught concretely. Action* solved the problem in this way.

The children gathered data about what happens when you make a conscious effort to design and throw a paper airplane so as to make it travel the greatest possible distance. How to use a rubber band to permit it to give the greatest distance to a projectile was also explored. What happens to ice and water when they interact was studied, and

Figure 8–11 Children fly paper airplanes to gain the experience they need to be introduced to the idea of energy in the *Learning Science Program.* (Photograph courtesy of Benziger Bruce & Glencoe, Encino, California.)

data were gathered about how far various sizes of spheres will push a chalkboard eraser to which various sized weights have been added when the spheres are rolled down inclined planes of varying heights. Fifteen separate, concrete, "Gathering Data" activities are completed before the children are presented with the idea of energy. They then meet this "Getting the Idea" page in the textbook.

GETTING THE IDEA
Now, let's review what your experiments have told you about action.

1. A person has to throw a paper airplane to make it go.
2. A rubber band has to be stretched before it can shoot an object.
3. When ice is put in water, the ice melts and the water gets cold.
4. The greater the height from which a sphere rolls down a ramp, the farther it will push an eraser.

The experiments you have done produced the results they did because of

energy.

The person gives the airplane *energy* when throwing it.
The rubber band gains *energy* when it is stretched.
Ice gains *energy* from the water and melts.
The sphere gains *energy* by rolling down the inclined plane.
When the sphere strikes the eraser, it gives the eraser *energy.*
The system giving the energy is the

energy source.

The system receiving the energy is the

energy receiver.

After the idea of energy has been invented for the children they next meet the following four questions, which have them think back through the experiments done during the "Gathering Data" phase.

EXPANDING THE IDEA

Understanding Energy

1. Think back upon the experiments in this chapter. What was the energy source in each experiment? What was the energy receiver?
2. What makes it possible for a bowling ball to knock over bowling pins?
3. What kind of energy causes ice to melt?
4. What is the energy source for a moving automobile?

The foregoing example is typical of the instructional design used in LSP to insure that the concepts which the students meet are concrete. There are no formal concepts which can only be presented at the formal level, such as the atom, in the LSP. Energy, of course, can be presented at a very formal level but the LSP presents it concretely. In the "Getting the Idea" phase of the learning cycle you just read, the children are told many things. Those statements, however, are merely summaries of what the children have already done and would not make sense to a concrete operational student who has not done the experiments. The reading the learners do in TLSP instructs them what to do or summarizes what they have already experienced.

In the LSP one learning cycle builds upon another. You just read the "Getting the Idea" phase of a learning cycle which invented the concept of energy for the reader. That was followed by the "Expanding the Idea" phase which helped the children expand not only the concept of energy but also the language used to communicate about energy. There follows a learning cycle that explores, invents, and expands additional energy-related concepts for the learner.

GATHERING DATA
As you have learned from doing experiments, an object receives energy from a source. You give a paper airplane energy when you throw it. You are a source of energy. The ball receives energy from the bat. The bat receives energy from the batter.

Figure 8–12 In the *Learning Science Program* children have experiences *before* the concept of the electric circuit is introduced to them.
(Photograph courtesy of Benziger Bruce & Glencoe, Encino, California.)

Read this symbol ⟶ as "gives energy to." Now read this diagram:

batter ⟶ bat ⟶ ball

First, one object receives energy. Then it gives energy to another receiver. There is an exchange of energy. You can observe many exchanges of energy in the happenings around you. For example, there is an exchange of energy when you boil water.

Observing Add water to a beaker or to a heatproof container. Put the water-filled beaker on a hot plate. Boil the water. Observe what is happening. Now read this diagram:

hot plate ⟶ water ⟶ air

GETTING THE IDEA
One object or system giving energy to another object or system is evidence of

energy transfer.

A diagram like the one you read on the batter, bat, and ball is called an

energy chain.

An energy chain tells you how the energy in a system is moving from the source to the receiver.

Energy from the sun makes water warm. The water *evaporates* or changes to a gas. Energy has been transferred from the sun to the water. The evidence of energy transfer is the change of state of the water. The water changes from the liquid state to the gaseous state.

The water gives some of its energy to the air. The air moves faster, making the wind blow. Moving air, or *wind,* is the evidence of energy transfer. The moving wind pushes the sail on a boat. The boat moves. This is evidence of energy transfer.

The sun is the energy source. The water is the energy receiver. The evaporation of the water is evidence of energy transfer. The water gives energy to the air. The air moves as wind. The wind pushes the sail of a boat and the boat moves. The air is the energy source. The boat is the energy receiver. The moving boat is evidence that energy has been transferred.

EXPANDING THE IDEA

1. Find the energy chain in an automobile.
2. Give evidence of energy transfer in an automobile.
3. The lights in your school get their energy from electricity. Find the energy chain that brings them energy.
4. Locate the energy chain when you ride a bicycle.
5. A jet airliner takes off. What is the energy receiver? What is the evidence of energy transfer?

The Energy Game Play the Energy Game. First, write the names of six sports on the chalkboard. Name the energy source of each sport. Name the energy receiver. Then explain the evidence of a transfer of energy in each sport. What action does the energy transfer produce in each sport?

Interpreting You did some experiments with energy sources and energy receivers in Chapter 7, "Systems in Action." Look at the pictures of some of those experiments. What evidence do you see that energy was transferred from one object to another?

Experimenting Line a match box with a paper towel or with blotting paper. Then fill the box with bean seeds. Cover the bean seeds with water. Put the cover on the match box. Then put the box in a sandwich bag. Put the bag in a warm, dark place. Leave it there for four days. Then look at the box. What action do you observe? Describe the action. Use the terms "energy source," "energy receiver," and "energy transfer."

Experimenting Try another experiment with bean seeds. Soak some bean seeds overnight. Then mix plaster of paris in a nut cup. Mix the plaster of paris until it is like heavy cream. Then push three bean

Figure 8–13 The community concept is taught at the fifth grade level in both the *Learning Science Program* and the materials designed by the *Science Curriculum Improvement Study.* (Photograph courtesy of Benziger Bruce & Glencoe, Encino, California.)

seeds just under the surface of the plaster. Observe the plaster of paris from day to day. What action is produced? Identify an energy source, an energy receiver, and the evidence of energy transfer.

The foregoing illustrates how the LSP overtly uses the learning cycle. The use of concrete concepts by the LSP, described earlier, and the use of the learning cycle—assimilation and accommodation—demonstrate that the LSP is based upon the learning and developmental models of Piaget. Furthermore, the materials included here demonstrate that a textbook can be used to guide student learning using inquiry, and need not be used to tell the students what the authors want them to know. The last learning cycle included here was taken from Chapter 8 of *Action*, which is entitled "Energy Chains." At the end of that chapter the following is found:

Information

People and Energy Chains: In 1820 the Reverend W. Cecil read a paper before a meeting of the Cambridge Philosophical Society in England. He described his experiments with a mixture of hydrogen and air. When exploded, these gases would make an engine run.

Reverend Cecil's engine is believed to be the earliest engine built. Many other people contributed to making an engine which used fuel to make an energy chain. The energy chain begins with the fuel. From the fuel, it goes to the engine. Then it moves on to the object which the engine runs. Finally, the energy chain goes to the air and the earth.

William Barnett, an Englishman, patented an engine in 1838. In 1860 Jean Lenoir, A Frenchman, built the first practical gas engine. The Germans Nikolaus Otto, Eugen Langen, and Gottlieb Daimler designed and patented engines between 1876 and 1885.

In the year 1885, Karl Benz, another German, developed a successful gas engine. The name Benz later became associated with the famous Mercedes-Benz automobile. The German mechanical engineer Rudolph Diesel (1858–1913) also designed an internal-combustion engine.

Earlier, the Scottish engineer, James Watt (1736–1819), spent much of his life working with steam. Watt developed the first practical steam engine. The energy chain in the steam engine goes from a fire to water. The water changes to steam. The steam pushes a piston, which moves a vehicle.

In the field of electricity, many people contributed to an energy chain—a chain that goes from an energy source to a practical use. One of the first of these people was a Frenchman named Alessandro Volta (1745–1827). Volta used chemicals to develop electrical energy. The device he built became known as the "voltaic pile." It was the ancestor of today's storage battery.

Hans Christian Oersted (1777–1851) discovered that magnetism is present when an electrical current runs through a wire. Michael Faraday

Figure 8–14   Actual experience seeing a lens focus an image of an object is essential to assimilating the meaning of the concept of focal length.

(1791–1867) then used the magnetic field to produce electrical current.[20]

Notice that what you just read had the general title "Information," but it was information involving the energy chain. Used in that way the "Information" passage is a legitimate part of the "Expanding the Idea" phase of the learning cycle. In grades three through six, the LSP uses information sections like the one you just read. Those sections are included to be a legitimate part of the last phase of the learning cycle.

As was stated earlier, the LSP is based upon the learning theories of Piaget. But the LSP also recognizes that a science curriculum must lead children to move toward achieving the central purpose of education—the development of the ability to think—and provides activities which provide the learners with the essential experiences of science described in Chapter 6. The diagram in Figure 8–15 demonstrates how all of this is accomplished.

Figure 8–15 shows that in the LSP the essential experiences discussed in Chapter 6 are used in the "Gathering Data" and "Expanding the Idea" phases of the learning cycle. But while learners are having

[20] John W. Renner, Don G. Stafford and Vivian Jensen Coulter, *Action,* Encino, California: Benziger Bruce & Glencoe, and New York: Macmillan, 1977, p. 185.

The Learning Cycle

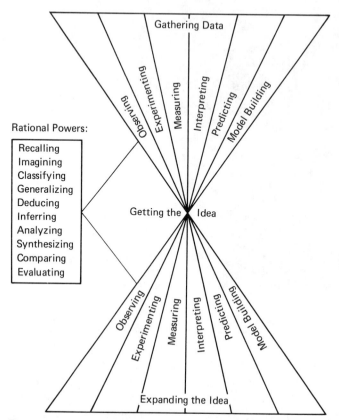

Figure 8–15   The rational powers (see Chapter 2) can be used with each of the essential science experiences (see Chapter 6) when children learn science through the learning cycle.

those experiences, they must use some or all of the rational powers with each experience. When students are experiencing interpreting, for example, they are classifying, comparing, analyzing, evaluating, deducing, synthesizing, and perhaps generalizing. Since the LSP overtly points out to the students—in grades one through six—what essential science experience each activity represents, it is also making provisions for rational power development. The philosophy base of the LSP, therefore, reflects educational purpose, the essential experiences of science, and a tested learning theory. That philosophy base also includes a definite position regarding what science actually is.

In Chapter 1 you met the quotation from Professor Duane Roller which states that "science is the quest for knowledge, not the knowledge." That quotation represents the position the authors of the LSP take with respect to science. The foregoing learning cycle examples demonstrate that the LSP is built around elementary school children learning what "a quest for knowledge" really is. But content is not neglected. The following description of the LSP shows that.[21]

Each of the student books covers three major content areas in the natural sciences. Or, to put it in structural terms, each book contains three major "content blocks." These content blocks are the physical, biological, and the earth sciences.

In the discipline of science, as in the environment itself, the physical, earth, and biological sciences are closely related. To ensure that the students will perceive these relationships and thus gain a true picture of their environment, four continuing themes, or content threads, run through each of the major content blocks. These content threads are:

Energy   Matter
Life, including human   The Ecosystem, in which energy,
    physiology   matter, and life interact to
                                    form a functioning whole.

In studying biological sciences at the fifth grade level, for example, students learn that the organs of the human body are made up of matter and that they must have energy in order to function. We obtain the energy we need from a special kind of matter known as food. This precious energy-containing matter is derived—through one or more energy transfers along a food chain—from plants. Using the energy contained in sunlight, plants can manufacture their own living matter from the nonliving matter supplied by soil, water, and the atmosphere.

Through such integrated learning experiences, made possible by the use of content threads, the students develop an understanding of the unity of the natural sciences and of the natural world that science studies. Perhaps even more importantly, they develop an understanding of the importance of preserving that natural unity on which all human life and activity depend.

The following is a short summary of the content of each book in the *Learning Science Program.*

BOOK 1: THINGS
First graders are preoccupied with learning the names of objects and investigating their properties. Learning that an object (or "thing") can be classified (or "named") according to its properties is an important concept which helps the students to organize their exploration of the environment and thus to make the transition from pre-operational to concrete-operational thought.

[21] The material describing the content of the LSP found here has been taken from the teachers guides to that program with the permission of the publisher.

BOOK 2: CHANGE
Second graders have just begun to employ concrete-operational thought. They have realized that the properties of many objects around them do not remain constant: plants change with the seasons, water changes when it is cooled or heated, the children themselves change as they grow. The concept of change—an essential concept in the study of science—is therefore the subject of Book 2.

BOOK 3: SYSTEMS
Whenever two or more objects are put together for some reason, they form a system. A dry cell, a wire, and a light bulb can form a system. If the objects in the system are put together in the right way, they interact to produce a change. The change—the lighting of the light bulb—is evidence of that interaction. Third graders are far enough into concrete thought to be able to make and manipulate simple systems and to study them for evidence of interaction.

BOOK 4: VARIATION
As a result of their experience in manipulating objects and observing the interactions among them, fourth grades have developed a more sophisticated interest in the concept of change. They begin to compare types and degrees of change. For example, they may notice that two plants of the same kind, planted at the same time, have grown to different heights, or that water in a pan will disappear very slowly if the pan is left on a table but rapidly if the pan is heated. Variables— the factors that produce variations in growth and change—therefore occupy a prominent place in Book 4.

BOOK 5: ACTION
By the fifth grade, students have realized that their own actions are an important variable in the changes that take place around them. They are able to understand that in interacting with an object to produce change—in throwing a ball, for example—they are imparting energy to the object. They can understand, too, that interactions among objects produce energy that they themselves can use. The energy transfers which make action possible are the subject of Book 5.

BOOK 6: MODELS
Sixth grade students are approaching the end of the concrete-operational thought period. Although their learning still must be based on concrete experience, they are able to understand the interaction of systems they cannot observe directly by gathering data about those systems and then constructing models of them. The behavior of electrical current, the operation of the human eye and the human lung, and the relationship between the earth and the sun all provide data that sixth graders can use to construct models.

Three criteria to be used to judge the quality of an elementary school science curriculum were given earlier in this chapter. Apply those three criteria to the *Learning Science Program.*

The title of this section is "Synthesizing Curricula." That title infers that the three models—SAPA, SCIS, and ESS—represent sources of ideas from which syntheses had been made. How does the LSP represent a synthesis of what was learned while developing SAPA, SCIS and ESS (the projects)?

The most important element from the projects included in the LSP is the common, underlying philosophy found in each. That philosophy demands that children learn scientific concepts through interacting with materials. In other words, children *must* be involved in the investigation.

The LSP obviously used the teaching procedure introduced by the SCIS—exploration, invention, and discovery, although with different titles for each phase. The learning cycles in the LSP are overtly labeled for the learners and are smaller in scope than those used by SCIS. But the LSP profited from the development of the learning cycle by the SCIS. The LSP took the learning cycle concept one step beyond where the SCIS advanced it and demonstrated the place for and the function of reading in a science program. Reading helps learners in the concrete operational stage to expand an idea they have been introduced to through the learning cycle.

The LSP is based upon the belief that there are certain process-type experiences children should have while studying science. While the number and names of such experiences are different in the LSP than in SAPA, the impact that SAPA had on the LSP is evident.

The ESS and the SCIS are each committed to first developing the content of science rather than the processes to be developed. Even though the LSP is overtly concerned with the processes of science, it quite obviously is designed from the content to the processes rather than the reverse. The SCIS program had a conceptual hierarchy upon which the content it selected was based. Quite evidently, the LSP has a similar hierarchy—the SCIS influence is evident.

The LSP, therefore, has drawn the strong characteristics from all three of the massive elementary school science curriculum projects of the 1960s. In addition, it added two new dimensions. The LSP put the directions and suggestions for investigations in a book. That dimension enables learners to work independently of the teacher without waiting for directions, but it does not hamper the learners from departing from the book and carrying on their own investigation. That feature is particularly important in the "Expanding the Idea" phase of the learning cycle.

The second new dimension introduced by the LSP was referred to earlier and is the place of reading in an inquiry-centered program. The LSP demands student reading in two cases. The students need to read the direction in order to carry out the investigations. If, however, reading is a problem, those directions can be read to them and a lack of reading ability has not hampered student achievement in science. The most important use of reading is made in the "Information" sections of the "Expanding the Idea" phase of the learning cycles. Using the "Information" sections at that point in the learning cycle puts reading in science in its proper perspective—concepts should be read about by learners in the concrete operational stage after they have been experienced. Reading about a concept before experiencing it does not allow the learners to experience assimiliation and the subsequent disequilibrium and accommodation.

The LSP is but one synthesis of the findings made by the SCIS, SAPA, and the ESS. Those efforts will probably influence the development of elementary school science curricula for many years, and that influence will generally be positive. There are other synthesis efforts[22] available, and no doubt still others will be forthcoming.

[22] Carl F. Berger, Glenn D. Berkheimer, L. E. Lewis, Jr., Harold T. Neuberger, and Elizabeth A. Woods, *Modular Activities Program in Science*, (Grades K-6), Boston, Houghton Mifflin, 1974.

Chapter 9
Evaluating Achievement in Elementary School Science

When evaluation is mentioned in connection with the educational enterprise, different meanings are immediately focused on by different people. To most students evaluation means grades and examination, and that is also certainly one of the meanings teachers focus on. Teachers, however, also think of evaluation in terms of the appropriateness of materials and the overall structure of the course they are teaching with respect to how accurately the particular science they are teaching is portrayed. Not infrequently teachers also think of evaluation as how well the course and its materials fit the particular students they are teaching. That is an extremely fine use of evaluation and one that every teacher should continuously perform.

The most significant use of evaluation in any field is to determine how well what was to be done has been done. Auto mechanics, for example, evaluate their work by asking themselves how well engines run after they finish with them; tailors asks themselves how well garments fit clients; physicians evaluate their efforts by how completely their patients are restored to physical or mental health, and lawyers by how adequately their clients are treated. In all cases, the evaluator has some objective to judge performance by. Mechanics compare the functioning of a newly repaired engine to, perhaps, a new one, and thus make allowances for the materials, that is, the old engines, being worked with. Physicians must judge their performances by the age and initial condition of their patients, and so on. In short, anyone evaluates completed work in terms of what that person set out to do—that is, that person's objectives. The results of that evaluation can be used to judge not only the effectiveness of what has been done, but also to furnish feedback to the persons doing the jobs, which will allow them to adjust the manner in which they discharge their responsibilities.

The foregoing, when applied to teaching, means that teachers have three distinct evaluations to make. They must:

1. Evaluate pupil performance.
2. Evaluate the programs being used.
3. Evaluate their own performances as classroom teachers.

In making these three evaluations, the teacher must, as does any person doing a job, use some evaluative criteria. For teachers, those criteria are the objectives of the field in which they are teaching. The three objectives of science teaching were discussed in Chapter 2. These objectives are to develop in each student:

1. A command of the rational powers.
2. The ability and confidence to inquire.
3. An understanding of the changing nature of the environment in terms of matter, life, energy, and their interactions.

Teachers must translate the content of the particular discipline being taught into evaluative tools that can be used to judge student performance, the programs used, and their own effectiveness in terms of the three general objectives of elementary school science. Any other objectives that might be constructed for a particular content area must lead directly to the three general objectives of science education. Suppose, for example, that the ability to explain the process of energy transfer is listed as an objective for fifth grade science. That is an important objective only if acquiring that ability assists in achieving one or more of the three general objectives. Such an objective would certainly require students to analyze, synthesize (two of the rational powers), and inquire into the relationships and interactions among matter. In judging students, understanding of energy transfer, their abilities to analyze, to synthesize, and to see interactions can be evaluated. However, the information they might use to answer a question might as easily come from rote memory as from their abilities to analyze, to synthesize, and to see relationships *if* the evaluative tool—the questions asked—permit this. Teachers must be able to perform evaluations that distinguish between rote memory and understanding. The latter leads to the achievement of objectives; the former does not.

EVALUATING STUDENTS

The best type of evaluation program to measure achievement in science—or any content area—is one that has been designed by the teachers actually working with the children. No outside evaluator knows the many factors that are influencing the achievement of the students in a teacher's classes. There are, however, some general principles for developing and selecting an evaluation program that may be useful.

The Evaluation Program Should Be Comprehensive

Because all phases of child development are interrelated, the teacher needs information about the social and attitudinal development of pupils as well as their academic progress. All too frequently in the past, evaluation has been confined to that which is most easily measured. Although measurement is an important phase of evaluation, it does not constitute the entire program. Measurement is concerned with the quantitative aspects of pupil progress, whereas evaluation is concerned with both the quantitative and the qualitative aspects. Achievement tests have in the past been too much concerned with recall of isolated bits of information about science. The new elementary school science programs require more emphasis on evaluation instruments and procedures designed to reveal pupil progress in understanding, in concept development, in attitudes, and in behavior.

Some instruments have been designed to measure important attitudinal and behavioral changes. Figure 9–1 is an instrument designed to help the teacher gain understanding of how the students view the science class. How the students perceive the class activities could cause teachers to continue or modify the teaching approach used in the classroom. An instrument like this should be used several times during the year. A teacher can also use this instrument to determine the kinds of activities students like best by asking them to cross out the activity they like least and encircle the one they like best, or rate the activities in the order they like them from best to least. Figure 9–2 can be used to help the teacher determine how the pupils feel about various activities. Collecting this information on the activities over a period of time enables the teacher to isolate those that are

Figure 9–1   "Our Science Class." Children are asked to encircle the picture that best shows what might go on in science class.

SOURCE: Science Curriculum Improvement Study, *Life Cycles Evaluation Supplement,* "Our Science Classes," © 1971, The Regents of the University of California, Berkeley, p. 13.

liked best by the children—those are probably the most productive.

Other attitudinal and behavioral evaluations can be made by direct observation by the teacher. The Science Curriculum Improvement Study group has identified, for purposes of evaluation, four attitude areas that are a part of scientific literacy, as well as various observable behaviors that are associated with these four areas. These

Figure 9–2 "Faces." The first time the students are asked to respond on the "Faces" pages, they are invited to describe the faces. The fact that the answer page has three rows of faces is pointed out. Each row is used to answer one question. By circling one face in each row, the students indicate how they feel about three activities.

SOURCE: Science Curriculum Improvement Study, *Life Cycles Evaluation Supplement*, "Faces," © 1971, The Regents of the University of California, Berkeley.

attitude areas and observable behaviors are as follows:[1]

1. *Curiosity.* Children who pay particular attention to an object or event and spontaneously wish to learn more about it are being curious. They may give evidence of curiosity by:

     Using several senses to explore organisms and materials.

     Asking questions about objects and events.

     Showing interest in the outcomes of experiments.

2. *Inventiveness.* Children who generate new ideas are being inventive. These children exhibit original thinking in their interpretations. They may give evidence of inventiveness through verbal statements or actions by:

     Using equipment in unusual and constructive ways.

     Suggesting new experiments.

     Describing novel conclusions from their observations.

[1] Science Curriculum Improvement Study, *Environments Evaluation Supplement,* "Attitudes in Science," © 1973, The Regents of the University of California, Berkeley.

3. *Critical thinking.* Children who can provide sound reasons for their suggestions, conclusions, and predictions are thinking critically. They may exhibit critical thinking by:

Using evidence to justify their conclusions.

Predicting the outcome of untried experiments.

Justifying their predictions in terms of past experience.

Changing their ideas in response to evidence or logical reasons.

Pointing out contradictions in reports by their classmates.

Investigating the effects of selected variables.

Solving brain teasers and providing explanations.

4. *Persistence.* Children who maintain an active interest in a problem or event for a longer period than their classmates are being persistent. They are not easily distracted from their activity. They may give evidence of persistence by:

Continuing to investigate materials after their novelty has worn off.

Repeating an experiment in spite of apparent failure.

Completing an activity even though their classmates have finished earlier.

Written Work in Pupil Evaluation

Another common student evaluation practice that can be used by teachers in upper elementary school, if done correctly, is written work that is "handed in." The teacher, in assigning such work makes the assumption (often valid) that by performing the assigned task the student will move closer to achieving the course objectives. Written work cannot be justified on any other basis. Requiring students to do written "busywork" is beneath comment, and the same is true for work assigned as a disciplinary measure. When teachers assign extra experiments to do or questions to answer as punishment, they are using the content vehicle that can lead students to achieve the objectives of science education in a manner that will eventually convince them that the principal purpose of the content is to discipline their social behavior. This is hardly a student attitude that will lead to achieving the ability and confidence to inquire.

Work that is given to the teacher for evaluation without the student being present, and written examinations, comprise the majority of the evaluation category of written work. From our frame of reference, daily written assignments and examinations must (and do) reflect the teaching and learning philosophies of the teacher. If teachers are leading students to learn by inquiry, they must evaluate the ability of the students to inquire and utilize the results of that inquiry. There is probably no action of teachers which reflects these basic beliefs about teaching and learning as accurately as the written work assigned to their classes. If teachers purport to believe in inquiry and evaluate students on their abilities to accumulate and memorize factual detail, no one, *most of all the students,* will take them seriously. Written work—whether out-of-class assignments, reports of experiments, investigation, or both, or examinations—which is intended to evaluate the results of an inquiry-centered learning experience, must reflect such characteristics of inquiry. *That is, the written work must require the learner to classify, analyze, evaluate, interpret, synthesize, predict, and generalize.*

The following three examples show how students must be given written assignments which question them exactly as they have been taught.

1. The students have gathered data which led them to the concept that sound is carried by a medium. They are asked to respond to the following question in writing.[2]

   A bell is placed in a big jar. The air is pumped out of the jar. The bell rings. What is happening?

   To answer the question the students must use the data they received from their experiments. Those data told them that a medium was necessary to carry sound. Since no air is present, there will be no sound.

2. The students have taken many different kinds of measurements. They have found that the greater the number of measurements taken by two or more persons, the greater the variations in those measurements will be. Here is the question they are asked to respond to in writing.[3]

   Suppose ten members of your class each measured the length of a chalkboard with a ruler 10 cm long. Ten other members of your class each measured the same chalkboard with a meter stick. Which group's data do you think would vary the most? Explain why you think so.

   The student who has learned the concept that an increased number of measurements increases the variation in reported measurements will have no trouble with this question.

[2] John W. Renner, Don G Stafford, and Vivian Jensen Coulter, *Models,* Beverly Hills, California: Benziger Bruce & Glencoe, and New York: Macmillan, 1977, p. 160.
[3] John W. Renner, Don G. Stafford, and Vivian Jensen Coulter, *Variation,* Beverly Hills, California: Benziger Bruce & Glencoe, and New York: Macmillan, 1977, p. 163.

3. An extensive investigation of how to hook together dry cells, wires, and flashlight bulbs has first been completed. Every student in the class has worked with the materials. They then have this question put to them.[4]

How must two dry cells be placed together in order to light a bulb?

The question is simple, direct and can be answered from evidence the students found during their investigation.

Another type of written problem which is profitable in evaluating student achievement is shown in Figure 9–3. Notice that four separate questions are asked and that all the data needed to answer them are given in the problem if the student understands the necessary processes. This assignment measures the ability to use those processes.

Imagine that you are one of thirty-five students who were each given a mimosa leaf.

←— leaflets

You were asked to count the leaflets on each leaf and record the number on the chalkboard at the front of the room. Here are the 35 values:

18, 22, 16, 20, 24, 26, 20, 18, 18,
16, 20, 22, 21, 18, 20, 20, 18, 22,
26, 16, 18, 20, 18, 18, 20, 22, 16,
14, 18, 20, 16, 18, 18, 22, 18.

1. State some general patterns from the data.
2. Organize the data into a histogram or some other classification scheme.
3. What predictions about mimosa leaves could you make based on the patterns you have isolated?
4. How would you test your predictions?

Figure 9–3   All the data needed to answer the four questions are contained in the problem if the student understands the necessary processes. This assignment measures the ability to use those processes.

There are some general criteria that we have found useful in preparing materials which can be used with students to evaluate their achievement from their written responses.

[4] John W. Renner, Don G. Stafford, and Vivian Jensen Coulter, *Systems,* Beverly Hills, California: Benziger Bruce & Glencoe, and New York: Macmillan, 1977, p. 127.

1. *Does the written work assigned allow—in fact, encourage—the learner to utilize the results of previous investigation?*

One of the basic axioms of learning is that we learn many "things" in terms of what we already know. Written work can provide the learners the opportunity to relate what they are presently doing to what they have already done; this experience can perhaps disequilibrate them and enlarge their concept of the environment. If students are expected to relate (synthesize) the results of two investigations, they should be reminded of the past investigation; that is, you are not evaluating their ability to remember the previous results.

2. *Does the written work lead the learner toward discovering a new investigation that needs to be done?*

Written work that satisfies this criterion is open ended (divergent); anything less is convergent. Summaries are convergent and a "list-the-properties" type of question is also convergent. Occasionally you need to use those kinds of questions, just to sharply focus the attention of the student upon a specific. Do not delude yourself that any rational powers are being developed (except perhaps recall) while you are focusing the attention of the class. But when the learners see the next step that needs to be taken, they are being led in a divergent path. That path will encourage them to enlarge their scope of content understanding and provide them a natural opportunity to develop their rational powers.

3. *Does the required written work provide the learners the opportunity to make their own interpretations of "things" as they see them; that is, are they provided an opportunity to use their imaginations?*

There is no doubt that use of the imagination is at the heart of creative thinking and is the natural outgrowth of the use by the learner of analysis, evaluation, synthesis, and the other rational powers. We believe, however, that if students are not provided the opportunity *and encouraged* to utilize the rational power of imagination they will most likely not make the trip. There is much evidence that suggests that the normal educational establishment does not encourage such trips.[5] Written work can provide part of the stimulus necessary to start the imagination and also provide teachers with a measure of how the activities of their classes are changing that behavior. Consider this exercise.

One of man's qualities, or attributes, which sets him apart from other living creatures is strong hands with opposable thumbs—that is, the thumb can push against the fingers of the same hand.

[5] See Charles E. Silberman, *Crisis in the Classroom: The Remaking in American Education,* New York: Random House, 1970.

1. What kinds of things does this allow man to do better than other animals?
2. List a special attribute of some other animal that allows him to do things that man cannot do as well.
3. Can you think of a special attribute which some animal has that makes him especially suited to live at certain places on the earth?

4. *Does written work allow the learners to work at their own levels rather than at some level that is nebulous to them?*

This evaluative criterion needs to be consciously applied by teachers to their *expectations* of the student. If permitted, students will work at their level and, in most cases, make a conscious effort to produce their best work. If the teacher consistently tells the learners that their written efforts are not acceptable, that written work is harmful. In Chapter 3 the developmental levels concept of Piaget was introduced. Knowing where your students stand in the developmental scheme will give you a frame of reference for what you can expect from them. Do not expect a learner in the concrete operational stage to do formal operational work.

Written work provides teachers the opportunity to watch the intellectual levels of students grow, but they must evaluate written work from a level of proper expectations and not from some absolute standard that reflects content mastery (often memorization).

· **Preparing and Scoring Written Work.** You have no doubt concluded that preparing written work such as that suggested by the foregoing five criteria can be an exacting task. Nor will the questions and exercises you prepare necessarily be exactly on target the first time you use them. If you evaluate the response of the pupil, you will find much guidance there to assist you in increasing the quality of written exercises. The length of sentences used, the language employed, and the specific details given and asked for are all factors that influence the quality of your evaluative instruments.

The phrase "written work" has been used here without reference to whether the exercise was a developmental exercise used in a daily class situation or in an examination. When examinations are focused on, there are many types of questions which can be used. True and false, multiple choice, matching, and essay questions are the major types of examination questions generally used. There are many specific factors which, if properly utilized, will increase the quality, validity, and educational soundness of your examination questions. Discussing those specific factors is not within the scope of this book. Many excellent books have been written on test construction. You are urged to consult such a reference.

If the essay-type question is utilized either as a test item or in a daily class situation, and employs the five criteria discussed here, not many such questions are necessary to gain an impression of how the student is growing intellectually. We believe that using only a few such questions frequently provides a better overview of the students' progress than does giving a long list of such questions at one time. When learners are dealing with only a few questions, they do not feel the pressure of hurrying through one in order to respond to all of the questions and finish the written work. Since this procedure limits the samples of the course which can be evaluated, the questions must be carefully constructed in order to determine the progress the learner is making toward the objective of the course and science education generally.

When completely objective-type written work is used, scoring is no problem—the student's response is either right or wrong. Only in the teacher-and-student dialogue about the answer can the teacher gain an insight into the logic that went into selecting the response that was made. It is for the foregoing reason that we do not feel that the evaluation of a student's progress should be made *only* on the basis of objective written work. Carefully constructed objective examinations that adhere to the previously given four criteria have a place in evaluation, but need to be used in conjunction with (though not necessarily at the same time as) essay-type written work. Such written work can be from a daily class situation or an examination. Essay-type written work allows the teacher to catch and evaluate the logic that went into the student's response. In scoring such written work, the only defensible criterion to use is the logic and inductive inference the student used. If the answer is given the greatest share of the weight in determining the student's performance, the teacher has contradicted the basic tenet of inquiry: the student has been judged on some predetermined absolute standard and not on the student's ability to make an inductive inference. If teachers are guilty of this breach of inquiry, the pupils in their classes will soon learn that getting the approved answer is the important thing. If that happens, leading learners to achieve the objectives of science education will become an impossibility.

Semiformal Pupil Interview in Evaluation

The term *semiformal* is used to distinguish between this type of evaluation and the informal interview that is conducted on a day-to-day basis as the teacher interacts with individuals or small groups in a class during a regular activity. During the semiformal interview, the teacher should have some predetermined tasks and questions with which the pupil interacts. This type of evaluation cannot be done very often for each pupil, but it can provide the teacher and pupil very valuable insight concerning the pupil's understanding of concepts or mastery of process skills.

Following is an example of an interview instrument that could be used to evaluate process skills.

Process Definitions[6]

The following definitions have been constructed to identify the processes which the tasks have been designed to assess. The reader must understand that each definition is specific to the process as it is used in this instrument.

• **Observing.** The process through which information is obtained, either directly or indirectly, with the intent of understanding more about an object or situation. This process is based on the utilization of the five senses—seeing, touching, hearing, smelling, and tasting, either partially or in totality in any specific situation.

• **Classifying.** The process of mentally or physically placing objects in groups which have systematic relationships. These relationships can occur among the objects of a specific group and among or between groups.

• **Measuring.** The process of obtaining the dimensions of an object by comparing the object to a standard unit. Any selected unit can serve as this standard.

• **Experimenting.** The process of recognizing and controlling variables while doing something in an attempt to solve a problem. The problem can be externally designed and presented to the experimenter or the problem can be structured internally by the experimenter.

• **Interpreting.** The process of searching for a meaningful understanding in accumulated data with the intent of utilizing the understanding in answering questions relative to the data.

[6] The sample questions here—one for each process—were taken from M. C. Weber, "The Influence of the Science Curriculum Improvement Study on the Learner's Operational Utilization of Science Processes." Unpublished doctoral dissertation, University of Oklahoma, 1971, pp. 64–76. The complete instrument contains 34 factors upon which to evaluate the interviewer.

• Predicting. The process of foretelling the behavior of an event from the available data which are currently at hand.

PROCESS—OBSERVING

TASK 1: NUMBERS 1–0 AND 2–0

Materials   A piece of clear, transparent plastic 8½ × 5¼ inches.

Administrative Procedure   Give the plastic to the child.

Instructions to the Child   Describe this object.

Score 1–0   Place a check in the acceptable[7] column if eight or more properties are given.

PROCESS—CLASSIFYING

TASK 4: NUMBERS 7–C AND 8–C

Materials   A collection of the following objects: two nails, one plastic spoon, 4 × 4 inch piece of aluminum foil, four marbles, one thumb tack, one wooden pencil, one index card (3 × 5 inches).

Administrative Procedure   Give the collection of objects to the child.

Instructions to the Child   Place these objects in groups so that the objects in each group are alike in some way and tell how they are alike.

Score: 7–C   Place a check in the acceptable column if the child places all the objects in logical groups.

Score: 8–C   Place a check in the acceptable column if the child properly identifies the characteristic of each group.

PROCESS—MEASURING

TASK 6: NUMBERS 11–M AND 12–M

Materials   A collection of the following: a strip of paper two inches by one-half inch, a marble, a nail, a button and twelve beans, and a 3 × 5 inch card. (No ruler.)

---

[7] Dr. Weber suggests that the test administrator score each response as acceptable or unacceptable. He used a sheet that listed 34 divisions, with space to check acceptable or unacceptable for each division.

Administrative Procedure Give the collection to the child. After he examines them, give him the 3 × 5 card.

Instructions to the Child Measure the length of this card.

Score: 11–M Place a check in the acceptable column if the child attempts to use any of the objects to measure the card's length.

Score: 12–M Place a check in the acceptable column if the child actually gives a measurement. Example—3½ nails long.

PROCESS—EXPERIMENTING

TASK 9: NUMBERS 17–E AND 18–E

Materials Solutions of salt water (A), water with phenolphthalein (B), and distilled water (C). The following dry powders: lead nitrate (1), calcium oxide (2), and sodium chloride (3). Straws to serve as droppers and scoops. Wax paper on which to mix. Powder papers and small paper cups to hold the liquids.

Administrative Procedure The solutions and the powders must be prepared before the test administration. Give the child about 25 milliliters of each solution and 5 grams of each powder. Also, a sheet of wax paper should be given for the mixing. The straws, cups, and powder papers should be discarded after each child is tested. In placing the materials before the child, make it a point not to order them (i.e., 1, 2, and 3 or A, B, and C).

Instructions to the Child A red color will be formed when one of these liquids and one of these powders are mixed. Find which two will give the color.

Score: 17–E Place a check in the acceptable column if the child approaches the task in a systematic manner, i.e., put powder 1 in liquid A, B, C, et cetera.

Score: 18–E Place a check in the acceptable column if the child finds powder 2 and liquid B will give the red color.

PROCESS—INTERPRETING

TASK 12: NUMBERS 23–I AND 24–I

Materials Four microscope slides and four water solutions of sodium chloride for each child.

Administrative Procedure The day before the task, the four slides must be prepared to insure the water will be evaporated.

Slide	Liquid	Water	Sodium Chloride
A	A	250 milliliters	1 teaspoonful
B	B	250 milliliters	5 teaspoonsful
C	C	250 milliliters	3 teaspoonsful
D	D	250 milliliters	10 teaspoonsful

Instructions to the Child These liquids were made by putting salt in water. Each bottle has a different amount of salt. These glass slides were prepared by placing a drop of liquid on the glass. The letter on the glass slide tells which bottle of liquid it came from. Which liquid has the most salt in it?

Score: 23–I Place a check in the acceptable column if the child attempts to correlate the amount of salt on the slide with the liquids.

Score: 24–I Place a check in the acceptable column if the child determines liquid D has the most salt.

PROCESS—PREDICTING

TASK 15: NUMBERS 29–P AND 30–P

Materials A rubber band, a small piece of stiff wire, a support stand, a ruler, graph paper, and four washers.

Administrative Procedure Give the materials to the child.

Instructions to the Child You have four washers here. How far will eight washers stretch this rubber band? I will ask you to tell how you found out.

Score: 29–P Place a check in the acceptable column if the child determines how far the four washers will stretch the rubber band.

Score: 30–P Place a check in the acceptable column if the child gives an answer for the stretch of eight washers as based on his data.

Instructions to the Child How did you find out?

Evaluation of Pupil Progress Should Be Continuous

Too frequently in the past, evaluation of student progress has been regarded as something that happens after students have completed a given science assignment or project—as something that takes place at stated intervals, such as the end of a 6-week period. It is obvious that evaluation of the type we have been discussing must be viewed as a continuing activity that is an integral part of the teaching-learning process rather than as an aftermath. To make a continuous evaluation meaningful, records must be maintained that will allow not only the teacher but the child and parent to understand what progress is being made. Examples of such records are graphs, diaries, checklists, individual and group profiles, teacher-pupil conferences, written work, and formal and informal observations of student behavior.

Evaluation of Pupil Progress Should Be a Cooperative Process

Learning to evaluate progress toward clearly defined goals is a vital phase of a child's education. Failure to develop in children both the desire and the ability to share in the evaluation of their own progress has unfortunate consequences. Evaluation can become a form of threat or coercion, and the temptation to try to deceive the teacher by cheating on examinations is great.

On the other hand, cooperative evaluation is rewarding to the individual pupil because it provides a means of gaining insight into strengths and weaknesses and indicates what steps need to be taken to accomplish the goals being pursued.

To use the evaluative procedures we have suggested, your grade book must be a looseleaf notebook. Perhaps the first page will be a class profile sheet that allows you to see at a glance how the class is progressing toward the goals you established. Following this page in some order will be the individual pupil records. Each pupil might have profile sheets indicating progress in concept, process, and attitude objectives. The entries on the sheets will come from informal observation, semiformal interview sessions, written work including examinations, and pencil and paper instruments designed to measure perception of the classroom activity or activity-type preference.

Is this type of evaluation subjective? Definitely! But who is better qualified to make a subjective evaluation than the teacher who is with the class over a long period of time and knows not only the children but the objectives being pursued. Teachers, as professionals, must be willing to rely to a great degree on subjective evaluation, and must have collected evidence on which to base their judgments.

Standardized Achievement Tests

Many school systems rely heavily on end-of-year standardized achievement tests to determine how well the pupils have learned science. An achievement test might be useful if, and only if, the test measures achievement of the objectives you were trying to accomplish. The achievement test can at best do only a very limited job of determining overall achievement—and, if the achievement test does not measure what you were trying to achieve, it is only an expensive exercise.

EVALUATING ELEMENTARY SCHOOL SCIENCE CURRICULA

Today's elementary schools may lack many of the features, facilities, and opportunities the modern educator would like to see in them, but after reading Chapter 8, you will no doubt agree that they do *not* lack science curricula to select from. But how does one know which curriculum to select? The answer to the foregoing question is that it depends on the purposes for which a particular subject is taught.

As we have stated previously, we believe that elementary school science should permit and encourage every child to develop:

1. The ability and confidence to inquire.
2. A command of the ten rational powers.
3. An understanding of the changing nature of the environment in terms of matter, life, energy, and their interactions.

What follows is a set of criteria which can be specifically used to evaluate an elementary school science curriculum to determine whether or not it can lead children to achieve the foregoing purposes.

Before using the criteria, there are a few basic ground rules which we feel are important enough to explain. You will observe that each criterion is written in the form of a question which must be answered "Yes," "No," or "Information to determine not available." This technique was used deliberately because we believe that any evaluation instrument should yield definite information. The criteria are mutually independent; just because one is answered negatively does not invalidate all the other criteria. Furthermore, your evaluation does not need to achieve only affirmative answers to provide information that can be used to allow you to make science-curriculum decisions.

1. *Does the unit emphasize the processes of science as well as the information acquired?*
Teach science as science is, and science is process.

2. *Are the students actively involved?*
a. Do the pupils do their own investigations?
b. Do the pupils gather their own data?
c. Are the pupils encouraged to perform experiments on their own?

    d. Are pupils led to form hypotheses?

    e. Is the primary responsibility for data interpretation and evaluation left to the pupils?

    3. *Do the learning activities allow use and potential development of the rational powers?*

    The central purpose of American education, as stated by the Educational Policies Commission in 1961, is to develop the ten rational powers, which the Commission described as "the essence of the ability to think."[8] The learning activities of the program under consideration should include activities in which the use and development of these powers is demanded. In looking through the programs, examples of these activities should be apparent; classification of bottle caps, buttons, seeds, animals or plants should be required. There should be evidence of the students being called upon to imagine, experiment, synthesize hypotheses, and analyze and evaluate the data the experiments produce. Also, instances of students comparing things such as animals, rocks, or any other variety of materials or data should be apparent. Students should be encouraged to generalize from their classroom experiences and experiments to out-of-class experience in order to discover the important relationships.

    Because of the nature of the processes of science if you are able to answer "Yes" to question number one, in most cases, you will be impelled to answer "Yes" to question number three.

    4. *Does the program fit the developmental level of the child?*

    The developmental level concept based on Jean Piaget's model of learning has been thoroughly discussed in Chapter 3.

    5. *Is the material presented in learning cycles or can it be arranged in learning cycles to be taught?*

    Learning begins with assimilation and structures are built or rebuilt through accommodation. Data must be gathered, ideas must be identified, and ideas are expanded during assimilation and accommodation. In other words, the learning cycle is used.

    6. *Does the unit contain a variety of "materials" which appear to interest the child?*

    Children should be given *concrete* objects which they can handle and experiment with. These materials allow the children to be involved as they analyze, compare, and otherwise develop their rational thinking.

---

[8] Educational Policies Commission, *The Central Purpose of American Education,* Washington, D.C.: NEA, 1961, p. 5. (See Appendix C.)

Figure 9–4 Much valuable evaluation can be made in the semiformal pupil interview.

7. *Does the unit contain a variety of "activities" which appear to interest the child?*

Activities that interest the child will greatly increase the frequency and consistency with which his needs are met as he participates in the learning experience (read → as "lead(s) to").

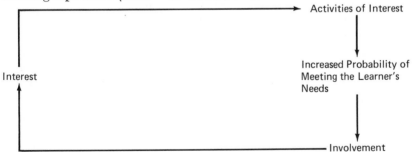

8. *Do the teachers' guides explain purpose and methodology?*

The nature of any guide is that it provides a skeletal outline of *what* is to be achieved and *how* those achievements are to be accomplished. A useful guide would include stated objectives with sample exercises discusssed and related activities given. Consequently, a useful teacher's guide must explain the what (purpose) and the how (meth-

287

Figure 9–5 Evaluation is a cooperative process.

odology). In other words, the guide should demonstrate how to use the learning cycle.

9. *Does the entire program have a conceptual framework?*

A conceptual framework is an expandable reference model (i.e., organizational scheme) which allows the learner to place and evaluate new information. We believe that a science program with a conceptual framework has a dimension that one lacking a conceptual framework does not have. That dimension adds depth to the program and allows the child to develop a structure in which to categorize ideas, concepts, and experiences. A conceptual framework gives direction to the ideas taught in the program and certainly gives the teacher added confidence in the materials and methods being used. In the *Learning Science Program*, for example, the conceptual structure of the program is composed of the concepts of matter, energy, the ecosystem, and human physiology.

10. *Does the program reflect the structure of the discipline?*

So many programs in the past and even today fall far short of the real goal of science education, which is to teach science. Remember that the data in Chapter 1 led to the generalization that science is the quest for knowledge, not the knowledge itself. Science, therefore, can and should be taught to help students think, solve problems, and become confident, but for a program to be truly successful it must remain true to the discipline. In teaching the quest for knowledge content identifiable as natural science must be used and the concepts must be the underlying concepts of the field, not trivial items of passing interest upon which so much of certain science textbooks are based.

11. *Are the concepts each unit purports to develop clearly stated?*

Since the teacher must have definite objectives in mind when selecting a science program, clear statements of the concepts of each unit will facilitate the selection process. In the teaching process, having the concepts of each unit clearly stated will allow the teacher to set goals and arrange priorities in order to utilize the unit to lead children to develop the basic concepts of the unit.

12. *Does the program encourage the teacher to accept all sincere student answers as valuable?*

A student's answer is always valuable even if that answer isn't "correct." That incorrect answer may lead to more questions and the teacher can guide (by questioning or by the children experimenting) the students to conclusions supported by evidence. In this way children learn by doing. The material provided for the teacher should give clues for questioning and suggestions for leading the children to experimenting rather than outlining specific facts to be mastered.

13. *Is the unit flexible enough to be adapted to the needs and interests of a particular class?*

The unit should allow rearrangement, expansion, condensation, tangent activities, and individual projects. Teachers should be encouraged to use their discretion in order to create the most dynamic learning situations and experiences for each individual child and the distinct (unique) class being taught. If the units are structured too formally or rigidly to allow them to maintain their effectiveness after necessary alterations are made, then they are not flexible enough to be adapted.

14. *Can a child with limited reading ability succeed in the program?*

Reading is extremely important, but achievement in science should not be dependent upon it.

15. *Are the teaching and resource materials carefully integrated into the program?*

If films, slides, or recordings are to be used with a lesson, the teacher needs to know what purpose these materials serve. Are they included to demonstrate something that can't be done by the class, or would be difficult to do successfully? Is it something that is needed at a particular time to make the lesson meaningful, or to allow the class to proceed with better understanding? Is the time that the material should be used for maximum effectiveness specified, or are the materials to be used at any convenient time? If the material has value, then there is a best time for it to be used, and the teacher needs to know when that time is.

16. *Is a format provided which allows the teacher to set up and teach each unit smoothly?*

17. *Is the cost, construction, mobility, durability, and availability of materials reasonable and practical?*

Whether or not the cost of a science program is reasonable and practical will be determined largely by the ability and willingness of the school to finance it. If the program requires the use of consumable items such as chemicals, seeds, and special solutions, their cost and availability must be considered. If the items are not common ones that the students can bring from home or that can be obtained locally, the price of the program is affected. With any elementary program the teacher, with a minimum of difficulty, should be able to handle and move from place to place the materials that will be used.

Do not attempt to produce some numerical score using the above criteria (although that could be done). Rather, after you have used the criteria on a particular science program, look at *which* of the criteria you have answered positively and which negatively. Then consult the purposes you have stated for teaching science. Only when you compare *your* purposes and the answers *you* gave to each criterion while evaluating a particular program will you know which "No" and "Yes" answers are most important to *you*. No one can evaluate a curriculum for you; that's your job. The foregoing criteria can help you focus your attention on those aspects of a curriculum that are important to you.

EVALUATING TEACHERS

There is probably no more inexact evaluation that can be made than that of teacher effectiveness. The literature of education contains the reports of many studies that have attempted to assess the value of teacher behavior in a classroom. Those studies will not be reviewed here, but if you are interested you are urged to investigate the literature. We believe that *teacher performance in the classroom should be evaluated in terms of what is done to further the accomplishment of the objectives of science education.* In other words, what specific, overt behaviors will be used by teachers who are using inquiry?

1. *They listen to the students.*

An inquiry-centered teacher listens to what the students have to say about an investigation or problem and utilizes their contributions in carrying the classroom activities forward. Utilizing the learner's contributions to the problem being considered establishes rapport, but it does much more; it tells the students that they, as well as the teacher, have a responsibility in carrying out the learning activities. A teacher who listens tells the learners that what they have to say is a valuable part of the investigation being conducted; this teacher behavior greatly contributes to developing student confidence to inquire.

2. *They accept the results which the student gets from an investigation.*

Too many times teachers will accept only experimental results that constitute the "right" answers. If a learner has honestly done an experiment and honestly contributes results to the class discussion, the teacher has the responsibility of accepting those results. What do you do if the results are completely unacceptable to science? Suggest other investigations that represent different ways of solving the same problem. The second investigation will probably produce results contradictory to the first. Now the students must make a decision regarding which set of results they will accept, and they will probably decide that one of the investigations (perhaps both) must be done again. If you had rejected their first set of results, the students would have simply tried to outguess you as to what results you would accept.

3. *An inquiry-centered teacher's questions will focus the students' attention on specific points in the investigation.*

Of extreme importance is the fact that questions are asked to find out what the students are thinking. Too many questions asked by teachers are simply "Can-you-guess-what-I'm-thinking" type questions. When the learners give honest replies, they must be accepted, and if those responses could lead them astray, other questions that will demand or allow them to refocus their attention should be asked.

4. *They are guides for students during an investigation.*

Asking questions, providing clues to those students either frustrated or on dead center, recommending reference books to consult and other investigations to perform, suggesting alternate ways of thinking about a problem, challenging results, and providing materials needed are all part of being a guide.

5. *More concern is shown for the type and quality of investigations that are done than with the number completed during a school year.*

The "we-must-finish-the-book" attitude has no place in a classroom that is concerned with achieving the objectives of science education.

6. *A teacher who believes that learning occurs by student involvement will utilize the full learning cycle.*

Many teachers who encounter the learning cycle will immediately remark that they allow students to gather information from many sources, provide the students with textbooks that give them information, and tell them much information. They conclude that they are using the learning cycle, and so they are—*partly.* They are no doubt providing their students with excellent opportunities to gather data about the area in which they are working. But for many teachers the learning cycle stops right there. The accumulated information has become their goal. They do not engage in, nor do they permit or encourage their students to engage in forming any new ideas from the information. Furthermore, the idea of sending students into a laboratory situation to expand newly required ideas is foreign to them. Teachers who use inquiry in an incomplete way also use the laboratory in an incomplete way. They send students to the laboratory to accumulate information—that is, to gather more data. We believe that much of what today is called science teaching is only the gathering of data, and that alone, as important as it is, will not lead students to achieve the objectives of science education. Even the most traditional of teachers, however, has taken the first step toward using the learning cycle (inquiry); they have allowed students to explore a given problem or area of science. When all teachers utilize the full sequence of gathering data, getting the idea and expanding the idea, science teaching will have begun to lead students toward achieving the goals of science education and the general goal of all education—the development of the ability to think.

Chapter 10
The Future

When we titled this chapter "The Future" we had in mind the work that still lies ahead of us in making science teaching truly scientific and intellectually centered, rather than an exercise in transmitting a few facts about science, a lot of facts about technology, and a few disconnected, and in many cases erroneous, tales about the history of science. We feel that science teaching has a good start. For the next few pages we will comment upon those emerging ideas which we believe will represent the most fruitful ones to concentrate on during the ensuing years. As you read the next few pages bear in mind that we are not stating any answers—just questions and hypotheses.

PIAGET AND SCIENCE TEACHING

The results, and the interpretation of those results, of the researches of Jean Piaget have a great deal to say to the science teacher which we do not feel has yet been heard by that group. Pupils in the elementary school are entering into the state of concrete operations, during which logical operations must deal with immediate, present reality.

Data from our research clearly show that students remain in the concrete operational stage for some time.

During 1976, 422 students in grade ten, 529 in grade eleven, and 362 in grade twelve—a total of 1313—were interviewed using the tasks shown in Appendix D. Only 22 percent of those students could be classified as reasoning at the formal operational level. Thirty-nine percent reasoned *only* at the concrete operational level and 39 percent reasoned mostly at the concrete level but *occasionally* showed evidence of reasoning at the formal level.

When those data are employed by secondary schools to select or build curricula, or both, those schools have no choice except to assume that an entire class must be treated as though they function on the concrete operational level. Furthermore, the data presented in Chapter 8 shows that when concrete teaching procedures are employed with groups of mixed formal and concrete thinkers,[1] concrete teaching produces the better results in content achievement, intellectual development and shifts in I.Q.

With the exception of a few sixth grade students who have just barely begun to enter the formal reasoning period—about 10 percent— children in the elementary school are in the concrete operational stage. All elementary school classes, therefore, should be taught only with concrete instructional procedures.

Think about some of the topics that are introduced in many elementary school science courses in the primary grades. We refer to such topics as the atom, the solar system, conservation of mass and energy, and genetics. Most assuredly each of the foregoing topics represents a hypothetical proposition—the essence of formal reasoning. In fact much of what is today presented in conventional elementary school science could be characterized as highly abstract hypothetical propositions. Indeed, these topics are too abstract for most of today's secondary school students to deal with effectively, with understanding. At one time, we were tempted to think, "What a fortunate circumstance;" students were, according to Piaget's first data, entering the formal operational stage by age 11 and were quite well advanced by 15 years of age. This meant that science that deals with hypothetical propositions and quite abstract concepts could be dealt with in upper elementary and junior high school. We no longer believe, however, that even the majority of secondary school students are in the formal operational stage.

Our own research has shown us that when you present junior high school students with two identically sized and shaped cylinders of

[1] The student groups used in that research contained approximately 15 percent formal operational thinkers.

different weights, the majority of them believe the heavier one will push a water level up more than the lighter one (conservation of volume). When secondary school students in grades 7 through 12 are given a simple pendulum to experiment with, well over 70 percent of them cannot separate the variables of weight and length and then exclude weight as a relevant factor to the pendulum's motion. If they cannot think about their thinking to a degree that will let them solve such problems as the foregoing, how can we expect them to separate one theory from another and exclude one in favor of the other, or understand the relationships between laws, theories, and facts? How can we expect such students to make mental-operational models to explain regularities in nature?

Quite evidently the presence of concrete thought in the secondary school is of concern to us. That concern led us to investigate the reasoning levels of college freshmen. Our sample of seven colleges included junior colleges through universities that granted the doctorate. The data we collected demonstrated that 50 percent of entering college freshmen reason concretely; the sample was comprised of 185 students. We have also found that of 77 college juniors, 30 of them—40 percent—would have to be classed as using concrete operational reasoning patterns.

The college-level data are introduced here to demonstrate that the problem of concrete reasoning is not confined to any particular grade level. There is no educational level, from kindergarten through at least the first three years of college that can make the assumption that all the students being taught are at the formal operational stage and, therefore, that only the abstract mental models of the discipline of science need to be considered. Concrete experience for such a group, however, would augment the understandings developed through the abstractions.

Figure 5–1 in Chapter 5 demonstrates that students in the concrete operational stage of reasoning do not succeed with formal operational concepts. Our hope is that curriculum planners will become cognizant of that fact. That cognizance will require that the curriculum planners become thoroughly informed regarding the essential differences between concrete and formal thought. Understanding those differences will require that content be carefully examined to ascertain which science concepts are appropriate for which age groups.

At present, most school systems have three disconnected levels of science—elementary, intermediate, and senior high school—with little if any attempt or desire on the part of the teachers at the three levels to participate in the overall planning of the total science program. Science coordinators have helped the situation somewhat, but there is a long road ahead before a truly coordinated K-12 program emerges.

As a result of the attempts of science teachers to coordinate a K-12 science program, the need to establish specific objectives for each level will arise. One such objective for elementary school science could and should be to actuate the beginning level of hypothetical thinking (formal operations) by the end of the elementary school program. The successful completion of the conservation-of-volume task usually signals the *very early* beginnings of formal thought. Research needs to be conducted in the near future to determine just what kinds of experiences are needed in elementary school—experiences which our research indicates that pupils are not getting now—to actuate the level of formal operations. The formal operational level of thinking could be nourished by the intermediate and junior high school science programs and used in the senior high school program to make science and other programs meaningful. Other specific objectives for each level of the K-12 science program will arise naturally in the planning when the Piaget levels concept is used.

TEACHING METHODS AND INQUIRY

The teaching structure that has been presented to you in this book is based on the "Gathering Data," "Getting the Idea," and "Expanding the Idea" sequence—the learning cycle. *The learning cycle has been presented as inquiry*, and inquiry has been presented not as *a* method for science teaching but as *the* method. Certain procedures or techniques such as discussion, questioning, demonstration, and even short lectures in upper elementary education, have a definite place in the teaching method. We take the position, however, that everything that is learned is learned through the learning cycle. The aforementioned techniques are simply employed as a part of one of the three phases of the learning cycle. A short lecture, for example, can be used effectively in setting the stage for "Gathering Data" and is the principal technique for "Getting the Idea." During and following the "Gathering Data" phase and during the "Expanding the Idea" phase the teacher-student or small group discussions and questioning are especially fruitful. Demonstrations can be used effectively during the "Getting the Idea" and "Expanding the Idea" phases. One must keep in mind, however, that lecture, demonstration, questioning, discussion, and others such procedures are only techniques that enable one or all three phases of the learning cycle to move forward.

We predict that in the future all science teachers will come to look at teaching and inquiry as synonyms, and when they do, then the methods-phases-techniques concept will make sense to them. When that happens science education can begin to make its maximum and natural contribution to the central role of the school, namely the development of the ability to think.

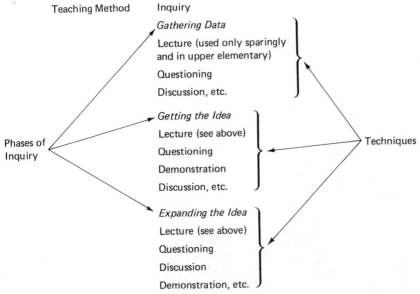

Teaching Method Inquiry

Gathering Data

Lecture (used only sparingly and in upper elementary)

Questioning

Discussion, etc.

Getting the Idea

Lecture (see above)

Questioning

Demonstration

Discussion, etc.

Expanding the Idea

Lecture (see above)

Questioning

Discussion

Demonstration, etc.

Phases of Inquiry

Techniques

Figure 10–1

THE SPIRIT OF SCIENCE

The future of science in the elementary school depends on only one person—you, the classroom teacher. If you elect to follow a course of action which introduces children to the factual side of science only, the future of science in the elementary school classrooms in this country is very bleak. From such an experience children will conclude that science is a static body of information which "the books" spell out for them and which they are expected "to know." These kinds of experiences will convince children that science is not really for them, and the truly exciting aspects of learning are found in other fields. If, however, you provide an educational environment for your students from which they learn that science is concerned with investigations, and that those investigations demand that minds be applied to the problem and continue to maintain that contact until the problem is solved, they will learn that science is a stimulating, productive enterprise which they enjoy. In other words, if children meet science as a dynamic enterprise—one in which they can participate, and through participation develop the spirit of science—its future in the elementary school is bright.[2]

---

[2] The "spirit of science" is defined by the Educational Policies Commission of the National Education Association in the bulletin, *Education and the Spirit of Science,* published 1966, as follows: "The spirit of rational inquiry, driven by a belief in its efficacy and by restless curiosity," p. 1.

Figure 10–2 Children of today will have to solve problems that haven't been identified using techniques that have not yet been invented. An inquiry science problem can assist a child in developing the creativity needed for such tasks.

TEACHING THE STRUCTURE OF SCIENCE AND SCIENTIFIC LITERACY

The citizens of tomorrow will encounter many problems, old and new, with which they will be unable to cope because today's schools cannot possibly provide them with specific information about the problems or specific techniques for solving them. By the time learners are in a position outside the school to put to use the information and techniques acquired in school, the chances are quite good that the techniques needed to solve the problems will have changed and the information they have will be obsolete or false. Our educational institutions are operating in an era when information is being produced so rapidly that even the specialists in any given field of science can barely keep abreast of the current developments. That staggering fact certainly tells us that we cannot expect our elementary schools to be teaching the latest factual information in science. But even if it were possible for a school to convey to its students—at the proper educational level—the latest in biophysics, space chemistry, and bionics, such a procedure would be educationally unsound.

Before such advanced ideas as DNA, the language of computers, and spectroscopy can be used, students have to possess a background (a structure) that will enable them to understand and appreciate such ideas. Not too many years ago the proper background for understanding the advanced ideas of science was thought to be the accumulation of all the information about a particular topic which could be amassed. We have learned that such educational experiences do not guarantee that a learner will be able to cope with advanced ideas in the future. Such heavy doses of factual content, often "learned" by rote memory, do not build for the students a conceptual structure of the discipline of science. They only provide students with an encyclopedic knowledge and if the new information does not fit the specific part of the encyclopedia with which they are familiar, they do not know what to do with it.

A conceptual framework of a discipline is constructed only by providing children with experiences in which they encounter the relationships that exist among things and which provide them ways of looking at various things. A conceptual structure of a discipline, in other words, is built only when students have the opportunity to learn *how* to look at a given item of information as well as having the opportunity to look *at* the information. If we consistently provide children with experiences in science which lead them to understand that science is investigation and that they must base their generalizations upon what they have observed, measured, and otherwise found, we will have provided them with a conceptual framework. They will develop the concept that science is the quest for knowledge. That understanding will cause them to continually ask such questions as "What do I know?", "How do I know it?" "How is what I know now different from what I felt I knew earlier?" In other words when students learn that their responsibility is the *quest* for knowledge, they will have developed that elusive conceptual structure of the discipline that is so often discussed but so rarely described.

The foregoing suggests that students must encounter all the essential experiences in science described in Chapter 6 and 7. But those experiences are carried out with content. That content must, of course, be at the proper intellectual level of the students and be selected from the basic concepts of the major subject areas of the discipline of science. The learners are then experiencing science as it is structured (the quest for knowledge) with subject matter that is representative of the natural world. Students having such an experience in science education have the opportunity to become *scientifically literate*. That is, they will be able to think rationally about matters that involve our environment and those in it. When one considers such problems as the energy crisis, the world's increasing population coupled with food production and distribution, the byproducts of nuclear fission, and environmental pollution, most certainly the need for the citizen of this country to be able to use observation, measurement, interpretation, experimentation, prediction, and model building becomes very real. In addition, the need for content about those areas is also a necessity. When that content can be used with the six processes, scientific literacy is present.

Too often, however, schools believe that just providing the content about the environment is sufficient. That point of view is naive and is probably one of the major reasons—maybe *the* major reason—why the foregoing problems exist today. Just providing the facts, laws, principles, and generalizations of science does not provide scientific literacy; no one would know their value or utility in solving a problem. The same applies to the six essential experiences listed earlier. As you have probably deduced, those processes do not apply to the field of natural science only; they have utility in several fields. What develops scientific literacy is experiencing the quest for knowledge with materials and ideas drawn from the natural world. All of the effort to develop scientific literacy is lost, however, if the students do not encounter content concepts that are on their intellectual level.

THE ELEMENTARY SCHOOL SCIENCE CURRICULUM OF THE FUTURE

The concept of the school—which is held by the majority of the citizens of this country—and the public concept of curriculum are synonymous. The general public believes that schools exist to teach "something" and that "something" they understand to be the curriculum. To a large degree the public is correct. Schools do exist to teach something. If we assign a rather divergent scope of activities to that something, then the views of the professionals and the public become one. The professional's view of curriculum, however, includes not only the specific topics the learner will encounter but also all the various activities in which he participates while encountering those specifics. Keeping before us the idea that curriculum involves not only the "what" to be encountered but also the "how" it is to be met is the unique responsibility of educators. They must be the persons who have the ability and courage to view the curricula that children experience, not only from the point of view of what is taught and how it is taught, but from the frame of reference of what should be taught and how it should be taught. The only person in a given classroom whose responsibility it is to resist the introduction of improper educational experiences for children is the *teacher*. With the support of the school administrator, however, the teacher can be more effective in making those decisions.

Pressures from the community and the nation with respect to what the elementary school science curriculum should contain must be accepted, evaluated, and acted upon by you, the classroom teacher. For many years such pressures were very difficult to reject because the existing curriculum for elementary school science did little more than give children experience in reading and, therefore, there was no logical defense against community, state, and national curriculum pressures. That void in the elementary school curriculum is rapidly being filled. At the present moment there are in existence curricula that will allow a teacher to develop such an attractive and efficient science program that the pressures from outside the school to adopt a "pet idea" of some group can be effectively neutralized. We do not mean to infer that offers of suggestions, guidance, and assistance from the community should be ignored. But, if an effective science program is under way, the attention it draws will motivate interested citizens to assist what is being done rather than to attempt to introduce something different.

In order for teachers to select the classroom curriculum, they must first know what is available. Every teacher must, therefore, keep abreast of the curriculum developments going on in science education. Professional periodicals, meetings, colleagues, and the science consultant of the system are the most important sources for keeping informed about the frontiers of science education. The services of a science consultant are consistently being made available to teachers by more and more school systems. Schools are realizing that individual teachers cannot plan their own programs independently of other teachers in the system. To have the learner develop a conceptual structure of science in which each year's experience will use the previous year's learnings and demand the information of the succeeding year demands that the program have someone who is coordinating all parts, testing the effectiveness of new ideas, and replacing portions of the program when necessary. This "someone" also can assist the teacher in introducing new ideas, trying new materials, or even using different or novel teaching techniques. Such a person is a science consultant. As school systems develop a complete understanding of what science contributes to the intellectual development of a child, the services of a science consultant will become more and more available to teachers and, of course, the improvement that results from those services will ultimately benefit the children. The primary function of the science consultant will be (and is) to assist the teachers in surveying the curricula available, selecting what is appropriate for a given school in a particular educational system in a certain geographical location, and implementing that selection.

Will enough and different curricula be available so the consultant and teachers will have sufficient choices? The trend is most certainly in that direction. At least two types of programs are available which will make the building of an integrated science program for the elementary schools feasible. Those two types of programs are the "sequential" and the "unit" plans. When a sequential program is adopted, the entire "package" should be implemented. In adopting such a program it is necessary that its purposes be understood because most such sequential programs are devoted to a set of purposes for elementary school science for which they faithfully produce materials to accomplish. The adopting of such a sequential program is very advantageous in many ways; for example, the problem of coordination is minimized, the introduction of a new teacher to the system by the science consultant and other teachers in the program is facilitated, and the materials problem follows the same pattern each year. There remains, however, the first hurdle that must be crossed in adopting a sequential program—its purposes and the purposes the school wishes the students to achieve through the study of science must be in harmony. The purposes of the newly developed sequential programs are in agreement with the purposes that have been emphasized in this book.

There have been developed by some curriculum development groups plans of study in elementary school science which conform to the accepted definition of a unit—a major understanding. Each of these units leads the child through an investigation of a given topic in some depth. The teacher and consultant are left with the decision of putting these units together into a teaching pattern. There is a degree of flexibility in this scheme of curriculum development which is not found in the sequential approach. There can be, however, serious lack of continuity that occurs automatically with the unit plan. The unit plan has specific objectives for each unit, and these must be completely accepted before any unit can be used in the classroom. While, in general, the units have different specific objectives, the overall purposes of the units developed by each development project are in complete harmony with purposes we have suggested for elementary school science.

There now exist adequate curricula from which a teacher and a consultant can select those experiences that are needed to implement the established purposes of elementary school science education. This development will give the elementary school teacher a degree of freedom not available in the past.

Teaching science by the inquiry approach is not easy. It requires the dedication of the classroom teacher, the support of the school's administration, and courage for a school to do what is best for the children in order to develop their rational powers—their ability to think—as well as to increase the complexity with which they think. A program in elementary school science which will accomplish all of the goals outlined in this book will require a considerable amount of time to plan and implement. But the program's goals will not be accomplished unless teachers and administrators select a starting point. So, as John F. Kennedy said in his 1961 inaugural address, "Let us begin!"

Appendix A
Case Studies in Inquiry

The following case studies show how three famous scientists employed the processes of science to solve problems. The commonly used word, hypothesis, is used in these case studies; as you will see, the process of hypothesizing is one aspect of "Getting the Idea." It is that aspect in which a possible pattern begins to emerge in the mind of the scientist. To propose the existence of such a pattern which can be experimentally supported or disproved is to hypothesize. An hypothesis can also refer to a possible explanation or model. We hope that these case studies will reinforce and refine the phases of the activities of the scientist proposed in Chapter 1.

CASE STUDY NUMBER ONE

In the year 1854 the University of Lille in the northern part of France employed a 32-year-old man as Dean of Sciences and Professor of Chemistry. This might seem to be an excessive amount of responsibility for a man of this age, but this was no ordinary young man. At age 25, while working for his doctoral degree, he had found a solution to a problem in the field of crystal structure which had escaped some of the finest scientific minds of the day. His name was Louis Pasteur.

Until his acceptance of the position at Lille, Pasteur had been a "pure" scientist, that is, he had not been concerned with the practical applications of his findings. Many people believed that the type of mind which functioned successfully in the field of pure science could not perform successfully or happily in the field of applied science. Not so, said Louis Pasteur, "There are not two different kinds of science; there is science and there are the applications of science."[1] Shortly after his arrival in Lille Pasteur set out to prove his hypothesis.

To explain why Pasteur approached the problem in Lille we must go back seven years, to 1847, when Pasteur was but 25 years old. He had just begun thinking about the research work that would be necessary to the completion of his doctoral degree in chemistry at the École Normale Supérieure in France when he heard a lecture describing the work of a German chemist, Mitscherlich, on the characteristics of certain crystals.

After long and critical study of the crystals[2] (call them crystals A and B) that were formed during the process of wine fermentation, the German had announced that those crystals were alike in every way in which he as a chemist could examine them except in the way they treated polarized light[3] that passed through them. Mitscherlich's work showed that crystal A rotated[4] the polarized light (turned it from the path it was following when it entered the crystal) and that crystal B did not.

These statements by an established chemist bothered the young Pasteur, and caused him to demonstrate what is probably the most basic characteristic of a scientist—curiosity. How, he probably asked himself, could two crystals be exactly alike in every chemical property

---

[1] Rene Dubos, *Pasteur and Modern Science*, Garden City, N.Y.: Doubleday Anchor Books, 1969, p. 41.

[2] These were the crystals of tartaric and paratartaric acid.

[3] Light from any source, say, a light bulb, moves out from it in all directions. There are, however, certain kinds of materials which will let light move in only one direction, e.g., up and down; when this happens the light is said to be plane polarized. Polarized light is very useful in many experiments because it lets the experimenter have definite control of it.

[4] When light is plane polarized, we can think of it as moving like this:

direction the light wave is vibrating — direction the light wave is moving

Notice that the light vibrates at a right angle (90°) to the direction the entire wave is moving. When the plane-polarized light is rotated, the angle between the direction the light wave is moving and the direction the light is vibrating is less than 90°.

and yet not treat polarized light in the same way? This was not logical; Pasteur was sure that there had to be some chemical differences between these crystals.

Pasteur had just performed two tasks that any scientist must perform at some time during his work; he had provided himself with a well-defined problem (why do crystals A and B treat polarized light differently when they seem to be chemically identical?), and he had advanced a probable answer—an hypothesis—to the problem. (These two crystals must have some basic structural differences because it is not logical to think that two chemicals can be alike in every way except the way in which they treat polarized light passing through them. The difference in the interaction between the crystals and polarized light must come from some basic chemical difference.) Notice that Pasteur had a reason for his hypothesis; it was not just a blind guess.

The young scientist decided that he would investigate this problem and see whether his beliefs and the data he would collect were better than Professor Mitscherlich's generalizations. Now you must remember that Mitscherlich had devoted a great deal of time and hard work to the study of crystals and this particular problem. He undoubtedly possessed much more factual material about the crystals than Pasteur did. In fact, at this point, Pasteur knew nothing about these particular crystals. He did not have at his command many of the facts about the problem he was undertaking that other chemists in Europe had at their fingertips. In other words, experts in the field of study would have said Pasteur's "knowledge" of this field was so limited that he would not be able to contribute to it.

This latter point often makes elementary school teachers reluctant to teach science in their classrooms; they do not believe they "know enough" science to teach it to children. What these teachers are really saying is that they don't know enough of the formalized facts of science to be able to communicate them to children in encyclopedic fashion. These teachers have selected as their primary reason for teaching science the acquainting of children with the facts of science. There can be no doubt that the facts of science are important, but is the acquisition of those facts the most important reason for its study? Are the facts of such importance that a classroom teacher should build students' entire educational experience around them? Had Pasteur confined his work to those areas where he possessed adequate factual information, his problem would never have been solved.

When a scientific problem is to be solved, the investigator must first know what the problem is. Pasteur had already defined his problem. He knew precisely what it was he wanted to investigate. His next task was to isolate all the specifics he could about the problem. He already knew of the work of Mitscherlich; that was the basis for the hypothesis he had advanced. So this left him with only one other source of information—the crystals themselves.

Pasteur was a skilled laboratory chemist and had already acquired through his previous inquiries a great deal of information about the field of chemistry. This is one aspect of the cumulative nature of science. Knowledge gained through previous exploration which is applicable to the current problem can and should be used. Using the information and his skills Pasteur prepared nineteen samples of the two crystals. These had to be his only sources of information—no one else could help him, he was on his own. What did he do? He observed! He spent many hours studying the two types of crystals under his microscope and his hours were fruitful. He discovered "a fact which had escaped the attention of other observers."[5]

When you look at a crystal—a diamond, for example—you notice that it has many small, plane surfaces. These surfaces are called "facets." Pasteur observed that on the A crystals all the facets were in the same position. Upon study of the B crystals he found that on some the facets were oriented just like the facets on the A crystals. But he also found that on many B crystals the facets were placed in exactly the opposite position to the facets on the A crystals. Here then was a basic, fundamental difference in the two types of crystals, which Pasteur's logic told him should be there, one that had not been detected in all studies by others. Pasteur had found it in a relatively short period of intensive study.

The men who had studied similar crystals before Pasteur had as much, and no doubt more, experience with them as he. We cannot, then, attribute this basic "find" of Pasteur's to the fact that he "knew more," that is, possessed more encyclopedic factual knowledge, about basic crystal structure than had his predecessors. The young scientist had acquired the abilities of critical observation, comparison, and classification, and these were among the talents he brought to his crystal study that made it possible for him to find what others had not found. In addition, he looked at the particular problem in a way that other investigators had not. He examined the crystals with regard to his hypothesis that a structural difference existed in them.

This discovery of the different orientation of facets on the crystals had given Pasteur a specific point to investigate. He had already found a fundamental difference in his crystals, and he had not as yet used what Mitscherlich had stated as the only fundamental difference between crystals A and B, that is, what happened to polarized light as it passed through them. When Pasteur passed polarized light through an A crystal, it rotated the light in one direction (let's say to the right),

[5] Dubos, op. cit., p. 26.

and when this light was passed through a B crystal whose facets were on the same side as they were on an A crystal, (say, the right), it rotated light in exactly the same way as had crystal A. When light was passed through a B crystal whose facets were on the other side (say, the left), it rotated the plane of polarized light in the opposite direction. This direction was, of course, exactly opposite to the direction in which the B crystal whose facets were on the right had rotated the light. Next, Pasteur mixed all the right and left crystals of B and let polarized light pass through the crystalline mixture. If light first went through a crystal which rotated it to the left, and then a crystal which rotated it to the right, it finally emerged from the crystals without being rotated at all. This is what Pasteur found. He could then sum up his work by saying that the German chemist Mitscherlich was not correct when he had stated that there were no fundamental differences between crystals A and B except the manner in which they treated polarized light.

But Pasteur's goal was not to prove that Mitscherlich was right or wrong. It was to solve a particular problem and in so doing he made a discovery. This discovery was thrilling to Pasteur; he met an associate of his in the hall and said, "I have just made a great discovery . . . I am so happy I am shaking all over . . ."[6] Motivated as he was, the 25-year-old Pasteur at that moment would have probably tackled any problem in science which he even vaguely understood.

If pupils in the elementary school could be provided the kind of motivation Pasteur had, they would see that learning is fun! You probably think that children cannot be expected to discover anything that about nature is new, different, or original—and you are right. But think of the world that surrounds a child which the child's teachers, but not the child, know. If we lead the child to discover this world, what he or she discovers will not be original or new to us, the teachers, but it will be new and original to the child. Think also of the fun the child will have in discovering the world, and of the mental abilities the child will use in these discoveries. Like Pasteur, your pupils will have to utilize the process of observation to carefully compare and classify basic information about the world around them in order to synthesize a satisfactory explanation for what they find, just as Pasteur compared and classified basic information about crystals in order to explain why crystal B did not rotate plant-polarized light.

Why is the example of Pasteur's discovery about these crystals important to you as a teacher of elementary school children? Most assuredly this example does not represent content that you are expected to teach children! The example of Pasteur's discovery is of importance

[6] Ibid., p. 28.

to those of us interested in the educative process because of what it demonstrates. Let us look critically at what Pasteur did.

1. He identified his problem.
2. He observed the objects in which he was interested to obtain data he could classify and compare. He then searched for a pattern among those data which would let him synthesize an answer to his problem.
3. He got an idea, or saw what he though might be the pattern (this is also called formulating an hypothesis).
4. He then submitted his idea or hypothesis to the most rigorous of tests; he tested his own laboratory findings. He experimented. We stated that he mixed the crystals to see if those which rotated polarized light to the left and the right would, when mixed, let light pass straight through unrotated.
5. His experiment verified his idea or hypothesis.

These are the processes that Pasteur used to make his first discovery, and that we would use to provide children meaningful learning experiences. But if we generalized from one case (one piece of data) that educational activity based on these processes would be good for children, we would be acting in a very unscientific manner. Let's investigate the solutions of other scientific problems.

Early in this chapter, we stated that Pasteur had been confronted with his first opportunity to apply the practices of the pure scientific laboratory to practical problems when he arrived a the University of Lille. One of the principal industries in Lille was the production of alcoholic beverages and, shortly after his arrival, Pasteur was called upon by Monsieur Bigo, who produced alcohol by the fermentation of beet juice. Bigo told Pasteur that in the process of producing alcohol there were many times when it became contaminated with unknown substances. According to Bigo, there was no satisfactory explanation for this contamination; the process of manufacture had been carried out in essentially the same manner each time; nevertheless, in many cases, the alcohol became so contaminated it could not be sold.

Pasteur had spent his prior years in the study of basic chemistry, and particularly in the study of crystals. He had absolutely no understanding about the process of alcoholic fermentation. He did have, however, the curiosity that distinguishes a scientist, and the problem that Monsieur Bigo presented him with was an intriguing one.

The fact that Pasteur did not know anything about the problem he was undertaking points out very clearly where the practice of hypothesis formation fits into the scientific process. Notice that we have not said that Pasteur stated an hypothesis to the problem; it would have been imprudent for him to have done so because he did not as yet know anything about it. Many times teachers of science urge pupils to formulate an hypothesis before they know anything about the problem. This is an extremely unwise educational procedure because it encourages wild guessing, and it is most certainly unscientific. Science has seen people who could look at a particular situation and immediately see the exact problem and a solution to it. Such "intuitive leaps" are rare in science and are reserved for the Newtons, the Boyles, and the Einsteins.

Most progress in solving problems, in science or any field, is made not by giant strides but rather by inching from one known fact to the next. After enough information has been gathered about the problem, the data are inspected to see whether or not a pattern of results can be seen. This pattern of results is the basis for the formulation of an hypothesis. A clearly stated hypothesis can and must be verified (or denied) by subjecting it to rigorous tests under conditions that are like those surrounding the problem being investigated. Pasteur did not form an hypothesis to the problem with which he was presented because any hypothesis at this point would have been a pure guess. Hypotheses are always based on experience with a problem; without such experience an hypothesis cannot be stated. Hypotheses are creative leaps of the mind as it "sees" a pattern emerging from the mass of factual data or an underlying structure in nature which produces this pattern.

Since Pasteur knew little about the problem, he had to go to the source of it, the alcohol factory, and learn. He spent a great deal of time at the factory and observed everything he could, but he was specifically interested in the product—fermenting beet juice. He took samples of the product back to his laboratory and continued his observations with his microscope, collecting all the data he could by carefully describing and drawing diagrams of what he saw. As Pasteur studied the fermenting beet juice under the microscope, he saw particles of yeast, but this was not unusual because these had been seen by investigators before him. At this particular time such noted chemists as the German Justus von Liebig and J. J. Berzelius of Sweden were convinced that yeast was just a very intricate chemical material that was present for the sole purpose of bringing about the conversion of sugar into alcohol without taking part in the reaction itself.[7] But in addition to the yeast particles, Pasteur also saw some other structures that did not look like yeast. These puzzled him because he had no idea what they were. The young investigator had acquired enough information

---

[7] Whenever a substance is responsible for promoting or bringing about a chemical reaction but does not take part in the reaction, that substance is said to be a "catalyst." This is exactly what the chemist of the mid-nineteenth century thought yeast was.

to make it necessary to ask some questions but not enough as yet to form an hypothesis.

One of the most trusted axioms of learning is that we learn in terms of what we already know and understand. What a person "sees" is probably influenced by the way in which that person looks at something, that is, the frame of reference and probably the degree to which that person's language system is developed. That person's frame of reference, however, is a result of previous experiences and understandings. This can also be said of a person's problem-solving approach. The approach that has proved successful in the past will very likely be used again. In teaching children science, this must never be forgotten. An idea is born, an hypothesis is advanced, or a problem is identified and framed in terms that the child (or the investigator) understands. Pasteur was no exception to this axiom. He had achieved great success in his work with crystals by studying their treatment of plane-polarized light. He put samples of the fermenting beet juice in his polarimeter (the instrument used to study the interaction between polarized light and a crystal) and found that the juice was optically active—that it would rotate the plane of the polarized light from the plane at which it had entered the crystal.[8] Earlier in his career as a chemist studying optical activity Pasteur had investigated whether or not all organic compounds were optically active. Perhaps you know that "organic" refers to living organisms; the dictionary defines "organic" as "of, relating to, or derived from living organisms."[9] For many years chemists thought that all organic compounds were from living organisms. Then, in 1824, the German chemist Friedrich Wohler artificially prepared the compound urea $CO(NH_2)_2$.

Following this discovery by Wohler, chemists became interested in the synthesis of organic compounds, a problem that, because of the prevailing paradigm[10] in biology—that organic compounds were produced only by living organisms—had been considered absurd. Since that time thousands of organic compounds have been synthesized. From his investigations, Pasteur observed a pattern—organic compounds that were optically active came from living things.

Here, then, was the basis for an hypothesis. Pasteur had found that the fermenting beet juice was optically active and that the alcohol he isolated from the ferment was also optically active.[11] He believed that optically active organic compounds came only from living or-

[8] A material is "optically active" when it rotates the plane of polarized light.
[9] *Webster's Seventh New Collegiate Dictionary,* Springfield, Massachusetts: Merriam-Webster, 1963, p. 594.
[10] Thomas S. Kuhn, *The Structure of Scientific Revolutions,* Chicago, Illinois: University of Chicago Press, 1962, p. 23.
[11] The alcohol he isolated was amyl alcohol.

ganisms and inferred that yeast was responsible for the production of alcohol in the fermentation process. What then could be hypothesized? Yeast found during the alcoholic fermentation process and all the other organic substances found during this process (such as the structures he found under his microscope with the yeast) were not lifeless, intricate chemicals that just brought about chemical reactions. Rather, said Pasteur, yeast and the other materials found in fermentation are living things. The sugar is turned into alcohol because it serves as food for these living things, and alcohol is the product given off during the metabolic processes of these living organisms (the yeast).

Here indeed was a revolutionary idea. But notice that Pasteur was careful to have adequate reasons for advancing it. He did not say, "I believe. . . ." Rather, he said, "I believe . . . because. . ." Pasteur's challenge of such scientific giants as Berzelius and Liebig was at that time about as acceptable as would be a challenge today of Einstein's famous $E = mc^2$ by a completely unknown scientist. For not only is challenging a highly regarded person in science difficult, challenging a widely accepted model or theory—one that has paradigm status—is also difficult. Such paradigms as the theory of universal gravitation, the Bohr model of the atom, and the theory of evolution are so widely accepted and have become so ingrained in scientists' thinking (and teaching) that explorations of nature using those models as guiding principles are considered normal science. A solution to a problem that cannot be explained within the prevailing paradigm is frequently rejected by scientists as no solution at all. This respect for established authority in science plays an important role. It is responsible for causing an investigator who would propose a new explanation of phenomena to investigate the problem thoroughly in order to give as much evidence as possible in support of his proposed explanation.

Pasteur had yet to verify his idea and then find ways to solve Monsieur Bigo's problem. But the problem of undersirable wine fermentation would not even have had an hypothesis proposed as its solution had not Pasteur been willing to rush out into areas where his factual knowledge was nonexistent while using the same methods of problem solving which had been previously successful for him. However, in order to make his hypothesis acceptable to the scientific community, it had to be verified. Verification, then, is an important part of the process of science, but it is only a part. It is that part during which the hypothesis, which is based on the facts collected, is rigorously tested with respect to whether or not it really can represent a solution to the problem. The investigator does experiments. Much science teaching in today's schools resembles the description just given of verification. The experiences the children have consist of studying the already known facts and then doing some type of an "experiment" to verify that what they have "learned" is true. That procedure is a part of the total picture of science, but only a part. The importance of verification to the progress of science can be seen by considering the hypothesis of Monsieur Pasteur that fermentation is a process caused and carried on by living things.

One thing on which scientists generally agreed at the time Pasteur proposed his hypothesis was that there are certain characteristics that distinguish living things from nonliving. Two of these characteristics were that living things can be made to grow by properly feeding them and can propagate themselves. If fermentation is caused by living things, these two criteria must be satisfied. Pasteur knew this and began to search for evidence that would satisfy himself as well as the critics. He needed a source of material which was readily available and in which fermentation takes place rapidly. Milk is such a material. Pasteur knew that milk soured (fermented) rapidly if left at room temperature for a period of time. In addition to being a material in which fermentation occurred rather rapidly, milk was also readily available for experimentation. Pasteur also knew that the sugar in the milk was converted to lactic acid during the fermentation process, producing the characteristic sour taste of acids. Pasteur showed that the lactic acid ferment in the sour milk consisted of a great many microscopic organisms that looked alike. He also showed that by feeding these organisms milk sugar they increased in number and that, if he moved the organisms to a new sugar solution, lactic acid was produced very rapidly. He had, therefore, demonstrated that the two criteria had been satisfied— the organisms increased by feeding them, and they could propagate and demonstrate their metabolic process in a new environment.

There is, however, another point that must be raised here. A fire, which is a chemical reaction, will also satisfy the criteria in question. Once a fire is burning it will keep burning if it is fed. Furthermore, fire can be moved from place to place and continue to burn if the environment is right. Hence these two criteria alone are not sufficient to distinguish "living things" from "nonliving things." We cannot know whether or not Pasteur or his critics concerned themselves with our fire example, but they did concern themselves with two other questions. They asked, "Where do these microorganisms come from?" and "If the microorganisms are living things, why can't they be killed?" What then had Pasteur accomplished by working with sour milk? Only this—that his microorganisms were found in places other than in fermenting mixtures which produced alcohol. He also established that the undesirable effects in fermenting beet juice were caused by organisms other than yeast, because yeast globules were always found in connection with fermentation which produced "healthy" alcohol, and the unknown organisms were found only when the fermenting beet juice had become contaminated. Pasteur also found unknown microorganisms in fermenting milk. From his evidence Pasteur concluded that yeast was a living plant that produced alcohol, and that the other, unknown life was the "culprit" that must be eradicated. Still to be faced, however, was the problem of where this undesirable form of life came from and how it could be killed.

Pasteur figured he had learned enough about the fermentation process to establish firmly that it was not a chemical process, as all the scientific giants of his time thought, but was, instead, a biological process. In 1857 he published his results. Just slightly more than two years had passed since he began working on a problem about which he had absolutely no knowledge, and in a field (fermentation) in which the authorities had concluded that the problem already had a definite explanation. Most certainly, then, the conclusion can be drawn that Pasteur was a success in his studies of fermentation not because of his encyclopedic knowledge of the field. Something else, then, was responsible for his success. It was Pasteur's ability to isolate a problem, gather information about it, state an hypothesis, and then verify it. Let us see how Pasteur verified his hypothesis that fermentation is caused by living things by answering the questions concerning from where the alien microorganisms came and how they could be killed.

In 1857 Pasteur returned to the institution that had granted him his doctorate, the École Normale Supérieure in Paris, and there he finally solved Monsieur Bigo's problem. In the summer of 1858 Pasteur was vacationing in that part of France in which he had grown up (Arbois), where he had many friends who had well-stocked wine cellars. He studied many different kinds of wines (Bordeaux, Champagne, Burgundy, et cetera), and without exception he found that in the good wines there were only yeast cells, whereas in the defective wines there were other microscopic cells mixed with the yeast cells. These were exactly the findings he had made when he had examined the fermenting beet juice, and finally the alcohol, from Bigo's distilling plant.

Pasteur was not content with confining his attention to wine. He knew that beer and vinegar were closely related to wine, so he studied them also. If his hypothesis was valid, the microscopic cells should be found in them too. This illustrates another facet of Pasteur's problem-solving techniques and one that is common to scientists. He looked around for similar situations in which his hypothesis could be disproved. Here is a characteristic that has been completely missing from science teaching in the elementary schools. We have not given pupils the opportunity to state hypotheses and then see if they could disprove them. We have been so concerned with making sure the pupil "gets the right answer," that we have not given the pupil the opportunity to have the learning experience of disproving (or verifying) an hypothesis. The learning activities that the child had been permitted to have, have been aimed at "doing" the problem, not "solving" it. Any time a pupil advances an idea which satisfies the pupils own need for an "explanation" of a problem, the pupil should immediately be asked, "Can you disprove your idea?" This procedure will show whether the pupil has obtained a functional understanding of the concepts the pupil is using to solve the problem, or if there has only been memoration of a lot of miscellaneous information about the problem, which the pupil can mentally spew forth at any time. "Factspewing" science does not provide a child with the kinds of learning experiences that are needed for stating and then verifying or disproving hypotheses. In fact, they give the child only one kind of experience—memorization; and as important as memorization is to the education of a child in science, it is secondary to the learning that results from actual hypothesis formulation and testing. Through this activity the child learns how much his understanding of a problem really advances if his hypothesis is a correct one. The child will also be able to discover his misunderstandings if his hypothesis is incorrect.

The value of disproof must not be overlooked in teaching children. They must always ask, "Can you be shown to be wrong?" and we, as teachers, must learn to accept wrong answers from children not as something to be frowned on but as something to be used to redirect a child's attention toward the objectives of the learning experiences. Children must be convinced that teachers are not always looking for what they feel is the correct answer to a question or problem. Learners must be made to feel that we want their own contribution to the problem being investigated. The classroom methodology for doing this is examined in Chapter 7.

When he investigated beer and vinegar, Pasteur was asking himself whether or not his hypothesis that the spoiling of wine was due to the microorganisms he found with yeast was correct. He was asking a question which, if answered "No" (i.e., the spoiled beer and vinegar did not have the small microorganisms appearing in them) would disintegrate his whole idea concerning the functioning of these microorganisms and render useless all of the work he had done. Here indeed is demonstrated the intensity with which a scientist feels the value of disproof. Pasteur had, with his fermentation experiments, entered a field in which his factual knowledge was virtually nonexistent. Many men in Europe had devoted their lives to studying what Pasteur had undertaken. But in a few short years he had made more progress than they. Why? Dr. John R. Platt summed up why Pasteur succeeded when he wrote: "We praise the 'lifetime of study' but in dozens of cases, in every field, what was needed was not a lifetime of study but rather a few short months or weeks of analytical inductive inference."[12] What Dr. Platt is saying is that problems in science are not to be solved by what he calls "encyclopedism" but rather by trying to disprove the hypotheses in advance with crucial experiments. We must not be afraid to be wrong, and we must teach our pupils the value of being wrong. Let's see what Pasteur gained by submitting his hypothesis to the arena of testing.

Imagine the joy the scientist felt when he looked through his microscope at spoiled beer and vinegar and actually saw his newly found microorganisms just as they had appeared in spoiled wine. Here indeed is a great reward for the self-discipline which must be imposed if an idea (i.e., optically active compounds come only from living things) is to be turned into an hypothesis (i.e., the spoiled wine was caused by living things), and finally verified when subjected to the rigor of possible disproof. This same joy of discovery will be felt by pupils if they are allowed to discover the facts, principles, and generalizations of science for themselves and are not fed those found interesting and important by the teacher. Remember that the discoveries that pupils make are not meant to be original discoveries. Teachers should not be nearly as interested in what the child learns as in how the child learns it. Even with his joy of discovery, however, Pasteur now faced an even bigger problem than he had faced before—how could he rid the wine of these microorganisms?

The many marvelous applications of exploration and identification of the problem, statement of hypotheses, design of experiments to gather information to exclude some of the hypotheses, selection of a tentative solution to the problem, and subjection of that tentative solution (really a refined hypothesis) to the rigor of disproof which Pasteur made will not be discussed in detail. He did find that when wort (a mixture of sugars often used as the basis for starting beer) which contained the microorganisms was heated, pure yeast added, and the entire mixture protected from the air, the resulting beer was free of spoilage. This told Pasteur two things—where those microorganisms come from, and how to get rid of them. From these experiments the process of pasteurization was developed and was applied not only to alcoholic beverages but also to milk. Pasteurization of milk has saved untold lives and human suffering; this was a "bonus" to the principal problem Pasteur set out to solve.

[12] John R. Platt, "Strong Inference," *Science,* October 16, 1964, p. 351.

Appendix B
Methods of Organizing Data

METHODS OF ORGANIZING DATA[1]

The following section is included to provide the teacher with an overview of the methods of organizing data used in the *Learning Science Program*.

There are several techniques that people use to organize information, or data. Data may be organized for many different purposes, but there are two reasons which apply in almost every case:

> Organized data are easier to collect and to store than facts that are gathered and recorded at random.
>
> Organized data are easier to use because they permit a person to see patterns and relationships that are not apparent in unorganized data. Those patterns and relationships may then serve as a basis for generalization and prediction.

The organizational schemes discussed in this section are serial order, classification, tables, and graphs.

[1] John W. Renner, Don G. Stafford, and Vivian Jensen Coulter, *Variation, Teacher's Guide*, Encino, California: Benziger Bruce & Glencoe, 1977, pp. 126–131.

Serial Order

Serial order is the arrangement of objects in a series according to a property, attribute, or performance criterion. Objects may be arranged in a series from shortest to longest; foods may be put in order from those one likes best to those one likes least; people in a race may be listed in order of finish; and so on. The list of examples could be extended almost indefinitely.

Students are introduced to the serial-ordering technique in Book 1 of the *Learning Science Program* and continue to make use of it throughout the program.

Classification

Classification is the process of putting things that are alike in some way into groups, subdividing those groups into smaller groups, then subdividing the resulting groups into still smaller groups. As an example, Figure B-1 represents a possible classification scheme for a collection of writing instruments.

No doubt you can think of another way, and perhaps a better way, to classify the collection of writing instruments. Any collection of objects may be classified in several different ways. The divisions are arbitrary, made by the person developing the system, and represent only one way of grouping the objects in the collection. This is true even of systems—such as that developed by Linnaeus for the classification of flora and fauna—which have been in universal use for a great many years.

Students begin their practice of classification in Book 1 by putting objects into groups on the basis of property. In Book 3 they are formally introduced to the concept as well as to the term "classification." They

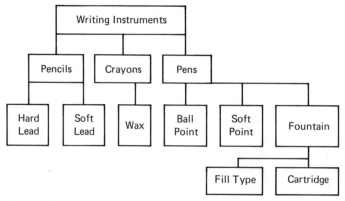

Figure B–1

will, of course, refine their ability to classify as they progress through the program.

Tables

Tables are a convenient way of recording data, and they have the additional advantage of enabling the user to perceive a pattern or trend.

Quite often in the *Learning Science Program,* the teacher is asked to place headings on the chalkboard. The students then make measurements and enter them under the appropriate headings. This approach is used in Books 2 through 6. Table B–1 provides an example. This table allows the students to compare the relationship between two measurements, circumference and diameter, in a variety of objects.

After the data have been recorded in table form, the measurements may be numbered from smallest to largest. A new table may then be constructed in which the objects are listed in serial order according to size. Even though the students' measurements may not be exact, the new table will reveal a consistent relationship between diameter and circumference which can be easily seen and studied.

Another table might show the variations within a group of objects or people. For example Table B–2 records the heights of children in one fourth-grade class. When the data are organized into a table, the distribution in height may be clearly observed.

Table B–1

NAME OF OBJECT	DISTANCE AROUND THE OBJECT (CIRCUMFERENCE)	DISTANCE ACROSS THE OBJECT (DIAMETER)
Plate	63	20
Bicycle Wheel	188	60
Top of a Cup	22	7
Bottom of a Waste Basket	94.2	30
Pencil	2.5	0.8

Table B–2

NUMBER OF CHILDREN	HEIGHT IN CENTIMETERS
2	121–125
7	126–130
12	131–135
5	136–140
3	141–145
1	146–150

Graphs

· Circle Graphs. Several different types of graphs are used in the *Learning Science Program* in Books 4 through 6. In a very few cases, circle graphs are employed. The circle graph is most effective when it is used to show how a quantity is divided. For example, if the students wished to show the division of time in a typical day, they might construct a graph like Figure B–2.

· Histograms. Often a graph is more helpful than a table in showing how a measurement or property varies within a group of objects. Suppose, for example, that the students wish to determine the variation in color of the pencils in the classroom. After sorting and counting all the pencils, they find that two are red, twelve are yellow, six are blue, and four are green.

The students can organize their data by writing the names of the colors below a horizontal line and then placing a symbol (such as an "X") above the line for each pencil of a given color. The resulting graph would resemble Figure B–3. This type of graph is known technically as a frequency distribution chart, although the simpler term "histogram" is used in the *Learning Science Program*.

A vertical line showing the number or frequency of cases may be added to the simple histogram. Figure B–4 provides an example.

With an additional step, the distribution of color among the pencils in the sample may be represented in another form, the bar graph.

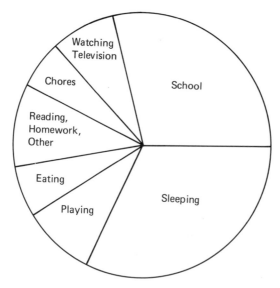

Figure B–2

```
                    X
                    X
                    X
                    X
                    X
                    X
                    X        X
                    X        X
                    X        X        X
                    X        X        X
     X              X        X        X
     X              X        X        X
   ─────────────────────────────────────────
     Red         Yellow     Blue     Green
```

Figure B–3

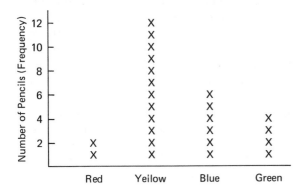

Figure B–4

To construct a bar graph, the students would simply make a bar indicating the number of pencils of each color. The top of the bar should
align with the appropriate number on the vertical (frequency) line, as
shown in Figure B–5.

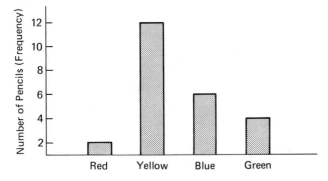

Figure B–5

Any of the three methods may be used to represent the distribution of a property within a group of objects. However, students of elementary school age generally find the simple histogram (Figure B–3) easiest to understand and use. This is the method that will be encountered most frequently in the *Learning Science Program.*

In Figures B–3–B–5, the horizontal line of the histogram was labeled with property words, it may also be labeled with measurements. Suppose, for example, that the students have measured and recorded the length of every pencil in the classroom. They now have the following data (in centimeters): 11, 12, 12, 8, 14, 13, 12, 10, 12, 9, 12, 10, 11, 10, 11, 13, 11, 12, 9, 14, 12, 10, 12.

In order to put their data into a histogram, the students would mark off the horizontal line with numbers, as in Figure B–6.

It is not necessary for the numbers on the horizontal line to begin at zero; in this case, seven or eight could be the starting point.

The range of the data is the numerical interval between the lowest and the highest result. If the range is narrow, the variation in the measurements is small. If the range is wide, the variation is great. In the example given, the range of variation in pencil length is 6 centimeters—from 8 to 14.

Inspection of a histogram reveals whether there is a cluster of tallies at or around a single value, or whether there is a large spread. Histograms may also be used for making generalizations and predictions. For example, the data contained in Figures B–3 and B–6 would allow the students to make the following generalization: Every pencil in the classroom is either red, yellow, blue, or green and is between 8 and 14 centimeters in length. The following prediction would also be possible: A pencil selected at random from the classroom collection is more likely to be yellow than any other color and is more likely to be 12 centimeters long than any other length.

Histograms are informally used in Books 1 and 2 of the program. They are formally introduced in Book 3, *Systems*, and are reviewed and reinforced in Book 4, *Variation.*

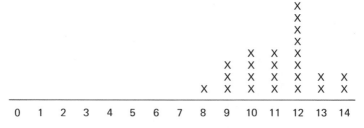

Length of Pencils in Centimeters

Figure B–6

· **Line Graphs.** The line graph is used to show a relationship between two measurements, such as time and distance, weight and volume, number of turns of wire around a magnet and number of paper clips picked up, and so on. One measurement is represented by a point on a vertical line, or axis, known as the ordinate (Y); the other measurement is represented by a point on the horizontal axis, or abscissa (S). Figure B–7 shows the positioning of the two axes.

The axes are number lines. The intervals between the numbers used on each axis depend upon the measurements or data involved. For example, an axis representing centimeters might be divided into intervals of 1, 2, 3, 4, 5, or 50, 100, 150, 200, 250. Figure B–8 shows some of the divisions that might be made. A good rule is to use from five to ten divisions on each axis. Notice, too, that the divisions on an axis are always equal.

Suppose that the students have made two sets of related measurements which they have organized into a table like that shown in Table B–3.

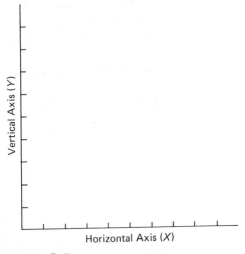

Figure B–7

Table B–3

Y	X
1	5
2	10
3	15
4	20
5	25

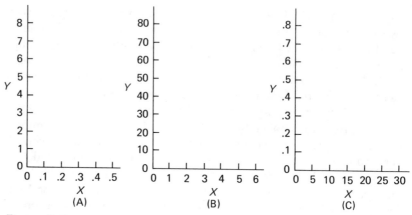

Figure B–8

After setting up and dividing off the axes, the students would place each related pair of values in its appropriate place. For example, the related pair of values $y = 1$, $x = 5$ would be placed at the point where a line drawn from the "1" mark on the Y axis intersects a line drawn from the "5" mark on the X axis. All five pairs of related measurments have been placed in the graph shown in Figure B–9. The related pairs of data are called coordinates.

A line graph is produced when the data points are connected with a smooth line or curve, as shown in Figure B–10.

When the line graph is completed, it will reveal the relationship

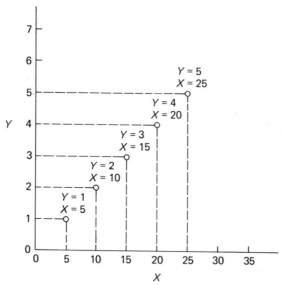

Figure B–9

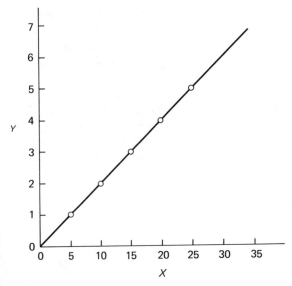

Figure B–10

between two measurements. For example, the line graph in Figure B–11 shows the relationship between centimeters and inches.

This graph reveals that as the number of inches increases, the number of centimeters increases proportionally. Thus the students could use the graph to determine the number of centimeters in a given number of inches, or the number of inches in a given number of centimeters. All of these values are "stored" in the line graph.

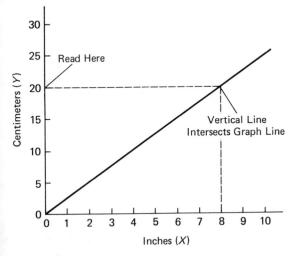

Figure B–11

Suppose the students want to find out how many centimeters there are in 8 inches. By extending a vertical line from the "8" mark on the X axis until it intersects the graph line, and by extending a horizontal line from that point to theY axis, the students will find the answer: approximately 20.3 centimeters.

Line graphs are used in Books 5 and 6 of the program.

The four types of organizing schemes discussed here are used in the *Learning Science Program* as tools for organizing, storing, and interpreting data. These tools are used by practicing scientists in all branches of the natural sciences, and thus they represent an important learning area for the students.

Appendix C
The Presence of Concrete and Formal Thought in Senior High School Students

For many years researchers interested in intellectual development have used tasks designed by Piaget and Inhelder to assess the presence of concrete and formal reasoning in junior and senior high school students. The second edition of this book contained a report of the data we collected from interviewing students from grades seven through twelve in 1971.

During 1976 the National Science Foundation provided funds which enabled the Science Education Center of the University of Oklahoma to prepare science-centered problems which can be used to measure intellectual development.[1] One of the activities of that project consisted of individually interviewing 1313 tenth, eleventh, and twelfth grade students with the four tasks described in Appendix D. One of those tasks—the conservation of volume—does not require the use of the IIIB level of formal thought; the IIIA level is adequate

---

[1] John W. Renner, Dianna K. Prickett, and Michael J. Renner, *Evaluating Intellectual Development Using Written Responses to Selected Science Problems*, Norman, Oklahoma: University of Oklahoma, 1977.

to solve the problem. Complete solutions to the other three tasks shown in Appendix D require the IIIB level of thought.

We believe that in order to construct a complete and accurate picture of the types of thought of which the 1313 interviewees were capable, each of those students would have to have had the opportunity to demonstrate the IIIB level of thought on each task completed. That belief dictated that the data obtained from interviewing students with the conservation-of-volume task be dropped from consideration. In other words, the data included in this analysis consisted of the rankings each of the 1313 students received on three tasks, each of which requires the IIIB level of thought for complete solution. The data, therefore, include a total of 3939 (3 tasks × 1313 students) *thought demonstrations*. The data from these 1313 student interviews are shown in Table C–1.

In studying Table C–1 you must remember that numbers and percentages shown do not represent individual interviewees. For example, 492 IIIA thought demonstrations were found among the eleventh grade students in the study. Do not interpret that number as meaning that the eleventh grade student sample in the study contained 492 students who reasoned at level IIIA. The extreme right-hand column in Table C–1 gives the total number of thought demonstrations per grade.

First consider the data found in the thought-type columns in Table C–1. In column IIA, 23 percent of the thought of tenth graders, 17 percent of eleventh grade thought, and 15 percent of twelfth grade thought is found. That thought level represents the *first* level of thought above pre-operational reasoning. We urge you to analyze each column in Table C–1 in the way just done for column IIA. The results are revealing and disappointing to us.

Examining the grade-level rows in Table C–1 is also informative. Consider the ramifications of analyzing the tenth grade row. A total of 69 percent of the tenth grade reasoning found in the sample is at

Table C–1   TYPES OF THOUGHT OF SENIOR HIGH SCHOOL STUDENTS

GRADE	STUDENT SAMPLE SIZE	IIA	IIB	IIIA	IIIB	TOTAL THOUGHT TYPE SAMPLE
10	422	289	587	341	49	1266
Percent	32	23	46	27	4	32
11	529	275	681	492	139	1587
Percent	40	17	43	31	9	40
12	362	159	427	339	161	1086
Percent	28	15	39	31	15	28
Totals	1313	18%	43%	30%	9%	3939

the concrete level. One of the subjects usually studied in the tenth grade is geometry. Now geometry is based on axioms and postulates—the consideration of the possible, and not the real. That description also applies to formal reasoning. Just possibly the geometry taught at the tenth grade level represents the most formal subject matter encountered in senior high school. That formal subject matter is taught to a group of students whose thought is 69 percent concrete. In other words, 69 percent of the thought present at the tenth grade level can function *only* with reality. Geometry most certainly does not deal with reality.

We urge you to take data about other levels from Table C–1 and compare it to the subject matter taught at that level. Be sure that you do not make the mistake of saying, for example, that 54 percent of the twelfth graders in the sample think on a concrete level. *That is not what the data in Table C–1 are saying.* The data in Table C–2 are showing that 54 percent of the thought found at the twelfth grade level is concrete.

Consider these data from Table C–1:

1. IIA thought decreases from 23 to 15 percent—8 percent—during senior high school.
2. IIB thought decreases from 46 to 39 percent—7 percent—during senior high school.
3. IIIA thought increases from 27 to 31 percent—4 percent—during senior high school.
4. IIIB thought increases from 4 percent to 15 percent—4 percent—during senior high school.

The very small decreases in concrete thought and increases in formal thought—15 percent—must lead to questions regarding the intellectual value of senior high school. These students have been following school-designed and directed activities that are purported to ready young people for a society that requires their participation at an abstract level. Voting is a process that requires the construction of mental models without concrete data. The small increases in formal reasoning become even more important when the large number of students who remain at the concrete level is considered. Since the increase in abstract thought among the sample of students studied is so small, the inference that the senior high school is not meeting the intellectual needs of its clientele is nearly irresistible. The question regarding the intellectual effectiveness of the intervention of the senior high school into the lives of teenagers must be asked.

Appendix D
Interviewing Protocols for Formal Operational Tasks

Critics of using student performance on the Piagetian tasks as a measure of intellectual development frequently state that those who have had school experiences in science—and particulary physics—have an advantage on those tasks. Anton E. Lawson and Anthony J. D. Blake in their article "Concrete and Formal Thinking Abilities in High School Biology Students as Measured by Three Separate Instruments"[*] state that their research led them to the conclusion that "the Piagetian tasks are relatively content free and can serve as realistic indicators of concrete and formal thinking abilities."

[*] *Journal of Research in Science Teaching*, 13 (3): 227–235, 1976.

INTERVIEWING PROTOCOLS FOR TASKS TO DETERMINE LEVELS OF THOUGHT[1]

Cognitive Analysis Project

COLLEGE OF EDUCATION
UNIVERSITY OF OKLAHOMA
1976

John W. Renner
Robert F. Bibens
Gene D. Shepherd
Rosalie Grant
Joan N. Sutherland
Mitchel R. Axsom
Robert L. Bibens
Caren I. Cook
S. Margaret Kennedy
Dianna Prickett
Michael J. Renner

[1] Adapted from Jean Piaget and Barbel Inhelder, *The Growth of Logical Thinking*, New York: Basic Books, 1958; and Jean Piaget, Barbel Inhelder and Alina Szeminska, *The Child's Concept of Geometry*, New York: Harper & Row, 1960.

The Cognitive Analysis Project has been supported by a grant from the National Science Foundation.

Contents

PREFACE

During the calendar year of 1976, approximately 1000 students in grades ten through twelve from the public and private schools in Oklahoma were interviewed to determine their levels of intellectual development. The interviews ocnsisted of having each student respond to four specific tasks which were originally designed by Jean Piaget and Barbel Inhelder. The protocols used to conduct those interviews were first adapted from the work of Piaget and Inhelder by the staff of the Cognitive Analysis Project in January 1976. Approximately 200 students were interviewed using those protocols. At that point the staff again studied the task protocols and made changes which made the descriptions reflect what was actually done during each interview.

Each task protocol is meant to reflect the criteria Inhelder and Piaget[2] used in establishing concrete and formal operational subcategories. The ratings assigned to student responses, therefore, are those established by Piaget and Inhelder. The current protocols, however, do not reflect criteria for the preoperational stage (Class I). Any Class I responses were rated as early concrete operational, Class IIA. Any additional exceptions to the Piaget-Inhelder established responses will be explained in the specific tasks to which they apply.

GENERAL INTRODUCTION TO THE INTERVIEW

The interviewer begins with the following statements:

"I am _____ (the interviewer states name). We are working on a research project at the University of Oklahoma to gather information to be used in developing classroom materials for high schools. We are interested in how high school students react to some tasks that we have. Don't worry about your answers being right or wrong; this is not a test. There are several different ways to approach these tasks. We are most interested in how you do the tasks, so please answer as honestly and completely as you can. Some of these tasks may be more difficult for you than others, but there are no 'trick' questions. What you do will not be shown to anyone in your school, so it will not influence your grades. We need an accurate record of what we talk about and I can't possibly remember it all, so do you mind if I record our conversation?"

---

[2] Ibid.

CONSERVATION OF VOLUME[3]

The materials are placed in front of the student. The interviewer uses a dialogue such as the following:

"Here are two test tubes that are exactly the same, and the level of water in them should be the same. Make sure you are satisfied that the water levels are the same in both tubes. If you need to change one of the levels you may use the medicine dropper to make them equal.

"Here are two metal cylinders that are the same size. You will notice one is just as big around and just as tall as the other." (Demonstrate this.) "Hold one of them in each hand and tell me how they are obviously different." (The answer should be weight.)

"We are going to put one cylinder in each tube. Each cylinder will sink all the way to the bottom of its tube. What will happen to the level of the liquid when the cylinders are submerged in the tubes?" (The answer should be that the water levels will rise.)

1. The interviewer then asks: "Will the heavier cylinder raise the water level more? Will the lighter cylinder raise the water level more? Or will both cylinders raise the water level the same?"
2. The interviewer asks why the subject believes as he or she does, and has the subject explain the answer he or she chose.
3. The interviewer lowers the lighter of the two cylinders into a tube.
4. The interviewer then has the subject lower the heavier cylinder into a tube and observe the water level.
5. If the subject predicts incorrectly (or correctly giving the wrong reason) the interviewer asks what he or she thinks caused the levels to come out equally.

Scoring

IIA The subject makes an incorrect prediction or predicts correctly and gives the incorrect reason; can't explain the results when he or she sees the experiment performed.

IIB The subject makes an incorrect prediction or predicts correctly and gives the incorrect reason (as in IIA); however, when the subject sees the experiment performed he or she realizes the correct explanation.

[3] *Piaget's Theory: Conservation*, San Francisco, California: John Davidson Film Corporation; and Jean Piaget, Barbel Inhelder and Alina Szeminska, *The Child's Concept of Geometry*, New York: Harper & Row, 1960, op. cit., chapter 14.

IIIA The subject predicts correctly and gives a correct reason.

IIIB This task does not require IIIB level of thought.

SEPARATION OF VARIABLES: BENDING RODS[4]

The apparatus is placed in front of the subject and the interviewer uses a dialogue such as the following:

"I have an apparatus and I want to show you how it works. I can pull the rods back and forth and make them as long or as short as I want. The effective length is from here out." (Demonstrate.) "The screws must be loosened in order to move the rods." The interviewer allows the subject a few moments to explore with the apparatus, and makes sure the subject understands that adjusting the lengths of the rods is permitted.

The interviewer says: "Look at the rods and tell me as many ways as you can how the rods are different." The interviewer leads the subject to state the three ways the rods are different, and explains that these differences are called variables. If the subject does not find all the variables, the interviewer explains what they are. At this point the weights are introduced, and the subject is shown how the weights will bend the rods. The interviewer now restates the four variables.

The interviewer next says: "Do some experiments to show me the effect of each one of the four variables on how much the rods bend." The interviewer is inviting the subject to demonstrate at least one experiment to show the influence of one of the variables on the bending of the rods. That is a category IIIA characteristic.

If the subject does not reach the IIIA level, the interviewer should provide the opportunity to reach the IIB level. A good question to lead back to IIB is: "Take one thick rod and one thin rod and make them bend the same amount, using two equal or identical weights." The subject in category IIB solves this problem by logical multiplication and explains why. The intuitive feeling is present that long and thick balances short and thin. The IIA student does not demonstrate logical multiplication.

A good question to use in leading the subject after one experiment controlling variables has been done, and after the subject is established at the level IIIA, is: "What else can you do to test the other variables?" The interviewer may precede this question with: "There are three more variables. Do you remember what they are?"

A good question to lead the subject during the task, but not before an opportunity to set up *an* experiment has been provided, is: "What

[4] Barbel Inhelder and Jean Piaget, *The Growth of Logical Thinking*, New York: Basic Books, 1958, chapter 3.

can you do to prove that the material (or length, or shape, or diameter) of the rod is important in determining how much it will bend?"

A good question to conclude the interview for this task is: "Is there anything else you want to do with this apparatus?"

Questions to be asked during the entire interview after each experiment the subject attempts are:

"What are you showing with that experiment?"
"What variable is your experiment dealing with?"
"How does your experiment show what variable you are testing?"   •

Scoring

IIA   The subject cannot explain logical multiplication.

IIB   The subject can explain logical multiplication (intuitive feeling that long and thin balances short and heavy).

IIIA   The subject does at least one experiment that proves the effect of at least one variable.

IIIB   The subject solves the entire problem.

EQUILIBRIUM IN THE BALANCE[5]

The apparatus is placed in front of the student. The following dialogue is begun:

"Here is a bar which is balanced at the center. Notice that there are 17 evenly spaced hooks on each side of the balance point on which to hang weights. We are going to do some balance tasks. I'll hang a weight on one side and ask you to balance the bar by hanging a weight or weights on the other side. You can hang weights on different hooks or on the same hook if you wish. The weights can be hooked together to suspend them from the same hook.

The interviewer proceeds with the following steps:

1. "First, I'm going to hang a 100 gram weight on the sixth hook." (Count from center.) "I want you to place a 100 gram weight on the other side to make the bar balance." The interviewer holds the bar level while the subject is hanging the weight, and before releasing it asks this question: "Why did you hang the weight on the _____ hook?"

2. "I'm going to leave my 100 gram weight on the sixth hook and give you two 50 gram weights. Where will you hang your 50 gram weight to balance my 100 gram weight?" The interviewer

[5] Ibid., chapter 11.

holds the bar level while the subject decides where to place the two 50 gram weights and places them. Before releasing the bar, the interviewer asks: "Why did you hang the 50 gram weights on the _____ hook (or hooks)?"

3. "Now, I'm going to hang a 100 gram weight on the sixth hook." (Count from center.) "I want you to take a 50 gram weight and hang it on the other side to balance the bar." The interviewer holds the bar level while the subject is placing the weight. While holding the bar level, the interviewer asks: "Why did you hang the weight on the _____ hook?"

4. "Next, I'm going to hang a 120 gram weight on the third hook." (Count from center.) "Hang a 40 gram weight on the other side to make the bar balance." The interviewer holds the bar level while the subject is placing the weight. Still holding the bar level, the interviewer asks: "Why did you hang the weight on the _____ hook?"

5. "Now, I'm going to hang a 70 gram weight on the tenth hook." (Count from center.) "Hang a 100 gram weight on the other side to make the bar balance." The interviewer holds the bar level while the subject is placing the weight. Still holding the bar level, the interviewer asks: "Why did you hang the weight on the _____ hook?"

If the interviewer is unsure of his or her judgement after using the 70/100 weight combination, a good way to test that judgement is to place a 60 gram weight on the sixth hook and give the subject 40 grams. The dialogue followed is the same as that given above.

Suggested Amendments—Balance

The magnitude of the weights and distances can be changed, provided the proportions of 1:1, 1:2, 1:3, and a more complex one (e.g., 3:2, 7:10) are retained.

Scoring

IIA   The subject is not successful with anything beyond Step Two.

IIB   The subject is successful with the two-to-one[6] proportions of

[6] Piaget and Inhelder infer (*Growth of Logical Thinking*, chapter 11) that the successful completion of the 2:1 proportion task is a characteristic of the IIIA category. Warren Wollman and Robert Karplus ("Intellectual Development Beyond Elementary School V: Using Ratio in Differing Tasks," *School Science and Mathematics*, Vol. LXXIV, No. 7, November 1974, pp. 593–611) have shown the 2:1 proportion concept to be attainable at the IIB level.

Step Three. The explanation must include the use of the proportion concept.

IIIA   The subject is successful in balancing the bar using the weights and distances outlined in Step Four. The explanation must include the proportion concept.

IIIB   The subject is successful in balancing the bar using the weights and distances outlined in Step Five. The explanation must include the proportion concept. A student who solves the problem using a rule such as weight times distance on one side equals weight times distance on the other side is using an algorithm, without necessarily using a proportion. If this is evident, the subject is asked, "Can you give me another solution using weight and distance in some other way?" If the student cannot satisfactorily explain this using proportions, a lower score is given, depending upon the last level for which a satisfactory explanation was given.

COMBINATIONS OF COLORLESS CHEMICAL LIQUIDS[7]

A rack of small test tubes and five bottles labeled "1," "2," "3," "4," and "g" are placed in front of the subject. Bottle 1 contains dilute sulfuric acid, Bottle 2 contains distilled water, Bottle 3 contains hydrogen peroxide (1.5 percent), Bottle 4 contains sodium thiosulfate (0.16 molar), and Bottle g contains potassium iodide (0.14 molar). Piaget and Inhelder explain the chemical reactions as follows:

. . . hydrogen peroxide oxidizes potassium iodide in the acid medium. This mixture (1 and 3 and g) will yield a yellow color. The water (2) is neutral, so that adding it will not change the color, whereas the thiosulfate (4) will bleach the mixture (1 and 3 and g).[8]

A dialogue such as the following is used:
"Here are two test tubes, and each contains a clear liquid. Each of those liquids is from one of these bottles or from a combination of two, three or all four. There is a different liquid in each bottle. Here is a fifth bottle, labeled "g." The liquid in it is different from the others. I will add some of Bottle g to each test tube of liquid.

I would like for you to do as many experiments as you need to in order to reproduce that yellow color change in as many different ways

---

[7] Barbel Inhelder and Jean Piaget, *The Growth of Logical Thinking*, op. cit., chapter 7.
[8] Ibid., p. 109.

as you can. You may use as many test tubes as you need to use. As you add the liquids, please state the number or letter of the liquid you used so the tape recorder will record it."

Scoring

IIA The subject who simply attempts combinations of a single liquid with g or all four with g, without any other combinations, is in substage IIA. Any hypothesis formed will be quantitative (too much water or too little water) dealing only with serial ordering or correspondence. If the color is achieved, it will be fortuitous and the color will be attributed to a single liquid rather than a combination.

IIB Substage IIB is characterized by the same basic reactions, with the addition of some n $\times$ n combinations with g, or n $\times$ n $\times$ n combinations with g. The IIB subject will "begin by multiplying each element by g or taking them all at once, but finally they spontaneously use two-by-two or three-by-three combinations (each time with g)."[9] The upper limit of Substage IIB is determined by the fact that a IIB subject's system will be empirical and the color will still be attributed to one particular liquid. At Substage IIB the subject will not continue to experiment without reasonable prompting.

IIIA The two innovations which appear at Substage IIIA are the introduction of a systematic method in the use of n $\times$ n combinations and an understanding that the color is a result of a combination rather than coming from one of the liquids. A subject at this substage, when finding a color-producing combination, does not stop there, but goes on. The subject tests other combinations in order to complete the combinatorial system.

IIIB The difference between Substage IIIB and the earlier one (IIIA) "is only one of degree."[10] The combinations and proofs are organized in a more systematic fashion with the experiment organized from the start with the intent to find proof. "Thus, the only innovation appearing at Substage IIIB is the greater speed with which the subject understands the use he may make of these substitutions and additions in the determination of the respective effects of the elements during the actual construction

[9] Ibid., p. 115.
[10] Ibid., p. 120.

of these combinations."[11] The subject can determine the role of the water and sodium thiosulfate solution in the combinations. The subject may have to be questioned to ensure that he or she effectively demonstrates some form of proof for the role of those liquids.

[11] Ibid., p. 121.

Index